Figured Out

 THE UNIVERSITY OF
WINCHESTER

Figured Out

Typology and Providence
in Christian Scripture

Christopher R. Seitz

Westminster John Knox Press
LOUISVILLE
LONDON • LEIDEN

Scripture quotations from the New Revised Standard Version of the Bible are copyright © 1989 by the Division of Christian Education of the National Council of the Churches of Christ in the U.S.A. and are used by permission.

Book design by Sharon Adams
Cover design by Mark Abrams

First edition
Published by Westminster John Knox Press
Louisville, Kentucky

This book is printed on acid-free paper that meets the American National Standards Institute Z39.48 standard. ∞

PRINTED IN THE UNITED STATES OF AMERICA

01 02 03 04 05 06 07 08 09 10 — 10 9 8 7 6 5 4 3 2 1

Library of Congress Cataloging-in-Publication Data

Seitz, Christopher R.
    Figured out : typology and providence in Christian Scripture / Christopher R. Seitz.—1st ed.
        p. cm.
    Includes bibliographical references and indexes.
    ISBN 0-664-22268-4 (alk. paper)
    1. Typology (Theology)—History of doctrines. 2. Bible—Criticism, interpretation, etc.—History. I. Title.

BS478 .S45 2001
220.6′4—dc21   2001026177

Contents

Preface

In recent days, there has been a lively and, for the most part, genuinely illuminating reappraisal of typology and allegory—for now, call it the figural interpretation of scripture. In a period when historical-critical reading is casting its own historical shadow, fragmenting into this or that subdivision, or simply dying a slow death, it is remarkable to note an area of exegetical investigation that is both vigorous and promising.

Fresh questions and angles of vision are being set forth.

1. Are typology and allegory to be sharply contrasted?
2. Is "typology" in truth a modern term, thought to be congruent with Enlightenment notions of "history" but, if so, actually distant from the figural readings of the early church?
3. Has the breadth and range of Origen's exegetical practice been properly assessed, over and above the scattered remarks he makes in *On First Principles*?
4. What is the actual exegetical practice of the Church Fathers and what do the terms they use—literal sense, spiritual sense, anagogy, scope, mind, hypothesis—imply? How are these to be coordinated, if at all, with concern for historical reference as this has latterly been the focus of biblical studies?
5. Is exegesis closer to doctrine than one might have thought, obscured, however, by an emphasis on historical differentiation and innocent or aggressive insistence upon variety within the biblical witness, as that feature most characteristic of the two-testament Christian witness?

This book does not treat these questions directly, though concern about them informs what I have written. This book is more like Hezekiah's tunnel.[1] We are trying to find a way from one zone of concern (historical modes of reading scripture, in their academic and ecclesial guises) to another—that is, with how the two testaments of Christian scripture can be reconnected without harm to their literal or plain sense, as this term has been used in the prior history of interpretation. The first part of the book offers examples of how scripture has been "figured out." The examples are drawn from the history of ideas (and a specific configuration of these on my part) and from the down-to-earth struggles of Christian churches *to hear any word at all from the witness of the Bible*. That an investigation of this latter context brings me into the fraught and parlous world of Anglican Christianity does not mean that the discussion is parochial and irrelevant. Indeed, we are talking about the post-Christian world throwing up challenge after successive challenge and the response of Christian bodies in the form of accommodation, resistance, nostalgia, or great enthusiasm. Naturally, the Bible lives in this world of upheaval, and its Word cannot be said to be caught off guard by it.

The second part of the book consists of readings of holy scripture with implications for how the instincts of figural reading might be recovered in our own day. Anyone reading these essays will see this is not a project in retrieval or nostalgia; I am fully a product of historical-critical assumptions, not to say of the category of "history" itself. This category was famously thrust upon us by the late-eighteenth-century desire for religious tolerance, rational truths, conscience, and an objective account of "what has happened in time"—all this considered apart from a view of Providence or scripture's history-creating Word, yet holding on to the teaching of Jesus or the feelings of religion natural to all humanity.[2]

One trajectory that emerges, though it is not discussed directly in either main section, is our general abandonment in time. The loss of figural reading is not the loss of an exegetical technique. It is the loss of location in time under God. Certain forms of allegorical reading, it has been claimed, are ahistorical and must be cast out of the church's academic (or ecclesial) reading of the Bible.[3] Ironically, however, those readings most interested in historical reference are the same ones that cannot make any accounting of the church's place in time and so resort to homiletical analogies of the most spiritualizing and moralizing sort in order to let the Bible have some sort of say after all the historical heavy lifting is over. And one might well question whether all spiritual reading was as temporally disinterested as modern historically minded folk have thought. At issue is likely a different order of temporality, not a spiritual-versus-historical frame of reference. In the final section of the introduction is a brief word about this.

This book is offered in sincere provisionality. Maybe the tunnel will turn up sounds of tapping on another side, but that is for the God who orders all time to say. My only prayer is that Christ's body will be "figured in" to his glorious body and that the scriptures would illumine him in his threefold mystery and give the church a place in time again.

Lent 2001

FIGURAL READING OF SCRIPTURE: A SELECTION

J. Barr, "Allegory and Typology," in *Old and New in Interpretation* (New York: Harper & Row, 1966) 103–48.

B. S. Childs, "Allegory and Typology within Biblical Interpretation" (unpublished paper delivered at the University of St Andrews, April 2000).

H. Crouzel, "The Interpretation of Scripture," in *Origen* (ET; Edinburgh: T&T Clark, 1989).

R. Greer, *Theodore of Mopsuestia: Exegete and Theologian* (Westminster: The Faith Press, 1961).

———, *Broken Lights and Mended Lives* (University Park, Pa.: Pennsylvania State University Press, 1986).

A. Louth, *Discerning the Mystery* (Oxford, 1983).

T. E. Pollard, "The Exegesis of Scripture and the Arian Controversy," *BJRL* 41 (1958–9), 414–29.

M. Simonetti, *Biblical Interpretation in the Early Church* (Edinburgh: T&T Clark, 1994).

K. Torjesen, *Hermeneutical Procedure and Theological Method* (Berlin: de Gruyter, 1986).

J. W. Trigg, *Origen: The Bible and Philosophy in the Third-Century* (London: SCM, 1985).

———, "Allegory," in *Encyclopedia of Early Christianity* (2d ed.; New York and London: Garland, 1998).

Frances Young, "Exegetical Method and Scriptural Proof: The Bible in Doctrinal Debate," *Studia Patristica* 29 (1989) 291–304.

———, "Allegory and the Ethics of Reading," in *The Open Text. New Directions for Biblical Studies?* (F. Watson, ed.; London: SPCK, 1993) 103–20.

———, "Typology," in *Crossing the Boundaries: Essays in Biblical Interpretation in Honour of Michael D. Goulder* (S. E. Porter, P. Joyce, D. E. Orton, eds.; Leiden, New York, Koln: E. J. Brill, 1994) 29–48.

———, *Biblical Exegesis and the Formation of Christian Culture* (Cambridge: CUP, 1997).

Acknowledgments

While reading Ephraim Radner's brilliant doctoral thesis on Jansenism, I struggled to enter a very different universe of scriptural interpretation and temporal perspective. Yet I sensed something had gone missing in much modern academic reading of the Old Testament and New Testament. It was not just that biblical scholarship was going the wrong way—that has been said and will always be said by some. It was that biblical interpretation had lost something: a general confidence that the Bible was truly anticipating the church and its times, long before we showed up and started to deploy this or that reading strategy.

This book is indebted to many very bright, very insightful, very disciplined Christian minds, all of whom are trying to understand and perhaps even reinstate the something that has gone missing. Alongside Radner I will mention Kathryn Greene-McCreight, David Yeago, Rusty Reno, George Sumner, and Phil Turner. It is not accidental that all of these folk are ertswhile Yale colleagues and friends who continue to prod and influence my thinking through the work of Scholarly Engagement with Anglican Doctrine (SEAD). We have held biannual conferences in Charleston, South Carolina, Toronto, and Washington, D.C. over the past several years. Papers read at these events typically seek to look around the corner at what God may be doing in a church attending to his word, especially at times when he falls silent to his own sovereign end. The commitment of SEAD to disciplined thought and prayer and fellowship focused on scripture and theology has stimulated and enriched my own reflections. The form they take in this book is obviously my own responsibility. Nevertheless I wish to acknowledge the gladsome fact that I have been able to think in the context of Christian friendship, mission, and praise.

Within this same circle of Christian fellowship I acknowledge especially the support of Fitz Allison, Martha Bailey, Gil Greggs, Gary Anderson, Richard Hays, Kendall Harmon, and those several churches in the United States where I have been asked to speak and have been the one doing the learning. The Diocese of South Carolina has been a second home for me during my travels, and the Bishop and Dean have been good friends and steady hands at the helm. Lutheran friends and The Abbey of Mepkin round out the South Carolina circle of support.

It seems to be the way of things that much of this writing has taken place in hotel rooms, particularly at the finishing stages. I have had *Figured Out* in my mind's eye for at least three years of thinking and speaking and reflecting. Many of these chapters were occasioned by public lectures given at King's College London, Asbury Seminary, North Park Seminary, Wheaton College, Hamilton College, Wycliff College Toronto, Selwyn College Cambridge, The Divinity School, Cambridge, and the SEAD conferences in Charleston and Washington, D.C. My hosts and interlocutors have included Klyne Snodgrass, Colin Gunton, Scott Hafemann, Richard Schultz, Ben Witherington, Lawson Stone, Richard Longenecker, Craig Bartholomew, Alan Hays, Dan Hardy, and Liesl Amos. I acknowledge with gratitude their patience, support, and wise counsel.

Like many people I am finding the Internet and e-mail communication a very mixed blessing. Things that happen rapidly can make us happen rapidly. This book has been edited and re-edited by electronic shipments. I cannot adequately express my appreciation to Carey Newman for his encouragement, and for his incisive and decisive judgments. The same must be said for Tiffany Taylor, whose hard work I am pleased to acknowledge here. I thank them both deeply. The book would not have come to form without their hard labor. I would also be remiss if I did not acknowledge that some of the material in this book has appeared (or will appear) elsewhere. I wish to thank the respective editors and presses for their kind permission to use it here, though in some cases much of the material has been altered. In specific, chapter 2, "Scripture Becomes Religion(s): The Theological Crisis of Serious Biblical Interpretation in the Twentieth Century," appears in *Renewing Biblical Interpretation*, ed. Craig Bartholomew (Grand Rapids: Zondervan, 2000). Chapter 8, "Of Mortal Appearance: The Earthly Jesus and Isaiah as a Type of Christian Scripture," appeared in *Ex Auditu* 14 (1998), 31–41. Chapter 10, "Handing over the Name: Christian Reflection on the Divine Name YHWH," appeared in *Trinity, Time and Church: A Response to the Theology of Robert W. Jenson*, ed. Colin Gunton (Grand Rapids: Eerdmans, 2000). Chapter 12, "Prayer in the Old Testament or Hebrew Bible," will appear in *Into God's Presence: Prayer in the New Testament*, ed. Richard N. Longenecker (Grand Rapids: Eerdmans, forthcoming).

On a personal note I want to thank John and Laura Barr for their friendship, prayers, and good fellowship during the period when this book was being conceived and written. My brother Mark has been an invaluable support and friend, and together with his wife Kathleen and children Amy and Matthew,

I thank them for all they have done while this book has been taking form. If every family has a designated computer czar, Mark has been that for me.

Brevard Childs remains an extraordinary pioneer. Conversations with him are unfailingly stimulating. No sooner had he finished his Isaiah commentary, he lectured at St. Andrews on figural reading and indicated he had decided to revisit the early Church's vast interpretative exploration into Isaiah. Always the student seeking to learn more, Childs has been a true Christian witness, and I wish to acknowledge his ongoing impact on my own thinking.

My mother taught me by playing the piano and organ. In some ways, hymns carry on the work of theological construction better than books, even as each has its place. In my reflections in the Conclusion, I was aware of how much the hymns of the church had influenced my thinking on figuration and I acknowledge my mother Jan as the bearer of these musical gifts. This book is dedicated to her.

Christopher R. Seitz
Pentecost 2001

Part One

Introduction

1

Introduction

GOD TRIUNELY FIGURED

In the middle of the twentieth century, Jürgen Moltmann made popular the phrase "the crucified God."[1] With this phrase, he wished to stress the full divinity of Christ and the full participation of the Father in the death of the Son. A recently published Christology by Richard Bauckham emphasizes the same thing.[2] Jesus Christ is the Son of God Crucified, not because his death was squared with a rigid monotheism in some theologically ingenious way but because of the identity of the God of Israel in the truest and deepest sense. This identity is manifested, in essence, in Jesus' death on a cross. The systematic theologian Robert Jenson has struck some of these same notes in his recently published two-volume work.[3]

One senses in these two more recent efforts—one from the side of biblical studies and the other from the side of systematic theology—the conjunction of existentialist apologetic and exegetical realism. That is, the letter of scripture is taken with utmost seriousness; it is not the accident of a metaphysical substance. At the same time, God is figured and accessible to the eyes of faith at the maximal depths of human sinful existence, including death and corruption itself.

By "figured" is here meant coherently and sovereignly one, even as God is three in his economy and in his self-identity. His figural manifestation comes as the One God who raised Israel from the dead of Egypt and exile,[4] who raised the Son from the grave, and who sent the Holy Spirit. Figuration entails the trustworthy and truthful witness of the scriptures of Israel to the One Lord (YHWH, the "I am who I am in my disclosure of myself with Israel") toward which the New Testament's proclamation of Jesus as Lord is "in accordance" (1 Cor. 15:3).[5] Figuration means that God is providentially and eternally

3

truthful in his disclosure of himself and that when we call upon him as "the Father and the Son and the Holy Spirit" we can be sure he knows himself to be addressed and has urged this address in the first place by the prevenient work of the Holy Spirit, present and lively in the church's worship, prayer, and praise.[6]

On this figural view, the cross of Christ is not an unfortunate mistake but is the eternal will of God for himself, in his disclosure as righteous, holy, and loving. The cross is the figure of God, adumbrated in Israel's testimony to God's identity, manifested in the flesh and blood of the Son, breathed forth in forgiveness and true judgment in the Holy Spirit, until "all things are put in subjection" to Christ and the Son "himself will also be subjected to the one who put all things in subjection under him, so that God may be all in all" (1 Cor. 15:27–28). This confession is figural because it is rooted in God's eternal word to Israel, finds full accordance in the cross and empty tomb of Christ, and covers all time under God's full providence and eternal purpose, enclosing our own day—if even under purposed, configured judgment.[7]

THE DISFIGURED GOD

In the 1960s, the cautionary voice of one of the period's strongest biblical scholars was heard, anticipating the theological concerns of those who later would prove unpersuaded by America's so-called Biblical Theology Movement.[8] At stake were basic theological issues, not adequately covered by the (then) popular themes of "the mighty acts of God," "Greek versus Hebrew thought," "history as the primary arena of God's action," or "theology as etymology, or word study." The problem with historical criticism was that it had failed to do constructive theological work involving the identity of God in the most basic sense. By focusing on how Israel thought about God; how Israel's religion issued forth into New Testament religion (or how, with Bultmann, it did not); how traditions changed and shifted focus over time, redactors then getting the final word; or what Jesus said about the kingdom or who he thought he was (the stock-in-trade of historical-critical theologizing), how might it then be possible to speak of God as one, as three, and as disclosed in a unique way in Israel's testimony from the Old Testament?[9] All the focus on history, God's actions, religion, traditions, differentiation within the canon, and the like made for much complex reflection and a particular brand of close reading. But could it be said that God could speak, in time and space or through the canonical deposit of prophets and apostles, as had been assumed throughout the history of interpretation before the rise of "history" (historicism) as a non-negotiable category of significance? Could it be said that God's identity was uniquely disclosed in the testimony to him in Israel's scriptures, or were we just "on the way" to knowledge of God somehow brokered in purer form, for Christians, in "historical Jesus" as he could be reconstructed behind the Gospel witness? A nineteenth-century alternative to this sought revelation in the apostolic testimony to Jesus as "divine" or partaking of divinity in some religio-historical sense.[10]

The words spoken in 1964 must have had a curious, isolated ring, given the trends set loose by the American effort to popularize historical-critical labor (and preach it or enlist it in Sunday school curricula, as well).

> All Christian use of the Old Testament seems to depend on the belief that the One God who is the God of Israel is also the God and Father of Jesus Christ.

Note what a remedial and clear statement this is, theologically.

> All our use of the Old Testament goes back to this belief. What is said there that relates to "God" relates to our God. Consequently, that which can be known of our God is known only when we consider the Old Testament as a place in which he is known.

Note here how the privileged character of Israel's witness—quite apart from how we are to use it—is made central. Then the developmental logic of so much historical-critical thinking is exposed, especially as it took a virulent "Christian" turn in the understanding of Christian scripture as entailing two distinct witnesses, an old (or Hebrew/Jewish) and a new (Christian) witness.

> It is an illusory position to think of ourselves as in a position where the New Testament is clear, is known, and is accepted, and where there-fore from this secure position we start out to explore the much more doubtful and dangerous territory of the Old Testament. . . . [This] is not possible, for quite theological reasons. . . . Insofar as a position is Christian, it is related to the Old Testament from the beginning.

In this portion of the quote, all of the more recent objections to the limits of historical inquiry into the scriptures of the Old and New Testaments are antic-ipated. Theology, in the basic sense of the word, concerns the identity of God. It could never be simply about using one understanding allegedly disclosed at a later period as a sort of Geiger counter to assess prior statements. This is to misunderstand the subject matter under discussion: God as he is and as he has disclosed his identity in Israel and Jesus. The developmental model (with its Kantian epistemology and apparatus) cannot be sufficiently conjoined to the scriptures' own plain-sense presentation of the theological subject matter that lies at its heart and is its own point of origin and disclosure.

The relevant quote concludes, "In this sense, if one wishes to express the argument in terms of classic theology, our approach to the Old Testament is Trinitarian rather than Christological. The direction of thought is from God to Christ, from Father to Son, and not from Christ to God." And then, to illustrate proper caution, given the figural reality of God described previously, the author rightly concludes, "It should also be noted that, where we have a Trinitarian structure, we can proceed to a Christological one."

These prescient remarks on the relationship between a properly theological handling of Christian scripture—given the figural identity of the Triune God, and our own present Christian God-talk—were delivered in the Currie Lectures at Austin Presbyterian Seminary at the height of the Biblical Theology Movement. The prophetic voice was, ironically, that of James Barr.[11]

FIGURED OUT: CAN A TWO-TESTAMENT WITNESS TO GOD FIND PROVIDENTIAL SPEECH FOR OUR DAY?

The essays in this book all operate with an assumption about the rule of faith as constructive and essential to theological work. The rule of faith is assumed by historians to be a principle at work in the early church.[12] Some believe it was a sort of credal deposit or précis of the apostolic faith (derived from early baptismal interrogatories?) that guided Christian interpreters toward ascertaining when scripture's word was being heard and applied in a proportional way, as consistent with the literal sense, both in the parts and in the whole of scripture.[13] We are aware of proto-rabbinic and inner-exegetical principles that grew up over time and aided the faithful in hearing the full counsel of scripture's word, all the while attending very closely to the letter of the text under specific discussion.[14] The rule of faith is a mature, explicitly Christian, trinitarian development from these prior inner-biblical instincts. The focus for our present purposes is on the explicitly *theological character of the rule and its hermeneutical consequences, chief among them, that as the Son and the Father are one, so, too, is the witness to them from the Old and New Testaments, which witness is perceived by eyes of faith through the work of the Holy Spirit.* As the persons of the Godhead are not divided, even as they exist in differentiated order (*taxis*), so, too, the Old Testament is not to be heard apart from the New, or the New apart from the Old, whether in the name of literalism, historicism, spiritualism, or crass supercessionism.

If this is a fair, general depiction of the rule of faith, it helps to explain why frequency of citation, a flat "concordance logic," or appeal to external metaphysical criteria (the material world is evil; God cannot be mysteriously three yet one; a son of God cannot be a creature, or must be) never gained catholic (universal) assent in matters of dispute in the church insofar as constructive application of scripture was concerned.

Now, each age must confront the scriptures with concern for the challenges of the day. For our day, the chief of these is *historicism*. The questions of historical reference or the intention of the human author are not new ones. One can see in the Antiochenes (Diodore of Tarsus, Theodore of Mopsuestia) concern with what we might call historical or diachronic matters (how is David author of the Psalms? Why are the Psalms or the Book of the Twelve in their present order? What effect did the Exile have?), and in many ways no one read the Bible more literally than Origen (Where is the mountain from which all the kingdoms of the world can be viewed? Why does the law condemn eating vultures when no one would do this anyway?). What is different about historicism is its appeal to the human dimension of scripture to such a degree that the actual form and structure of the literary witness is eclipsed, in a manner that Origen's spiritual exegesis avoided.[15] That such an appeal began with a highly theological justification (inspiration required an accounting of the *real* human author) is made all the more tepid when one observes the capacity of historical reconstructions to continue unabated and unconcerned with any large-scale theological justification. Things are simply out there to be discovered, and novelty is demanded in the nature of the enterprise.

Or again, some of the more theologically conservative handlings of the "historical Jesus" still view the New Testament as a collection of information to be put to use in reconstructions of what Jesus thought—elegantly and, on occasion, persuasively argued—so that the information of the New Testament might be trusted.[16] What becomes unclear, however, is what theological significance the *form* of the Gospels, in their present fourfold presentation, might have.[17] This is no mere quibble. Once the New Testament as canon is used for (maximal or minimal) historical presentations of Jesus, it becomes very difficult to comprehend how the Old Testament functions as scripture for the church's ongoing life and not just as (important) historical background to be viewed from the standpoint of the "historical Jesus" interpretation of it.[18]

The contrast with the exegesis of the early church could not be starker. What is at issue in the early church is not the scriptures of Israel as normative theological witness. What is at issue is how such a witness is to be heard, given the appearance of a second testament and its witness to Jesus Christ as Son of God. The pressure is on letting the first witness sound forth its notes in an appropriate manner, not on recovering a historical Jesus behind the witness of the second, such recovering then being used to assess the first. Rather, at issue is an account of the character of God that is faithful to both witnesses. It would be simply inconceivable to speak of a "development" from one testament to

the next that avoids, rejects, or minimizes the ongoing role of the Old Testament as first-order theological talk. Only Gnostics or literalists working outside the rule of faith could consider such an option acceptable.

To say that "historicism" is the challenge of our day is to name a certain sort
of historical inquiry; not all forms of inquiry into the past are the same. The
Bible is a human witness, and the human dimension is to be handled carefully
and not obscured by spiritualism, moralism, or a modern anagogy blind to the
details of the word (as ironically so much experiential or thematic preaching
has become, built on the foundations of historical-critical training in respect
of the Bible). What is at stake is retention of the actual form of the witness.
The final form of scripture has theological significance. To refer to Moses as
"author" of the Torah, David as the voice of the Psalms, Solomon as collector
of Proverbs, or the Paul or James or John of the New Testament with the literatures associated with them need not carry with it the burden of historicism.
Rather, such reference coheres with the plain sense of scripture's presentation
and must be considered a piece of historical datum not to be cast off by historicist quests for this or that datum behind the witness. To repeat, I refer here
to a concrete, historical reality and not some vague spiritual truth about scripture. History is more than origins; it is effects as well. That the church or synagogue heard the Torah and spoke of Moses, or of Paul and spoke of the letters
associated with him, is a piece of historical fact every much as deserving of our
attention as a new date for the Yahwist or confidence about this or that "Jesus
tradition." The burden may need to shift toward the justification of a single
sort of historical quest as prioritized and disproportionately claiming our
attention.

Exhaustion or restlessness with forms of historicist reading have given rise
to a concern with the social location of the modern reader or meaning as tied
to the reading process itself.[19] What we see in figural reading in the history of
interpretation is recognition of kindred influences. These are, however,
closely tied up with ecclesial ascesis and the rule of faith, this latter providing
its own exegetical guardrails concerning the relationship between texts of the
one scriptural witness in two-testament form. Appeals to general hermeneutics or the pressures of culture would probably have been regarded as tooth-
less (or worse) in the face of an overriding concern to hear scripture speak for
itself in its own dynamic key. Concern with the figural linguistic world of scripture did not mean single-meaning exegesis! No one reading Justin, Irenaeus,
Clement, Origen, the Antiochenes, or Athanasius should expect anything like
uniformity, yet all of them, including even Origen, bear a decided family
resemblance. The dynamic character of scripture in its two-testament form
does not allow for propositional or technical flattening, given that this witness
is received in faith, under the guidance of the Holy Spirit, disciplined by

prayer, eucharistic fellowship, and the teaching of the church in its baptismal interrogatories and credal affirmations.

Then, finally, there is the matter of providence. Allegory and typology were not strictly distinguished as types of figural reading, and, indeed, "typology" is not a formal term in the same manner as the terms enclosed within the broad spectrum of literal, plain, and spiritual reading ("mind," "scope," "hypothesis," "theoria," "historia").[20] One can spot a tension within the range of figural reading having to do with temporality, both in terms of the referential character of the scriptures in the past and also in terms of the eschatological force of the divine word to the church in the future, right up until the curtain of time is brought down and God is all in all. Taken as a broad statement, it might be said that Origen is more concerned with a present spiritual anagogy than with comprehending God's temporal grasp of Israel in the past, or the church in and through time, under the lordship of one God who orders and disposes time itself. But it would be saying too much to claim that he ignored this reality altogether. And that is all the more true of figural reading in its more literal or reality-concerned guises.

Historicism has given us a Bible that points beyond itself to a vast, complex, developmental, ever-changing continuum in time and space. Historicism insists the past become truly *past*, distinguished from the present, except by means of human analogy, ingenious application, or a piety resistant to historicism's acids. Our place in time is accidental and without clear divine anchor. God is not ordering our days, and our times are not in his (or her) hands. Anachronism has become a problem to observe and correct, for everything belongs in its proper historical location, even if the connections between locations are as speculative as the locations themselves. Theological explanations for this state of affairs have been given, some more convincing—if not also more disturbing—than others.[21] The fallout may not be immediately available to our senses. One example taken up in several chapters in this book will suffice—namely, the one having to do with human sexuality and Christian teaching from scripture.

In the early days of modern reconsideration of biblical teaching, the Bible was thought to be amenable to a different interpretation than the "traditional" one with respect to a "new sexual ethic."[22] What was at fault was the history of interpretation, from which we could sever ourselves in the name of reconnecting (a long leap in time though it be) with the true word of scripture. Various historicist essays and monographs sought to show that the world of the Israelites or emergent Christianity had been misunderstood. Paul was against certain specious forms of same-sex conduct. The men of Sodom were guilty of inhospitality (even the Old Testament's internal references to the episode, so it was argued, confirmed this). As for Jesus, he was silent on the subject.

Recently, however, this sort of constraint, under which the Bible was shown to be better than its history of interpretation (this keeping us with some tenuous sense of providence), has receded in favor of another approach. The Bible simply knows nothing of our day. In modern homosexual behavior and states of nature, we find the equivalent of a Walkman or zip drive; that is, we have a modern sexual theme the Bible can know nothing about. The Bible is locked in its (important, religiously prior) day. Jesus is locked there, too, and the God of the Old Testament was locked there before him. Because Jesus is silent about our *novum*, we can imagine him to be sympathetic, in contrast to Paul or James, who were loud and too ambitious, en route to the wisdom of our own day. The Holy Spirit, we are told, is about leading us into new truths and toppling old taboos, be they in the form of Jewish vestige or early Christian caution.[23]

The price to be paid for this, theologically, is sustainable, or so it would seem. The Holy Spirit can inspire Moses; after him, James; and after him, us in our new day, in ways that are internally contradictory and mutually corrosive. More than this, the Holy Spirit's life in genuine subsistence with the Father and the Son boils down to absorption of them both in the name of living in providential care for a new day neither could have seen, at least as reported in the witness of the two testaments of Christian scripture that tell us who they are and convey their present life with us, in the very first place. It should be emphasized that the Holy Spirit, on this account, "updates" us on the law of Moses (a topic that is a matter of considerable nuance and significance, in equal measure, in the New Testament's plain sense). But more than this, the Holy Spirit updates us on a new truth nowhere to be found in the New Testament and, indeed, at odds with major portions of it (as had always been seen in the history of interpretation).

In sum, figural reading, under the rule of faith, ensured that the arena within which the Holy Spirit could speak to the church from the witness of prophets and apostles was not confused or its boundaries removed in the name of conforming to an age outside God's own providential ordering. Figural reading is not an exegetical technique. It is an effort to hear the two-testament witness to God in Christ, taking seriously its plain sense, in conjunction with apostolic teaching. This teaching is guided by the conviction that the persons of the Trinity are to be seen in their fundamental unity, as the Father, the Son, and the Holy Ghost, one God. And this teaching is derived from the two-testament witness itself. This reciprocating character of authority means that literalism, propositionalism, historicism, and the new spiritualism are ruled out, so that the figural word of Holy Scripture might be heard afresh in each new generation of faith, until the providentially ordered new creation descends with its risen and eternal Lord, to the glory of God the Father.

Part Two

*Christian Scripture,
Figured Out*

2

Scripture Becomes Religion(s)

The Theological Crisis of Serious Biblical Interpretation in the Twentieth Century

INTRODUCTION

I will begin by making several preliminary remarks, so that you will have a right to anticipate some focus in what could otherwise be an enormous and unwieldy topic.

People today speak of a "crisis in biblical hermeneutics." Undoubtedly, as the twenty-first century dawns, biblical scholars, church members, and the general public could agree that something like a crisis exists. Naturally, they are concerned about this and feel the pressure of it in different ways, and so their reactions differ as well.

I appreciate the use of the term "hermeneutics" to locate the crisis, but I want to be sure we agree what we mean by that. In the works of Vanhoozer and Wolterstorff, for example, we see an effort to address topics such as divine speech, inspiration, and authorship.[1] This is done from the perspective of general hermeneutics (the philosophy of language; speech-act theory), and in both cases the engagement is sustained and intelligent. It is less clear to me that other works, such as Francis Watson's two recent contributions, emerged to address what might be called a crisis in hermeneutics in the same sense as Vanhoozer's and Wolterstorff's efforts.[2] A good way to illustrate the difference is in noting whether the long-standing problem of relating the two testaments of Christian scripture is seen as central. Hermeneutics as a science of reading and interpretation could simply speak about matters of authorship, reader, text, inspiration, divine speech, and so forth, in the manner of Vanhoozer or Wolterstorff, and never once address the difference between Old and New Testaments on historical, theological, canonical, literary/genre, or specified audience/ecclesial grounds. The Bible would be one big book, whatever its differences, and the problems of talking about author or reader or text could go on in general terms without much regard for the divide separating two distinct literatures (Old Testament, or Tanak, and New Testament). And we could still plausibly argue that a hermeneutical crisis existed and buffeted the field, and not be wrong.

When we look at the discipline of formal biblical studies, however, from the mid-nineteenth century through to the postwar years, in British, North American, and Continental contexts, it would be difficult to speak of a hermeneutical crisis as we may now mean it, and yet crisis there was, and crises there have been. This *series* of crises focused not on general hermeneutics (text, reader, author, world) but on quite specific matters: the historicality of individual writings, literary methods and their compatibility, dating texts properly, social-historical reconstruction, the history of religion, and so forth. Always sitting close to these questions were serious subsidiary or even more up-front concerns. Is there a unity to Christian scripture? How is the Old Testament Christian scripture? In what way does the New Testament function as scripture, especially given its fourfold gospel record and what would come to be known as "quests of historical Jesus" behind this fourfold account?[3]

These questions—even when covered up with matters of historical and literary science so detailed as to numb the mind—persisted and were never competely banished from the field. It is proper, in my judgment, to call these theological and not just hermeneutical questions. They have to do with the way in which the testaments, each in its own specific historical and canonical way, bear witness to God. In the middle of the previous century and for many decades into our own, these questions did not just hover near the fray but were first-order questions demanding first-order answers if the discipline was to have any integrity as a historically oriented one still tuned to the life of the church and an earlier history of interpretation. What may have happened in recent years is that the central theological questions receded as the discipline, historically oriented as it has been, simply never ceased to find new historical questions to occupy itself with and chose to focus on them as though the theological matters would somehow fall into place when all was said and done.[4] Qumran and Nag Hammadi freshly enriched our historical options, and we should not have been surprised that yet another quest for "historical Jesus" would give New Testament scholars something to preoccupy themselves with, in line with previous inquiry.[5]

The turn to hermeneutics as a general discipline, then, has not so much offered a resolution of older theological questions, historically considered, as it has changed the subject. We may wish to judge that a good thing, but in so doing there would have to be an admission that what has counted in the history of biblical studies for the past century and a half as central was misguided from the start. The field posed the wrong questions, it would have to be concluded, and therefore got wrong answers and ended up in its present desuetude—call it a "hermeneutical crisis"—as a consequence. A cursory comparison with Westermann's *Essays on Old Testament Hermeneutics*,[6] produced at a period of general critical (methodological) consensus, shows an array of concerns untouched in recent hermeneutical discussions,[7] and any accounting of our present crisis is obliged to say why this is so.

A BRIEF WORD ABOUT MY CHAPTER'S TITLE

My title should reveal several things. First, my overview will be historical; that is, it will seek to examine biblical studies in the twentieth century to make general classifications as a new century (and millennium) approaches. Since the mid to late nineteenth century witnessed the battle over the "new science" of biblical criticism in intense form in the United Kingdom, the survey must begin there.

Second, my area of interest is what shall be called, with all appropriate overtones, "serious biblical interpretation." By this I do not mean hymnody, sermons, church trials over interpretation, or intramural denominational uses of scripture (lectionaries, Roman Catholic encyclicals, heresy trials at seminaries, the scriptural defense of gay Christianity, popular church journals and newspapers), even as I would argue these are in some ways more manifest markers of scripture's hold on our century than serious biblical interpretation. By serious biblical interpretation is meant academic formulations and debates about scripture. As we shall see, in the late nineteenth century, the integers Watson has named "text, church and world"[8] were still spinning on one axis, and academics had yet to discover they could carve out their own special domain of inquiry. This was by no means self-evident in the nineteenth century. Pusey's defense of Daniel's authorship engaged "text, church and world" with just as much seriousness as something later to be called specialized "academic discourse."

Third, "theological crisis" means those aspects of biblical studies manifestly connected to constructive and normative statements about God and the nature of God, whether Jewish or Christian in origin.

Finally, "scripture becomes religion or religions" refers to what I will argue is a disfigurement of scripture in the name of relating the testaments developmentally. This has been the hallmark of the twentieth-century "serious biblical interpretation." There is an emphasis on what I will call here testamentalism—that is, a decision that gradualness, process in religious growth and understanding, tradition-historical development, or some such historical index is central to comprehending the unity of Christian scripture in the light of an otherwise incontrovertible and manifest diversity. The present turn to general hermeneutics, to the degree that it seeks to work with scripture independently of testamentalism, ignores a very real problem that must be faced. Christian scripture is twofold in its very essence. This character cannot be undone, ignored, or historicized, for the twofoldness is part and parcel of serious theological convictions, convictions that Jews and Christians share but that also divide them. These divisions are not anthropological or religious alone but belong to the nature of the God confessed, as he is seen to be disclosed by scriptures, the first testament of which is shared by both groups.[9]

I will argue here that testamentalism is, in the nature of the thing, an interest in religion, even when that interest proceeds to inquire about normative God statements as central to what makes scripture unique and worthy of the denotation. Ironically, the twentieth century had already at its inception inherited a religious outlook, and for all the diversity of approaches that emerged over the next hundred years, it never really offered any genuine alternatives to the religious orientation of the mid to late nineteenth century. Several recent exceptions prove the rule.

For this reason our inquiry starts with the transition from Pusey to Gore. In my judgment, permutations in approach in the twentieth century still operate within the range established by the work of these two figures of the nineteenth century.

PUSEY

Childs remarks in his section on Daniel that S. R. Driver's commentary of 1900 "broke the back of the conservative opposition."[10] What is meant by this? At the threshold of the twentieth century, how was the back of opposition broken and what had it amounted to?

In his treatment of Daniel,[11] Pusey is clearly offended by four things in Daniel interpretation. One reads the polemic from Pusey today and cannot miss the seriousness of the scholarship deployed and the level of concern for proper interpretation. It is hard to imagine a debate comparable to it in the twentieth century for sheer comprehensiveness of concern.

Pusey is concerned about continental Daniel scholarship, and its British counterpart, to such an extent that Childs can accurately conclude, "Pusey was willing to rest the validity of the whole Christian faith upon the sixth-century dating of Daniel."[12] I am not interested here in the arguments for the sixth-century date of Daniel. I am interested in why Childs's characterization is accurate (which I believe it is).

The four areas of concern manifested in Pusey's writing on Daniel relate to (1) piety, or true, expressly Christian, believing; (2) a religious conception, involving prophecy and how it works; (3) the New Testament as interpreter of the Old; and (4) his appeal to what he calls "Our Lord." Pusey is concerned about text, church, and world. His interlocutors are not locked in one academic domain but are conceivably every interested person (this is clear in his footnotes and manner of citing opponents; the debate went on at this period in popular journals and newspaper articles).

Pusey's project is the opposite of what now counts for academic specialization, a fact made all the more ironic by the erudition and almost impenetrable rationalism he deployed. If one piece of argument cannot be integrated with another in a much larger universe of meaning, then the whole thing is foul. "Text" for Pusey is the Old and New Testaments of one Christian scripture. The nonspecialized comprehensiveness of his concern is most obvious in the rhetorical totalitarianism he works with. He speaks of the debate over the dating of Daniel in this way: "it admits of no half-measures. It is either Divine or an imposture. . . . The writer, were he not Daniel, must have lied on a most frightful scale." Here we see the absolutely moral nature of the debate, and we can say this without thereby declaring Pusey right or wrong. Nor was he an isolated figure who happened to have had a bad temper and a ready pen.

Theology, in this realm of Daniel disputation, involved matters in front of the text (piety leading to proper belief), a religious conception (prophets predict things miraculously), the interrelationship between texts (how the New Testament hears the Old, at once confirming and constraining its literal sense), and a specific doctrine of Christ (he tells the truth and is a privileged witness, not to God but to proper biblical interpretation for the church and world). Theology is not a doctrine about God as the Old Testament discloses this, in the primary sense, but a discipline arising from core, unimpeachable religious truths concerning prophecy, Jesus, the believing heart, and the New's hearing of the Old Testament as determinative and totalizing. In other words, Daniel's theological truth had to cohere with a wide range of religious concepts imported from the New Testament, or it failed as Christian scripture to be a reliable vehicle of God's truth. Pusey felt he was arguing in defense of the literal sense of Daniel, but there was much more on the table.

If any part of this bundle of religious convictions is disturbed, then a threat is felt for which there can be no remedy. Striking here is not so much whether Pusey's view could be sustained—Driver did indeed "break the back" of an opposition for which Pusey was representative, and the Maccabean dating of Daniel's later chapters was generally accepted in the twentieth century. Could a satisfactory position be set forth that adjusted Pusey's dating scheme without sacrificing his bundle of religious convictions? Pusey was facing a view of Daniel, in British and continental scholarship, without obvious precedent, and where precedent was available (Porphyry and eighteenth-century Deist revivals), it tended to manifest, to his mind, the same irreligion he credited to his nineteenth-century interlocutors.

It is not easy to shift this debate in the late nineteenth century into the realm of general hermeneutical crisis. All sorts of manifestly religious notions inhabit the debate. When Pusey speaks of unbelief and other matters of impiety in front of the text, he is not talking about options of a hermeneutics of either suspicion or assent (see Stuhlmacher and the popularizing of suspicion models).[13] When he speaks of "our Lord," we cannot properly imagine the aftershocks of Renan, with whom he is familiar, as these registered in waves of quests in the twentieth century, culminating in "the Jesus seminar." When he speaks about the New Testament's hearing of the Old, we cannot draw a straight line to the general concerns of hermeneutical appraisals of "text" by Wolterstorff or Vanhoozer. And yet we can sense that in this debate much more is at stake than dating Daniel. Christian faith, insofar as it is reliant on scripture's two-testament presentation, is under massive and unprecedented assault, and Pusey is standing on a fault line of enormous proportions.

GORE

I was struck by a remark made at the Theology Seminar at the University of St. Andrews, that for all of hindsight's classification of the Tractarians together with succeeding Anglo-Catholic generations, Pusey would have found unrecognizable (or offensive) Gore's "catholic" view of scripture.

It will be important to read Gore's views on scripture very closely. In him, we see emerging the lineaments of a position on scripture completely twentieth century. The transition from Pusey to Gore is, however, not surprising. Above all, it is Pusey's attachment of theology to general religious concepts, together with an incipient testamentalism, that paved the way for Gore's full accommodation of continental biblical scholarship, buttressed in his own inimitable way by appeals to the Fathers, church tradition, and Anglo-Catholicism's special mixture of piety, ritualism, and Hegelian idealism.

Gore's views on scripture are provided in his contributions to *Lux Mundi*, in prefaces and in his original essay on the Holy Spirit.[14] This alone is worthy of reflection; that is, *Lux Mundi* offers no independent essay on scripture. *Lux Mundi* purports to be a book about "the religion of the incarnation," and within such a universe, where religion is manifestly central, one cannot talk about Holy Scripture without beginning with general, anthropologically conceived notions of inspiration that will in turn, it follows, give rise to, or find formal expression within, scripture.

It is obvious that Gore's essay was one of the more—if not the most—controversial of the volume (he says so himself in subsequent prefaces), though it was not clear at this period that the culprit was the innocent sounding "religion of the incarnation" approach. Lindbeck's recent classifications (cognitive/propositional, experiential/expressive, linguistic)[15] would clearly find a "religion of the incarnation" approach located in the second category, and I suspect Gore would have inhabited that realm with pride. The category of experience, in this instance seen from the standpoint of certain theological convictions about the Holy Spirit, is what guides Gore's reflections on the Bible.[16] There is a measure of overlap, here, between Gore and Pusey. What counted for "unbelief," however, in Pusey has become much less sharply profiled in Gore's own expansive treatment. Indeed, Gore concludes the essay on a much more optimistic note, regarding the insights of the biblical criticism gaining such strength in his day. Yet even here, we find the same language as in Pusey, when Gore speaks of being able to distinguish between "what is reasonable and reverent, and what is high-handed and irreligious."

At the end of the day, however, Pusey's concern for comprehensiveness has been replaced by admission that "in all probability there will always remain more than one school of legitimate opinion on the subject" of inspiration and that it is better to speak of what can "without real loss be conceded," not what one might accept on the grounds of what he terms "irrationality." One should be able to see here the slippery slope of an appeal to experience (in this case, not within but in front of scripture), as words such as "irrational" are made to sit astride "reverent" with very little in the way of clarification as to when one is being one and not the other.

Testamentalism

For Pusey, the scriptures in their entirety required a consistent view of prophecy and miracle, on the one hand, and on the other, the record of the second testament was used as a guide to the proper interpretation of the first. What Jesus said about Daniel in the narratives of the New Testament was indispensable, indeed central, for how we were to read and interpret Daniel. The OT's per se voice had to be consistent with its voice in *novo receptum*.

This is the first place where the testamentalism of Gore differs from that of Pusey. In Gore's universe, the expectation of intertestamental congruence (even one where the New's hearing of the Old creates a potential imbalance) has been replaced with a decidedly Hegelian appeal to gradualness as the means to comprehend the scriptures' unity. In this universe, the OT has a per

se voice detachable from the NT, but it must be assessed within a larger developmental schema designed with criteria for what counts for a maximal convergence of spirit and reality. Gore uses this Hegelian dialectic and glosses it
with his understanding, not of spirit (*geist*) in general but of the Christian Holy
Spirit. The consequences for a unified Christian scripture are enormous.

After describing a split between spirit and flesh, faith and experience, and
yet the church's need "for unity in all things," Gore would need to account for
the fact that the Old Testament, in his words, "presented a most unspiritual
appearance." He therefore speaks of "the gradualness of the Spirit's method"
as the response given by "the Church" (he does not cite his sources here) to
the problem of Old Testament religion. The frankness of his assessment is
startling.

> It is of the essence of the New Testament, as the religion of the Incar-
> nation, to be final and catholic; on the other hand, it is of the essence
> of the Old Testament to be imperfect.[17]

Two things should be noted here. First, Gore collapses the entire New Testament into a category of religion, thereby making an enormous form-critical
assumption about the character of the New Testament as a canonical document. Second, insofar as it has a religion, it is a higher religion, "final and
catholic." Throughout the essay, Gore speaks of the "Jews" in the Old Testament and of the distinctiveness of their race. This anachronism is to be
explained as consistent with the Hegelianism of his schema, whereby one religion gives way to another, and the scriptures are records of religions differentiated by the testaments. (Compare the language in the title of the popular,
critical treatment of the day, "The Old Testament in the Jewish Church" by
W. Robertson Smith).

When, at another point, Gore ponders the special character of the religion
of the Old Testament Jews (*sic*), over against other races, he wants to emphasize that all peoples have their inspired thoughts and inspired individuals.
What is special about "the Jews" of the Old Testament is that "the inspiration
is both in itself more direct and more intense." The graded character of inspi-
raton fits nicely with the notion of a gradual movement from OT religion to
higher incarnation (NT) religion. Revelation comes in different grades and
intensities.

One potential problem in this schema is how to account for the movement
from NT religion to the church as a postbiblical reality. On the continent,
Hegelianism was given maximal freedom at this juncture. The NT scriptures
could not be conflated with a single religion, just as surely as the OT scriptures did not reflect one religion either. Many religions existed within the NT,

and some of these evolved in positive directions, so the theory held, and others less so. "Early Catholicism," for example, was seen as a retrograde development. Measured against Pauline Christianity, James was found wanting, for a whole host of reasons. This is too familiar territory to require comment.

Here, with hindsight, we can see that Gore was prepared to sacrifice the Old Testament as scripture on an altar of religious gradualness, because he thought the NT and creeds presented a firewall for Christian faith (his "Religion of the Incarnation"). He is adamant about this at one juncture. The New Testament and Old Testament represent not just different religions; they have completely different tolerances for the "idealizing element."

> . . . we may maintain with considerable assurance that there is nothing in the doctrine of inspiration to prevent our recognizing a considerable idealizing element in the Old Testament history. The reason is of course obvious enough why what can be admitted in the Old Testament, could not, without results disastrous to the Christian Creed, be admitted in the New.[18]

"Our Lord"

The ghost of Pusey rumbles at this point, because the New Testament is used, in the case of Daniel, as the chief defense of its miraculous nature. Did not Jesus accept Daniel in a way that criticism was calling into question? How could Gore avoid this problem, with his very different accounting of the unity of a two-testament scripture? Was not Jesus himself hopelessly tied up with this "religion of the Jews," even in a New Testament record Gore conflates with a "Religion of the Incarnation"? And in that record, according to Pusey, a Jesus appeared who stated that the scriptures of Israel had such and such an authority, not limited to a lower religion evolving into a higher one. In short, Pusey was well aware that Jesus functioned with a distinction between scripture ("it is written") and "religion" and that in many ways it is this distinction that lies at the heart of Christian theology (whose creeds speak of a death and raising in accordance with scriptural claims—namely, the OT as divine word of figural truth, not a "lower religion" or one with "more direct or intense" racial inspiration than another). The relationship between the testaments would have to be comprehended on terms other than revelatory intensity or grades of religion, or one would run up against the second testament's differentiation of Jewish religion(s) and the word of the Old Testament as divine word.

Gore's response at this point is breathtaking. He wishes to see maximal, if reverent, use of critical tools to reconstruct the religion of the Jews, en route to the higher religion of the New Testament. A commitment to gradualism will mean far greater tolerance for the Old Testament being recast into this or that critical reconstruction, because the New Testament neither requires or anticipates such a handling.

Yet with such a high view of the New Testament and of what both he and Pusey called "our Lord," why was the true picture of Israel's religion, emerging into the light of day as a consequence of nineteenth-century labors, not capable of integration with what "our Lord" actually said about the scriptures he inherited?

Religious Conception

The answer is to be found in a competing religious conception, which ranks higher for Gore than Pusey's conception of prophecy in his handling of Daniel and "Our Lord."

The problem is obvious. If the religion of the incarnation is higher than its precedent "idealization" and yet the Incarnate One used the scriptures of Israel as an authority over against his (Jewish and Gentile) culture, and in that use he was obviously departing quite radically from the critical theory of the day accepted by Gore, what would prevent one from charging Gore with massive inconsistency? Should not a "final and catholic" higher religion centered on incarnation not be prepared to let Jesus lead the way in the handling of scripture? Or has some sort of *sachkritik* entered through Gore's otherwise solid NT and credal firewall?

The answer Gore gives is predictable even as it is curious, given the more radical historicism of continental NT scholarship. It belongs to the fact of kenosis, of the human limitations taken on by "our Lord," that he would not reproduce the findings of the Old Testament science of his (Gore's) day.

"Thus the utterances of Christ about the Old Testament do not seem to be nearly so definite or clear enough to allow our supposing that in this case he is departing from the general method of the incarnation, by bringing to bear the unveiled omniscience of the Godhead, to anticipate or foreclose a development of natural knowledge."[19]

It appears, therefore, that Gore is combining a certain historicism deeply indebted to Hegel's idealism, on the one hand, with larger credal convictions he accepts as unimpeachable, on the other. But can these two distinctly different realms of operation be combined? What is demanded, as we saw previously, is congruence between the NT and the creeds, on historical grounds, and that is the last thing that most historians of the day were willing to concede. Indeed, Gore does not establish this in his argument; rather, he demands that such and such congruence be in place, for functional reasons. It is a "fact of supreme importance," he opines, that there be "none of the ambiguity or remoteness which belongs to much of [how much of?] the record of the preparation," or else there would be "results disastrous to the Christian Creed."[20] True enough, perhaps, but lacking Gore's appeal to early catholicism, one would see the matter quite differently, and did.

Summary

What is refreshing in examining these figures of the nineteenth century is how directly and clearly they treat matters central to the use of scripture in the church and world. There is a concern for both testaments (not one apart from the other in areas of historical specialization). There is a concern for some accounting of the two testaments in one scripture. There is concern for emerging catholic Christianity. We have yet to see any balkanization of the discipline.

The other thing that is striking is how very few of these issues were resolved in the twentieth century on the strength of better or harder historical-critical labor. There is a degree of persistence in the questions faced by Gore and Pusey. This reality may have been ignored or considered resolved, but most treatments of biblical hermeneutics in the years that followed demonstrated the resilience and persistence of the four areas of concern in Pusey. This makes it now relatively easy to classify major movements in biblical theology and hermeneutics in the twentieth century.

ESSAYS CATHOLIC AND CRITICAL

Selwyn's 1926 collection establishes the final liberation of Anglican Catholicism from Pusey and his scriptural assumptions.[21] The four concerns of Pusey—piety, the OT in *novo receptum*, appeal to "our Lord," and prophecy as religious wonder—were transformed under the hand of Gore, leaving the next generation the simpler task of restating, reframing, and consolidating.

On the continent, the connection between scripture as "historical science," hermeneutics, and theology remained under pressure of clear coordination, in a way that ceased to prove so pressing for Anglo-Catholics. It is not clear whether what presented itself as confidence in historical-critical efforts was in reality that or was merely an excuse to leave its subtle or more entrenched problems to the side in a convenient division of labor. The "infallibility" of scripture is dismissed in a paragraph as "untenable" because of "the scientific development of the last century"[22] and now there is full acceptance that "competent scholars" will never "reach absolute unanimity as to the various problems which the scriptures present" because it belongs to "scientific thought that it should always contemplate the possibility of further progress."[23] It is as though a new office has emerged to replace the caricatured papal claims or the unscientific confessionalism of Protestants: Christian scholars making progress at something. At the same time as patristic figuration of the sort practiced, presumably, by an Origen merits the description, "allegorical interpretations of a rather desparate character," confessional statements "can only be regarded as the clear teaching of Scripture if it is admitted that the orthodox Catholic interpretation of the Scriptures on these matters in the first four centuries was in fact the correct one."[24] Obviously, the appeal to the Fathers over against Rome would have to be selective, and Origen's allegories did not measure up to what was needful in the light of biblical science.

The effort to coordinate historical-critical progress with appeal to the Fathers, against both Roman Catholic claims and Protestant confessionalism, reaches its zenith in *Essays Catholic and Critical*. We are told that authority must be verifiable, never mechanical or merely external, and the term "oracular" is used to characterize both the claims of the Roman church and a doctrine of scripture likely to have caught Pusey in its grasp. Instead, "the final appeal is to the spiritual, intellectual and historical content of divine revelation, *as verifiable at the three-fold bar of history, reason and spiritual experience*"—the sort of bold abstraction that is never clarified, except insofar as historical-critical methods, in the hands of progressing competent scholars, are somewhere out there generating this.

WALTER EICHRODT

Eichrodt was able to work at the history-of-religions questions posed by criticism on the basis of more thorough comparative resources, subtler literary methodology, and simply more time to reflect on the traditional problems of scripture's unified authority in the light of "the new science."

At the level of comparative work, he accepted the sort of notion posited by Gore, of something "more direct and more intense" going on within Israel of old, and then refined this considerably.[25] Israel, it was argued, was truly in possession of a unique perspective in the realm of "religion," over against its ancient Near Eastern neighbors, and this finding at once enhanced the authority of the Old Testament for Christians and made it far easier to reconsider something like continuity across the two testaments, linking them at the level of a shared "higher religion" (to use the language of *Lux Mundi* and *Essays Catholic and Critical*).

Central to Eichrodt's understanding was the concept of covenant. Covenant was the datum establishing continuity between Old and New Testaments. But what covenant meant for Eichrodt was not chiefly to be located in the final literary presentation of the Old Testament, where from creation to Noah to

Abraham to Moses to David to Zion, and back to creation again (Isaiah 66), it (covenant) was indeed famously crucial—a cruciality also registered without further ado in the literal sense of the New Testament. Rather, covenant was central insofar as Eichrodt was competent to establish this as a historical reality in Israel, early on, and vis-à-vis other historically verifiable religions and cultures in the ancient Near East. This left the way open for other scholars to challenge the theological centrality of covenant as historically untenable, and such was the challenge that emerged (Perlitt's demolition).[26] The debate between Eissfeldt[27] and Eichrodt over an independent biblical theology was in large measure a debate over history-of-religions methods propping up theological realities or aspirations of literary coherence in scripture's full form. Bultmann's later challenge to Israel's "sacred history" was only a mopping-up effort, seen from this perspective, though a particularly effective one, it must be conceded, because of his rhetorical skills (Socrates drank the hemlock in the same way as Israel's deliverance could be said to be, without further ado, *pro nobis*).[28]

GERHARD VON RAD

The attack on "sacred history" from Bultmann also had another front toward which its salvos were directed. This was the tradition-history approach of Gerhard von Rad. Von Rad explicitly rejected an approach based upon "religion"—of either the "thick" Eichrodt or the "thin" Anglo-Catholic versions. Instead, he sought to isolate "Israel's own explicit statements" about Yahweh (*sic*) by using a very sophisticated combination of literary and form criticism.[29]

What Israel said about YHWH was not self-evident, in terms of the canonical presentation, but would have to be reconstructed with historical tools. Only in this way could one successfully plot the theological movement that governed Israel's history as a people and that in turn gave rise to its literary legacy in the Old Testament. At no point could it be said that the final literary form was itself a setting-in-order of a previous history of tradition, thus making a qualitative distinction operative between tradition-history and scripture, as a literary reality of theological integrity in its final form. Von Rad knew there was something called a combination of P and J in Genesis, but this combination was not amenable to the same sort of theological reading as P and J themselves.[30] For tradition-history to make complete sense, there was a need for the traditions to remain aloof from any literary stabilization in the final form— or, better, any stabilization with separate theological integrity. The reason for this is complex. On the one hand, there was the actual legacy of historical-criticism that von Rad sought to honor, and whose inner tensions he sought to resolve (see now Rendtorff's challenge to von Rad and Noth's combination of source and form criticism).[31] On the other hand, tradition-history appeared to represent for von Rad a respecter of historical Israel, unsullied by Christian *nach*-interpretation.

What this required for von Rad, however, was some sense that the typological potential of traditions was actively moving toward a denouement in the New Testament that did not dishonor his historical "Israel making explicit statements about YHWH." Ironically, this required him to believe that tradition-history manifestly misdrew historical data in the name of *credenda* (Gore's idealizing element) so that an eschatological reality yet to unfold came into play. To my mind, what this meant was that historical Israel was separated, not from a critically reconstructed tradition-history of manifest misdrawing, but from the final form of its scriptures as theologically relevant. In so doing, he built a bridge of tradition from Old to New Testament that could then not account for the New Testament's own specific hearing of the Old in its final form. In the name of tradition-historical richness, and in the name of respecting "historical Israel," we got a theology neither the New Testament nor Judaism of the day recognized as "it is written."

FROM TRADITION-HISTORY TO UNRULY TRADITIONS: WALTER BRUEGGEMANN

In his chapter on authority for *Essays Catholic and Critical*, W. Knox referred to the collapse of confidence in the Bible as a "verbally inspired book, to which we can appeal with absolute certainty for infallible guidance in all matters of faith and conduct"—a bloated claim whose only point was to set up the higher-critical vis-à-vis. This consisted of determining "the exact meaning of its various parts and the authority which they can claim," a task to "be discussed by competent scholars," whose results would always be provisional, progress being what it is.[32]

Reference to "various parts" and their exact meanings was, in the decades to follow, to be given a highly theological profile in the tradition-historical, typological method of von Rad.

Walter Brueggemann, together with H. W. Wolff, popularized this tradition-historical approach in *The Vitality of Old Testament Traditions*.[33] The point of the book was to give an equally sharp and equally theological-homiletical reading of discrete sources, isolated from their narrative location and arrangement in the final form of the Old Testament and kept strictly separate from one another.

Here we may see the instincts that have recently come to full flower in Brueggemann's effort at theology. Shorn of their historicality, on the one hand,

and their capacity for being ranged on a typological trajectory, on the other, traditions in their diversity and in their contradictory manifestation have become the testimony to the unruliness of Israel's God. God has no longer any ontological status, in Brueggemann's estimate, but exists (as it were) strictly in Israel's rhetoric about God, which has likewise refused any effort from within to coordination or coherence; if any is found, it is put there by hegemonic interpreters (excepting, it is supposed, Brueggeman). If ontology and transcendence always mean for Brueggemann tidiness and power or control (there is no engagement with the history of interpretation on this matter, e.g., in the Eastern Church, where high doctrines of "procession" in the Godhead existed, but only sweeping and vast categorizing), then their decided absence from the field of the text is in proportion to God's strangeness and unpredictability. Methodological impasse, crisis, and disorder have become in Brueggemann's hands first-order theology. God is as messy and unpredictable as the methodologies of the now not-so-new biblical science.

HERMENEUTICS IN THE LION'S DEN: PUSEY REVISITED

It has been the argument of this paper that the mid-nineteenth-century debates give us a glimpse at a comprehensive biblical hermeneutic on the verge of collapse. Matters in front of the text (belief—but not a nineteenth-century version of "hermeneutics of assent"), in the text (the NT's hearing of the OT), in religious conceptuality (prophecy as miracle), and in the text's central subject matter (Jesus Christ as interpreter) all cooperated to produce this comprehensiveness, or the illusion of it, conjured up in the face of attacks without obvious precedent.

These "attacks" were coming from the new science of biblical criticism. The fragility of the comprehensive universe was likely the consequence of its genuine newness in the history of the church's handling of scripture, but Pusey could not have known that. Indeed, his comprehensive picture was closer to the traditional handling of scripture prior to the rise of historical science than the challenger was. Here, with hindsight, Pusey was right to defend his view against the new knowledge and especially against notions of progress inhabiting these. When Gore speaks of the advance of "natural knowledge" that "Our Lord" did not foreclose on, by revealing his (Jesus') awareness of J, E, D, P or the Maccabean date of Daniel 7–12, one is right to wonder what sort of theological defense of the advance of natural knowledge he could genuinely muster. Under what sort of explicit theological license were we to believe that the new science was gaining its proper place in Christian discourse? What is the "advance of natural knowledge" Jesus did not wish to foreclose on, specifically and theologically defended? To state it differently, what was required was a robust theology of reason, not one brought over from the earlier nineteenth and eighteenth centuries. Could theological accounts of "reason" keep apace with those mustered for "criticism"?

In traditional interpretation, concerns Pusey raised in his defense of Daniel were not handled in the same way, of course. Figuration and allegory stood ready to assure that the two testaments of Christian scripture could have something like a unified voice, and yet they did not engage the same forms of rationalism required for defense of the Bible's historicality evidenced in *Daniel the Prophet*. In part, this is because they understood, or were in a position to understand, prophecy differently than Pusey, as well as the relationship of the testaments. It cannot be gainsaid that rules of charity and truth had always been around and had often provided the main reason that scripture's "literal sense" was not perceived or obeyed by an interpreter lacking them; that is, Pusey was right to see that something was wrong about the attitude of the interpreter in the mode of the new science. He was wrong, however, in my judgment, to believe that this was the chief problem.

The Virtuous Reader

This locus is making a comeback in recent days. A prime example is Stephen Fowl's *Engaging Scripture*.[34] Hauerwas, Yoder, and others have flirted with this "in front of the text" solution to the problem of scripture at our end-of-the-millennium period. Less clear is whether MacIntyre and Milbank can be affiliated with this locus as well, with their call for conventicles of commensurable presuppositions.

I suspect that the initial reaction to the preface of Pusey, in our times, would be that it is too, well, moralistic or religious. We hear of "a tide of skepticism," which quickly becomes "the unbelieving school," "criticism . . . subservient to unbelief," "avowedly infidel," "the unbelieving critics," and so forth. "Disbelief had been the parent, not the offspring of their criticism; their starting point, not the winning-post of their course." "Their teaching was said to be 'bold.' Too 'bold' alas! it was toward Almighty God." The examples are too many to list.

I would venture that the problem was not just lack of piety or reverence (Gore's later adaptation), but in some cases a thorough misunderstanding of the theological motivations of much continental biblical criticism afflicted English churchmen-theologians. Much nineteenth-century biblical criticism was not an adventure in impiety but turned on assumptions about the nature of revelation and its (tenuous) relationship to the canon (as a literarily shaped and coherent theological product). Wellhausen actually believed that his reconstruction of Israel's religion was necessary if one was to get at the true state of affairs. To be sure, at moments he spoke of manifest manipulation of the truth in the canon's presentation, but at other places he worked with almost religious awe (e.g., the wonders of Yahwism in the early period). The Bible's final literary form demanded an accounting such as Wellhausen and others were attempting, in their view, because its presentation was constrained by religious forces that obscured matters and that prevented more obvious, historically tuned movement from OT to NT.

But the more serious problem with this tack can be seen in Gore's accommodation article and in *Essays Catholic and Critical*. Simply define belief in a new way, and Pusey is reduced to being a crank. Suddenly, his moral outrage looks like intemperate ranting, and he is closed off from any ongoing discussion.

The problem with the virtuous reader approach can be seen in part in MacIntyre's "whose justice, which rationality" exposé.[35] Once scripture's literal sense is open to deconstruction and reconstruction, on such a massive scale, using historical tools, it is no longer obvious what moral outrage might mean. By the time of *Essays Catholic and Critical*, what was immoral was impeding human progress. One searches in vain in Stephen Fowl's recent work for any comprehensive, public, agreed-upon statement of what actually counts for virtue, such that we could see it and believe it was under God's providential care as it went about the business of "engaging scripture."

"Our Lord"

Gore's solution to this problem of using Jesus as a model for modern biblical interpretation is classic. Jesus cannot be expected to conform to the universe in which modern historical questions are posed. He lived with the conventions of his day.

This is true enough, of course, but what, in fact, are our options here? Gore makes it sound as if we have two. Jesus lives within the constraints of his time and therefore cannot be used to disqualify critical findings. There is the Jesus of his day and there are the findings of scholars working on the OT, of which he knows nothing. Let both go their own way.

To say this is, however, to leave unanswered just what purpose Jesus' use of scripture had for his own time. Gore relieves modern scholarship of having to answer this question, in the name of honoring critical findings that are manifestly not on the horizon for Jesus. But what *is* on the horizon for a Jesus using scripture in the New Testament portrayal? Surely it matters in a "higher religion" what use is made by its incarnate Lord of Israel's scriptures—not to give ground for criticism but, more positively, as expressive of assumptions Jesus may have had about scripture's capacity to render God and God's Word. This is a bottom-line theological concern, and if it cannot be coordinated in some meaningful way with newer critical findings, then a problem exists that cannot be ignored with appeals to kenotic accommodation or credal truth.

Pusey saw what was at stake, I believe, in divorcing Jesus from any positive, theologically constructive account of Israel's scriptures as the Word of God and not just as an evolving lower religion. The problem was that this involved for Pusey a hermeneutical gamble over conceptions about prophecy and the proper relationship between the testaments: "such definite prophecy as the minuter prophecies in Daniel, the foreground of more distant and larger prophecy, is in harmony with the whole system of prophecy, as well in the Old Testament as in the prophecies of our Lord."[36] As he himself put it, "Men, then, had no choice between believing all and disbelieving all."[37] Well, Gore gave them another choice, but in so doing he dismissed as essential an account of the theological force of the Old Testament, not just on "our Lord" but on the church catholic. By the time of *Essays Catholic and Critical*, no one even felt the loss anymore, as scripture became religions and religiosity, and church theologians could annex the field of critical biblical scholarship and wait as it produced its findings and made its progress.

DANIEL REVISITED:
THE FRESH APPROACH OF B. S. CHILDS

Childs conceded that with S. R. Driver's 1900 commentary, Daniel scholarship slipped out of Pusey's range of fire. Yet Childs did not offer one more historically sophisticated interpretation himself. It is hard to know what Pusey would have made of it. If Pusey would not have recognized Gore's use of scripture, it does not necessarily follow that Childs's effort would similarly disappoint him. This is not for reasons of proper piety, though many have seen an introduction to the Old Testament "as scripture" defined in such a way.[38] Rather, Childs produced readings of Daniel and other books that once again fit into a comprehensive view of scripture and Christian theology but did not do so on terms Pusey had felt were necessary, indeed obligatory.[39]

Childs asked an important question. He did not ask whether the final chapters belong to the Maccabean period. They manifestly did. Rather, he asked how was a subsequent reader, later than the Maccabean details to which the book had been so acutely attached by criticism, meant to hear Daniel's ongoing word? This small shift amounted to raising a question not about religion but about scripture, and at once a connection to a *Wirkungsgeschichte* that included the New Testament and "our Lord" opened up. In other words, a

Book of Daniel manifestly outfitted with Maccabean-era dress could still be a fraud but on different grounds: the grounds of false prophecy, or non-prophecy. Why did Daniel's pseudepigraphic additions not prove accurate? Or, even if partly fulfilled, was the book now just a tribute to something that happened (at least partially) in the past, and in that sense was not prophecy in the proper sense at all, its eschatological character having been voided through historicizing? Childs was asking a question about how Daniel continued to function as a vehicle of God's Word. Ironically, historical labors had given greater and greater focus to referentiality but stopped short of asking another historical question, tied to the history of reception. That stopping short was not accidental but was the logical consequence of locking a book into a historical setting and letting it describe only a moment in religious history now past.

Childs's appeal to "scripture" in some sense opened the way for a different understanding of prophecy, in larger terms. Prophecy had in "the new science" become speech to contemporaries (forthtelling). Predictions, where they did appear, became prophecies after the event, and they belonged, in terms of composition, to the periods in which their message was hoped for or deemed about to be fulfilled. Much nuance was required to keep this distinction fluid (and one need only look at Isaiah scholarship for the bulk of this century to see how complicated the nuancing became). Forthtelling was settled into one phase of religious or tradition-history, and the foretelling *vaticina ex eventu* found a (later) home in the same trajectory. Daniel took it hard because in its case the book was chopped into two with almost no way to link the halves— no matter that Daniel was not even prophecy in any typical sense and, indeed, was regarded by von Rad as wisdom and by the traditional Hebrew division as one of the Writings.

So long as the biblical books were divided up along lines like this and fitted into a general religious history, leaning toward, corrected by, aborted into the religion of the New Testament, the expectation disappeared that such books could actually function as scripture in their own literary presentation.

Childs succeeded in connecting the two halves of Daniel by deploying a midrashic approach. Later chapters were serial efforts to hear earlier parts of the book, especially chapter 2. Though Daniel appeared as a figure in these later chapters, as he had in the first chapters, what was at issue was God's prior word pressing for fulfillment, beyond the moment of its original utterance or seeming reception, and this high view of God's word did not require anything more than obedience to it—even when it seemed, for it could only seem, to remain unfulfilled. Having joined the two halves of the book, not on a prophecy-fulfillment model overly constrained by historicism but by attention to the dynamic of God's accomplishing word, the way was also open to continue to see Daniel as scripture beyond the timetables at the end of the book and long after the details of Maccabean persecution were past and gone.

Too much attention to locating Daniel in distant phases of a religious history, as well as the defense of locating him in exile as a predictor of major divine endowment (Pusey), meant that Daniel as scripture forfeited its capacity to declare God's word, from within but also without the circumstances of its composition—as understood by critical theory or a defense prophecy as miracle.

CONCLUSION: "TOO 'BOLD' ALAS! IT WAS TOWARD ALMIGHTY GOD"

Figural interpretation has assumed there is a surplus of intended meaning in every divine revelation. This assumption has a basic theological grounding, involving a doctrine of providence and sovereignty. God remains custodian of the word he speaks and can by the Holy Spirit effect things through a word delivered once upon a time, heeded or unheeded, at yet a later time. When Christians confess God raised Jesus from the dead "in accordance with the scriptures," they do not mean that Isaiah predicted the empty tomb but rather that God's word to Israel was figured in such a way as to accord with God's wrath and raising vis-à-vis his son.

Where Pusey was right to take umbrage involved not so much the emergence of a competing religious system, over against the one into which he had fitted Daniel and assumed had all likewise before him.

Pusey believed that the dissection of Daniel into two halves made Daniel a fraud and a liar, but he also felt—more intuitively—that something was being said about God himself that was wrong. One would search in vain for a distinct or sustained articulation of this concern. My view is that this has to do with a peculiarly Christian attitude, the consequence of Christian possession of a two-testament canon in which claims about Jesus and "final religion" would appear to tolerate any loose or confused or domesticating handling of the oracles of God entrusted to the Jews—that is, the Old Testament. In the preface to his lectures on Daniel, we see for the last time, I suspect, in Anglicanism a sincere concern that critical method, as a method of constructing religions, is somehow (it is not entirely clear in Pusey) an attack on the One who raised Jesus from the dead and who gave to him his own name, the name above every name (YHWH). This is not an attack on an evolving religion, which Gore's Hegelianism could tolerate better than Pusey's piety. It was an attack on the capacity of the Old Testament to render God and his word as normative for Christian believing.

When Reventlow can classify Miskotte and van Ruler in a separate category in his bibliographic survey of biblical theology and label it "The Superiority of the Old Testament,"[40] we should see how far the criticism Pusey worried about had advanced. "Superiority of the Old Testament" is of course nothing of the kind for these two Christian interpreters. Rather, both acknowledge in a way never fully lost in Dutch scholarship (see, e.g., Vriezen)[41] that the Old Testament is a theological book in the most basic sense of the word; that is, it speaks of God as God is and does this through its own literary form, without the necessity of the construction of religious history. Such a history was meant to connect the testaments in some way, but ironically it produced an Old Testament nowhere heard in the New, with a Hebrew G/god en route to finalization or correction in New Testament religion.

But the New Testament is clear even when New Testament and Old Testament scholars are not. "If they do not believe Moses and the Prophets, they will not be convinced if someone were raised from the dead." That is a statement of fact having to do with Christian theological convictions about a two-testament scripture and its capacity—indeed, design—for identifying God and allowing him to speak for himself. The Bible has been "figured out" in the last centuries, and there can be little wonder we have a crisis in hermeneutics. The crisis in hermeneutics is in reality a crisis involving God's providence, a proper ecclesiology and doctrine of the Holy Spirit.[42]

3

Two Testaments and the Failure
of One Tradition-History

INTRODUCTION

In an essay prepared for a volume on biblical theology,[1] I examined the tradition-historical method of Gerhard von Rad, especially his attempt to extend this modern approach into the realm of typological exegesis and biblical theology. I argued that von Rad's approach was flawed. Three matters seemed insufficiently addressed:

1. First, in what sense could his approach depend upon the historicality that it was the purpose of modern critical approaches to commend, when the traditioning process he was identifying and valorizing as theologically significant was manifestly misdrawing the historical legacy bequeathed to it? In the name of extruding what von Rad called the *doxa* of the tradition's sense of the events, the events were "manifestly misdrawn." The historical fundament was what von Rad sought to uncover under the rubric of "Israel's own statements about YHWH" as that which constituted the crude matter, or "basic stuff," of a genuinely theological inquiry into Israel's testimony in the Old Testament. And yet the traditioning process both carried forward and vetoed this historical legacy at the same time.[2]

2. Second, had von Rad not isolated a tradition-history or streams of tradition that, in the nature of the thing, were to be differentiated from the final form of the theological witness of the canon, and that existed in forms nowhere on offer for a New Testament reflection said to be about the business of continuing the OT's tradition process? Does the NT kerygma find its orientation vis-à-vis tradition-history (say, in its most contemporaneous phase) or vis-à-vis a stable textualized scripture? To put it another way, if the tradition-history of the Old Testament identified by von Rad ran so straightforwardly into the New Testament kerygma, with which it was to be likened in an evolutionary process model, why were

there two testaments at all, and not a continuous tradition-history in literary form, with a certain theological self-evidence to be acknowledged
by all, concerning its necessary direction toward Christian confession?

3. Third, was the restlessness of the traditioning process not a Christian
back-projection? After all, certain obvious arrangements of the literature
of the canon pointed not to a driving forward of restless traditions but to
an opposite tendency: the establishment of the past (especially Sinai) as
foundational and stable and constitutive. One thinks above all of the relationship between Law and Prophets as the major theological categories
of the present Tanak. The Torah is not seeking some fulfillment beyond
itself. If anything, it contains its own seconding and dynamic voice, in the
Book of Deuteronomy, and this witness looks backward and forward at
once, with no restlessness or eschatological pressure for completion by
later traditions.

Von Rad's approach to theologizing a reconstructed tradition-history belongs,
of course, within its own tradition-history of twentieth-century biblical scholarship. In this chapter, I want to examine the tradition-historical efforts to do
biblical theology represented by Hartmut Gese and Peter Stuhlmacher, as they
pick up where von Rad left off.[3] They have put their own special signatures on
the methodology of tradition-history and biblical theology. The indebtedness
of Stuhlmacher to von Rad is made especially clear in his recent volume 2.[4]

The second part of this chapter examines the problem of introducing a concept like tradition-history to link the testaments, theologically, when, on material grounds, the New Testament does not relate itself to "traditions" but to a
stable canon. My objection to von Rad's approach was largely substantive in
character (having to do with the relationship between history, tradition, and
the final form of the canonical OT witness). My analysis of Gese and
Stuhlmacher focuses more on material objections, stemming from their attenuated conception of the Old Testament canon (a conception not shared by von
Rad). Especially in Stuhlmacher's 1975 study, one gets the sense that critical
study of the Bible is inaugurated and finds its essential endorsement in the
New Testament itself, with its critical handling of the Old Testament traditions. I argue in this chapter that Stuhlmacher has confused the way the Old
Testament functions authoritatively in the formation of the New Testament
and that this confusion is based in part on a faulty understanding of the material form of the canon. The consequence of this confusion is that modern critical approaches to the Bible at large are conflated with very different
approaches, involving the appropriation of the Old Testament as canonical
scripture in the New Testament.

The third section of this chapter puts forth an alternative understanding of
the authority of the scriptures of Israel, as Christian scripture, both within the
New Testament itself and then in subsequent postscriptural use. I hope that

an alternative model to the tradition-historical emerges that better reflects the actual state of affairs in the earliest Christian usage and that can be safely differentiated from virtually all modern critical treatments, even those that claim to be an improvement because of a special piety (hermeneutics of consent) or a special deployment of so-called Reformation principles (justification by faith and the like).[5]

TRADITION-HISTORY: HARTMUT GESE'S APPROACH

"Revelation comes in the form of truth experienced in Israel's life processes" ("Tradition," 310). By this, Gese means approximately what von Rad meant when he sought to isolate "Israel's own explicit assertions about Jahweh." The final literary form of biblical books, the internal canonical arrangements and ordering of diverse traditions into a final literary statement, or similar arrangements of books and larger divisions in the canon are essentially meaningless, theologically. Gese speaks of the "lived life" of Israel's tradition process as "immeasurably diverse and even seemingly contradictory" (310). The end form of the biblical text is without meaning on a tradition-historical understanding, except as an organic, vibrant depository of diverse and "even contradictory" traditions once the process stopped—which, in fact, it did not do because traditioning cannot stop; traditions continue to "speak over the head" of any final literary statement. What is important is, therefore, the beginning of the process and the process itself, this latter emphasis being what differentiates a mature tradition-historical approach from nineteenth-century historicism. "The biblical text thus begins in the life process of Israel. And only the tradition-historical approach can constitute the method for tracing this dimension of a text back into the lived life of Israel."[6] The proximity to the concerns of von Rad should be obvious here.

Why does traditioning take place at all? Because past statements are meant to be seen, retrospectively, as providing a "point of orientation for present-understanding" (312). Here we have the dynamic dimension of von Rad and the priority of the process over the original credenda as static and authoritative, because self-understanding is always in flux. The "actualization of the text . . . opens it up to a totally new theological perception" (313). The earlier statements have not been suppressed, of course, or else we would struggle to valorize the modifications and transformations and contradictory adaptations of them, not knowing the earlier traditions against which they speak. No, according to tradition-history, the entire history of development is there, and what it bears witness to is endless pressure to change and adapt.

Of course, it is an empirical fact that the Old Testament is more than growing traditions and endless refabrication, or else it would forever resist literary
fixation in deference to movement and change and life processes. We would
have no container holding the diversity we seek to valorize, with a fixed form
and a delimited scope, if diversity and growth were ends unto themselves.

It is at this point critical to emphasize the *necessary* direction Gese's
approach will take in respect to the canon. After he sets out his tradition-
historical conception and traces the processes of growth and adaptation, he
concludes with a discussion of the canon. One could well ask, Why is there
any final, stable form to the Old Testament? Why indeed can we speak of a
threefold (or fourfold) canon of the Old Testament literature in the basic
sense of the word, if it bears witness to an ongoing process of tradition extend-
ing into the New Testament without interruption? The answer Gese gives is
that there is no such stable form. The canon is open. The end is not closed.
The New Testament relates to traditions in motion, not to a closed canonical literature with a given form. There is no given form that "speaks over
the head" of intertestamental traditions, and so there is also no given form
within the Law and Prophets that "speaks over the head" of a reconstructed
tradition-history of "explicit statements about YHWH" extracted from the
canon's form.

It should be emphasized that the movement to a discussion of the canon is
critical to Gese's treatment in a way that goes beyond von Rad's approach.
(Stuhlmacher quotes Trebolle Barrera in defense of von Rad vis-à-vis Childs,
but it is genuinely unclear to me if von Rad would have lined up with Childs
on the question of the material form of the canon or with Trebolle Barrera; it
is striking that von Rad's tradition-historical method did not depend on a wider
or open canon for its logic in coordination with the New Testament kerygma).[7]
Gese asserts that the New Testament is "familiar only with the law and the
prophets" (321) as canonical literature, "a third part of the canon was in the
process of being formed in the period of the New Testament," (321) and
"without Sir. 24 logos-Christology is cut off from older wisdom theology"
(325). This is because for Gese, "we can really speak of only one single tradition process at the end and goal of which the New Testament appears"
(322). To state it differently, for Gese, the New Testament ushers in a critical
period when the limits of the Old Testament canon are under negotiation. As
such, one could not speak about a stable scripture speaking a word over the
tradition-process, not even in the case of parts one and two (Law and
Prophets).[8] Christian tradition handles the traditions of the Old Testament in
a critical manner, and the "open canon" is the warrant for its approach to the
evaluation of scripture's word. So, it is appropriate to adapt our title in radical

ways if we wish to appreciate Gese's approach: "one tradition history and the failure of two testaments."

In Stuhlmacher's 1975 treatment, this larger picture of Gese (and, less so, von Rad) appears to be in place without comment. "In the same measure as Jesus' appearances and behavior were violently disputed in his lifetime," Stuhlmacher writes, "he unfailingly leads his disciples into a process of critical scripture exposition" (23). The "beginning of critical exposition," Stuhlmacher states, has to do with the existence of an Old Testament needing to be sorted out and critically evaluated. Far from speaking a direct word as Christian scripture, through its per se voice, we must look to Jesus and the New Testament for interpretative moves over against the inherited traditions that "in essence determine the origin, formulation, and unfolding of the gospel of Jesus as the Christ of God" (22). Stuhlmacher points to the antitheses of the Sermon on the Mount as evidence of Jesus as "Messianic interpreter" and in this critical mode a harbinger of "a process of critical scripture exposition . . . which has not ceased to this day and may not be interrupted as long as the churches are oriented to scripture so as to preserve their identity" (23). This identity-preserving function of scripture is congruent with Gese's tradition-historical conceptuality but in Stuhlmacher finds further support in what he calls the "Protestant principle." Quoting Käsemann, "Historical criticism promises and guarantees proximity to reality" and "theologically, the right of historical criticism lies in its breaking through the Docetism which dominates the community" (64). This use of the term Docetism is a bold transfer of a conceptuality regarding the earthly and human character of Jesus, over against claims for his divinity, into the realm of historical research and claims for positivity in a history made proximate by a method that gets below the traditions to "reality."[9]

This chapter's purpose is not to analyze the appeal to a "Protestant principle," either along the lines of Käsemann or of the "justification by faith" rationality of Bultmann or Ebeling, except to say that, its rhetorical force notwithstanding, the imprecision regarding Docetism is telling. This begs the question, for example, of whether appeal to the canonical portrait of Jesus is any more or less an appeal to "reality" than a historically recovered "real Jesus." It is by no means clear how historical-critical retrieval of "reality" or of traditions brokering such a reality can be valorized over against the canonical portrayal itself, on theological or pneumatological grounds.[10] More confusing still is how Jesus and the New Testament can be appealed to for a justification of the historical-critical endeavor (even undertaken with proper respect) based on (1) the role of the Old Testament in the formation of Christian kerygma and (2) the eventual extension of the "critical exposition" to include the New Testament, whose plain sense is said to testify to its logic and necessity.

THE MATERIAL FORM OF THE OLD TESTAMENT

I have argued that, for Gese's approach, there must be a close and significant linkage of tradition-history as a theological process, on the one hand, and considerations of the form of the canon, on the other. This linkage is not incidental for Gese. As he sees it (and Stuhlmacher follows him here), for tradition-history to function as the bridge linking the witness of two testaments, the intervening period of tradition processing must be given equal weighting, or else we would misunderstand and wrongly emphasize the role of the canon and the impact of the Old Testament as scripture, not tradition, in the formation of the New Testament. When Gese says the traditions are still expanding, he means the Old Testament has no fixed form until Christians (or Jews) give it one. The Old Testament's status as scripture is a Christian bestowal.[11] Stuhlmacher makes the same point in his own way.[12]

With this larger conception and rationale in place, it is relatively easy to file objections to Gese's understanding of the material form of the canon.

Law and Prophets

For Gese and Stuhlmacher, this twofold and open designation serves the purpose of establishing a contrast with a threefold and closed designation, which the New Testament does not yet contemplate. The isolated phrase "Moses, the prophets, and the psalms" (Luke 24:44) does not alter but confirms the inchoate and unfinished character of part three. This is Gese's first main point.

The objections to this view can be quickly rehearsed:

1. The designation "writings" (*ketubim*) is a subsequent refinement of non-Mosaic books, and so says nothing about the extent of the canon at the time of the New Testament. David (Psalms) is prophetic, as is Solomon (Proverbs) and Daniel.[13]
2. Negatively, no book outside the traditional Hebrew canon (what Origen and others refer to as "the twenty-two") is cited as scripture in the New Testament (which points to the very issue at stake, Sirach functioning on a different level, in the nature of the thing, than, e.g., Proverbs or Ruth or Chronicles [from "the writings"] in the New Testament's world of reference).[14]
3. Beckwith has argued that the reference to slain prophets ("Abel to Zechariah") in Luke presupposes an order Genesis to 2 Chronicles, or one not unlike the tripartite and closed canon of the later Masoretic.[15]
4. Stuhlmacher speaks of the NT's quoting from Torah, Prophets, and Psalms, and he gives the figures for this.[16] Yet other books from the *ketubim* are obviously presupposed in the New Testament, including Ruth, Chronicles, Proverbs, and Song of Songs.[17] This makes his use of

"psalms" as a single referent misleading (as if Luke 24:44, following Sirach, knows of a truncated and open third section of a threefold canon). Moreover, it is simply false to say that Sirach is "quoted" in Mark and James (which it is not), and then represent the "writings" by the rubric "psalms" only. The effort to make Sirach and the *ketubim* equivalent is demanded by his (and Gese's) conception of tradition-history, but it lacks confirmation in the NT's literal sense. An argument that places subtle allusion to the apocrypha on an equal footing with massive and highly intentional citation of the Old Testament as scripture lacks proper proportion.

Gese's Second Main Point

The Old Testament of the New Testament's traditioning process is a wider Greek canon, including books indispensable (Sirach) for New Testament confession. The correlate of an open canon is the longer non-Hebrew list of books, if not also the priority of the Septuagint for a genuinely Christian biblical theology.

The objections to this view can again be simply listed:

1. The New Testament cites Old Testament passages from various languages, presumed orders, and listings; there is no single Septuagint to be contrasted with a single Hebrew exemplar, which is given priority in the New Testament on grounds of anything but convention and/or accommodation, as well as for reasons of specific, local theological argument.[18]
2. This finding also rules out a language-to-scope argument, as though the New Testament's use of Greek renderings of an original Hebrew said anything definitive about the scope of the canon as wider or open or fuller in terms of available traditions (e.g., Sirach's indispensability for Christology).
3. Bauckham and others have demonstrated the NT's use of Hebrew text-types alongside Greek text-types, the implication being that some early Christian communities were bilingual and used available text-types for reasons having nothing to do with recourse (or not) to a sole, favored tradition.[19]
4. Ellis has shown that lists of Old Testament books in the early church tend toward conservatism, even when non-Hebrew OT books are cited in the respective source's own exegesis.[20]
5. Ellis has also shown that the lists frustrate any simple parent-to-offspring logic; namely, there were not two choices vying for ascendency, one threefold and proto-Masoretic, one fourfold and septuagintal.[21] The orderings are too varied and demonstrate the lack of major theological significance assigned either to a "wider Greek" or "narrower Hebrew" option, in respect of internal order *grosso modo*.
6. Cross and others have shown, with the aid of the Dead Sea discoveries, early pressure toward constraining textual pluraformity in the direction of the proto-Masoretic Hebrew text-type. The later decision of Jerome

(*pace* Augustine) to defend the Hebrew textual tradition over the traditional Greek ecclesial usage, in matters of establishing the church's scripture, has its precedent in the *kaige* and proto-Lucian Greek recensions.[22]

7. Stuhlmacher speaks of Childs's attenuated treatment of Qumran and the
history of the Septuagint as damaging his canonical approach.[23] Yet Ellis
makes important note of an unpublished Qumran text that refers to "the
book of Moses [and in the words of the pro]phets and in Davi[d and in
the words of the days . . .]"—this latter reference being to Chronicles.
Here is a finding confirming that of Beckwith in his assessment of the
"Abel to Zechariah" delimitation of Luke (11:51). Ellis likewise sees Philo
and Josephus in agreement about a "Holy Scriptures" distinguishable
from "the ancestral philosophy" of the Therapeutae (for Philo) or "writings not deemed worthy of equal credit" (for Josephus).[24] The contrast
with Stuhlmacher's evaluation is obvious.

In other words, the material form of the canon cannot support the moves of
Gese (or Stuhlmacher) in the direction of valorizing a single tradition-history
over a two-testament form of scripture as critical to its inner logic, theologically. The Bible is not one continuous tradition-history, like a novel with a
beginning, a middle, and an end. Something stops, and a history of effects is
set in motion that testifies to the form of the original canon and the differentiation of traditions, of various sorts, from it.[25] Indeed, it has been argued that
Sirach is itself a witness to its own subsidiary status, over against "law and
prophets and other books."

Childs and others have noted that the roots of this perspective, whereby
traditions appear to reckon with a formal literary authority to which they give
testimony, is found within the Old Testament itself.[26] Zechariah speaks of the
words of former prophets "overtaking" generations after them, after their
death; Ecclesiastes speaks of the testimony of Qoheleth as limiting the scope
of proverbial sentences and of correlating wisdom and law; Deuteronomy
seeks to correlate law and prophecy; and Malachi sets a limit to prophetic textual authority beyond Zechariah.

Other understandings of the relationship between the testaments and a
proper conception of the theological form of Christian scripture can likewise
be ruled out.

First, Christian scripture is not a Christianizing of an original Hebrew
canon, by means of glosses, literary explanations, *vaticina ex eventu*, and era-
sure of the original languages themselves (Hebrew and Aramaic).[27] This would
have amounted to the production of a single testamental deposit, declaring
therewith (consistent with the logic of Barnabas and Justin) one book for one
people, the Jews having forfeited any claims to "copyright."

Neither is the relationship properly to be understood as between (a) a single delimited scripture ("inspired by God and useful for instruction"; "oracles

of God entrusted to the Jews"; "Law and Prophets") with a title retained from the New Testament's conventional language, to which has been appended (b) a secondary literary elaboration, in the form of aggadah, pesher, midrash, halakah and the like. Old is to New Testament not as Tanak is to Talmud. Instead, the concept of a literary canon, based on a covenantal relationship, is extended to a secondary, literarily distinctive deposit whose formation and rationale is developed on analogy to the first, with a new covenantal relationship at its heart.[28] The testaments are, of course, different, and they bear witness to the one subject matter of them both, in different ways. "Tanak to Talmud" may actually be more akin to what Gese means by "tradition-history," strictly speaking. When Stuhlmacher reckons with two tradition-historical choices, one ending in "Hebrew Bible" and another in "Christian Scripture," he fails to see how "Old Testament" and "Hebrew Bible" were competing concepts from the very beginning in the early church's use of the "scriptures" of the synagogue, "the oracles of God entrusted to the Jews." It remains meaningful that the terms "Old Testament" and "Tanak" are *both* postbiblical terms. Both require a commitment to a subsequent theological literature. Neither goes straightforwardly back to the scriptures of Israel without argument and defense.[29]

Finally, the relationship is also not merely germ to full flower, as could be implied by a tradition-historical or "Jesus as first critical expositor" model of development (so Stuhlmacher in the 1975 essay). The first testament is in the first instance a scriptural, authoritative witness and not a bundle of religious possibilities whose logic is not disclosed until an external agent is brought to bear on it. Here is my disagreement with Francis Watson's recent effort at christological reading.[30] Jesus sees the witness of the Old Testament to God and to himself in clear terms, from within the per se voice of the scriptures and not from the application of some external rationale or criteriology unknown or foreign to the witness itself. "If they do not listen to Moses and the prophets, neither will they be convinced even if someone rises from the dead." Luke is saying more here about the sufficiency and perspicuity of God's word spoken to Israel than about the challenge of resuscitation.

Watson also wrongly interprets 1 Peter 1:10 as saying the prophets had not the vaguest notion about what they were speaking, christologically considered. In similar fashion, he reads Luke 24 as if Jesus is showing the Old Testament to be about himself in ways that are foreign to its own warp and woof. He has, to my mind, also misunderstood the debate at issue in Justin. Justin is not working with a "Jewish scripture" and arguing for its genuine, though misperceived, christological correlatability. He is arguing that the scriptures of Israel preach Christ in their plain sense and that because "Judaism" (constituted for the first time in this sense) does not see or acknowledge this truth, the church is now the true Israel and the only intended referent of the scriptures' testimony to its only subject matter: God in Christ Jesus.

THE OLD TESTAMENT AS CHRISTIAN SCRIPTURE

The preceding section has established the main points of disagreement between the approach of Stuhlmacher-Gese, on the one hand, and a canonical approach, on the other. I have written elsewhere in detail on the implications of a canonical approach for a Christian handling of the Old Testament and will not cover all that ground here. My approach approximates that of Childs at many points, as the reviewers note. If anything, I have tried to underscore, perhaps more than Childs, the deference of the developing Christian kerygma to a scriptural (Old Testament) witness it assumes will continue to sound forth alongside it, as the New Testament writings develop and take their own canonical form. I have rejected the position of Hübner[31] (the Old Testament *in novo receptum*) in favor of an approach that has Christian confession, especially in the realm of eschatology, returning to the Old Testament to learn from its plain-sense voice (so, e.g., 1 Corinthians 15; Romans 9–11). Also, in the realm of ethics, I have argued that the decision of Acts 15 is rooted in a very subtle handling of the plain sense of Leviticus and Amos (both in its Greek and Hebrew text-forms), whereby the law of Moses has a perlocutionary force for Gentiles, who find themselves in the "midst of the house of Israel," and for Jews who confess Christ.[32]

It is striking, and worthy of our present reflection, how such a radically different view of the evidence for a stable Old Testament canon is presented in the tradition-historical conception of Gese and Stuhlmacher. It is as though scholars are working with an entirely different set of governing assumptions, which would in turn require confirmation of what would have to be completely different data. Or is it the case that the governing assumptions are themselves preempting a clear look at the relevant evidence? What would the explanation for that be?

One strong possibility is that a theological form of modalism has created a set of false choices for assessing the data regarding the material form of the canon; that is, a predilection for a certain understanding of the theological normativity of the Jesus kerygma, over against all other God-talk (even if rooted in the scriptures of Israel), has forced the conclusion that it is not possible to talk about God in any normative or abiding sense without immediate correction and correlation with talk about Jesus or Jesus' own (distinctive, different, unprecedented) talk about God. This latter talk must be regarded, in the nature of the thing, as different from what the canonical Old Testament brokers in its given form as scripture.

I believe Stuhlmacher sees to the very heart of the issue when he quotes (disapprovingly) from Childs on the problem with a tradition-historical approach, as follows, "the Old Testament has become a horizontal stream of tradition from the past whose witness has been limited to its effect on subsequent writers. The Old Testament has thus lost its vertical, existential dimension which as scripture of the church continues to bear its own witness within the context of the Christian Bible."[33] Stuhlmacher finds this assessment from Childs of himself and Gese "very disconcerting" (*höchst befremdlich*), but he fails to show how it is indeed a misjudgment on theological grounds of the tradition-historical approach. To say, as he does, that Gese sought to uncover genuine revelation through tradition-historical inquiry does not alter the objection that what Gese found was something other than the theological witness of the Old Testament in its form as scripture, a form everywhere presupposed by the New Testament. To call this historically retrieved tradition-process "revelatory" begs an entire range of questions as to what is meant by revelation in the first instance (Hans Frei's *The Eclipse of Biblical Narrative* is not cited by Stuhlmacher, and he seems largely unaffected by its thesis). Stuhlmacher appears to object to a portrayal of the Old Testament having a voice only when, as he puts it, it is "baptized" by the New, but the question remains: just how does that per se voice function for him in any normative Christian theological—indeed, trinitarian—sense.

To conclude, let me suggest several ways in which the Old Testament's per se voice functions normatively for Christian theological construction.

First of all, let us consider the antitheses of the Sermon on the Mount, where Stuhlmacher finds a critical instinct whose legacy survives, as he has it, in proper deployments of historical criticism by the Christian community, following Jesus' lead.

It is made clear in Matthew 19:4 and 22:29 that Jesus accepts the Old Testament as a divine word and not as "traditions of men." In the Sermon on the Mount, Jesus is contrasting his manner of teaching the Old Testament and the teaching of the Old Testament as received ("you have heard that it was said" is not a typical way of quoting scripture as such). "Jesus never understands Scripture," Ellis notes, "as words of the Bible in the abstract but as the message in its true meaning and application."[34] We see the same distinction at work in Mark 7:13, "thus making void the word of God through your tradition that you have handed on." What is at stake in Mark 7 and the Sermon on the Mount is the effort to perceive in God's word a general principle and then extrapolate this into the area of "washing pots" or Corban. A high view of the authority of scripture declares such logic vain and self-justifying, in distinction to true Torah-obedience.[35]

This point is further clarified in the antithesis concerning hating one's enemy—a text not found in Leviticus, though its supposed antithesis ("you

shall love your neighbor as yourself") is! An interpretation of the Bible in support of hating one's neighbor has been found at Qumran (1QS 1:3f), thus
showing the actual logic of the antithesis teaching of Jesus.

And finally, the canonical shape of the Sermon emphasizes the authority of
the law and prophets for Jesus in such a way as to constrain the reader against
drawing false conclusions about his own teaching authority ("do not think that
I have come to abolish the law or the prophets," Matthew 5:17).

In sum, the Christian judgment to hear the Decalogue as Christian moral
teaching, from the per se witness of the Old Testament, is grounded both in a
decision about the authority of God's word to Israel and the confirmation of
that perspective within the New Testament's plain-sense portrayal. To put it
another way, it is Jesus' acceptance of the authority of the Old Testament that
guides the church, not his declaration of its authority in the name of creating
a new Christian tradition theretofore without warrant.

A second example: In Romans 9–11, Paul constructs an elaborate theological program involving God's work in Israel, in Christ, and in the church, using
images of natural and unnatural branches. One could have imagined the narrative logic of Romans moving from creation, to justification, to sanctification,
to the new law for Christian life. The only explanation for such a detailed treatment of the eschatological tableau necessitated by the rejection by Jews of
Christ in chapters 9–11 is the plain-sense voice of the Old Testament, in which
irrevocable promises to Israel were made; that is, Christian teaching about the
relationship between the church and an emerging Judaism does not take its
bearings from christological teaching or from a developing tradition beyond
the plain sense of the Old Testament. Rather, Paul returns to the Old Testament to hear its theocentric and irrevocable word as interpreting the kerygma
in Christ. The Old Testament as scripture guides the church's Christian confession in ways that cannot be adequately captured in a tradition-historical
approach.

So, too, Harnack helpfully showed the way the Old Testament first functioned as the sole Christian scripture, as a venerable and privileged possession
used by Christians against paganism, nationalism, idolatry, and mythologies
of various sorts.[36] It took time for a rival testament to gain anything like the
same stature and high purpose for Christian apologetic and defense. Von
Campenhausen's much quoted dictim is consistent with this perspective.[37]
The problem for the early church was not what to do with the Old Testament.
Rather, in the light of a scripture whose authority and privileged status was
everywhere acknowledged, what was one to make of a crucified messiah and a
parting of the ways? It is this dimension of early Christian use of the Old Testament that is attenuated in tradition-historical approaches of the Gese-
Stuhlmacher variety. At stake is nothing less than an adequate Christian

doctrine of God. In the early church, the struggle was not so much with a low Christology of adoptionist stripes (which might be gleaned from a New Testament read apart from the Old) as with a high doctrine of God everywhere assumed, either on account of the witness of the Old Testament to YHWH, "the Maker of Heaven and Earth," or on account of Greek metaphysical reflections of the period.[38]

The witness of the Old Testament as Christian scripture is fundamentally a witness to the One who raised Israel from the dead, and who, in turn, raised Jesus from the dead. He thereby dramatically recalibrated reigning eschatological and pneumatological expectations, still in accordance with those self-same scriptures. The challenge of our day is not how to find in Jesus a model of critical exposition of the historical-critical type; those instincts are already well honed in modernity and late modernity. The challenge of our day is how to see in Jesus' death and raising actions truly in accordance with the scriptures of Israel. For that, we shall need to return to typological and figural senses once more keenly available in the church's handling of the "literal sense," before such a sense was conflated with the "historical sense." To the degree tradition-historical approaches attempt, as von Rad valiantly sought, to link historical recovery of the "real" with some larger governing universe of types, they will fail for reasons apparent, on the one side, to a Bultmann and, on another, to those who disparaged Goppelt in his day. Only when the literal sense is reencountered in our time, apart from a valorizing of "proximity to the real," in history or in tradition, will the way forward be found again for a Christian handling of Old and New Testaments as scripture for the church and world. This is what I am seeking under the rubric of a canonical approach to biblical theology.

4

Scripture and a Three-Legged Stool

*Is There a Coherent Account of the Authority
of Scripture for Anglicans after Lambeth 1998?*

What Scripture doth plainly deliver, to that the first place both of
credit and obedience is due; the next whereunto, is what any man
can necessarily conclude by force of Reason; after this, the voice of
the church succeedeth.
                    —Richard Hooker, *Laws of Ecclesiastical Polity, Vol. 5*

INTRODUCTION: LAMBETH CONFERENCE 1998
AND THE AUTHORITY OF SCRIPTURE

It is relatively easy to construct a short list of important Lambeth '98 resolutions. People who were there have shared anecdotes about how encouraged
they were to see the fresh face of Southern Hemisphere Anglicanism, to hear
stories of courageous Christian witness, to engage in Bible study, and to worship in new and moving ways. But for those of us who were not there, or
watched from afar on "the Bishop Cam," what stood out?

Four things should be mentioned: (1) A debate over cancellation of international debt; (2) a decision not to mandate women's orders; (3) a jurisdictional
resolution, calling for respect of boundaries, and restraint, with invitations into
dioceses being the proper procedure; and (4) a call of pastoral attention to same-
sex orientation and behavior, the latter judged "contrary to scripture." This last
resolution passed by an enormous margin (with a large number of U.S. Epis-
copalian bishops abstaining, including Frank Griswold and others on record as
having ordained active homosexuals or in some way "blessed" their unions).[1]

How was such a resounding statement made in the face of constant, well-
funded, highly organized pressure for change? In the West, being concerned

about homosexual behavior and its attendant systems of rationale is fundamentalism, ignorance, bigotry, and even, if one purports to be Christian, a sin against the Holy Spirit. At the close of 1998, in an astonishing public statement, the Bishop of Los Angeles reported that the Holy Spirit had not been truly present at the Lambeth Conference![2]

To be sure, one answer given was that in the Southern Hemisphere, in the struggle for Christian faith and identity, *cultural* pressure to resist homosexual behavior was paramount; that is, Christians needed to be able to appeal to some coherent moral code that distinguished them, or the mission of Christianity would be obscured and hindered. Seen in this way, objections to homosexual blessing had to do with a unique set of cultural factors. Stated otherwise, such objections were local and not of the essence of Christian faith and practice. Before Lambeth, the presiding bishop of the American Episcopal Church responded to a question on this matter by stating that in 1988 Lambeth had had to find a way to address polygamy, and so, too, homosexuality had a distinctive cultural expression in the United States and elsewhere.[3] Just as we had respected their cultural distinctiveness, the argument went, so they would be asked to respect our cultural distinctiveness.[4] Seen in this light, homosexuality is an aspect of cultural identity. There are no transcendent norms that might be applied to homosexuality, beyond the virtues of tolerance and human rights and promises to listen and so forth. These virtues could be regarded as distinctly Christian, for some, and for others their probative character is not exclusive to Christianity. General religious insight teaches us. To draw this to a close: Christian objection to homosexual expression is a cultural matter, and like left-handedness or slavery will be assessed differently in different places by Christians of good will. Of course, to talk like this calls into question what a Lambeth Conference is meant to do or be, as a catholic gathering of bishops who understand one faith, one lord, one baptism to be no bad thing and who must discern the degree to which local options on matters like sexual conduct is a coherent, non-self-contradictory Christian position.

So I believe one is forced to draw the conclusion that there was really only one reason for the resounding character of the resolution, and this reason also explains why homosexuality is attracting more attention in the long run than the other three resolutions I mentioned. The blessing of homosexual unions, some hold, is a lightning rod because of prejudice or ignorance or bad science or failure to attend to certain social rules (condom distribution and the like). This negative judgment might pertain to other cultures at other times and is undoubtedly true today, especially among non-Christians. The Greco-Roman literature on homosexuality, for example, reveals all sorts of objections to the behavior (medical, social, quasi-scientific), and one might fairly say that these objections reveal ignorance, prejudice, bad science, and so forth.[5] But Christians have categorically held homosexual behavior to be wrong for a different reason: it offends against God's own character. Like many other specific human behaviors or attitudes, homosexual behavior is wrong because it thwarts and opposes the good designs of the one true God and incurs in the nature of the thing God's judgment. This is what is called in the lexicon of Christianity "sin"—human rebellion in the face of God's good and holy self and will. Sin hands over men and women to a state every bit as determined and distinct as swimming is different than walking on dry land. To sin is to enter a zone of necessary estrangement and hurt. No one has described this better than Augustine.

Now, how does one get the notion that this particular behavior, like others, is not tolerated by God, offends against him, and places the individual in a position of grave forfeit? The Greeks drew their own conclusions, and it could be fairly said that Southern Hemisphere or Western Christians might draw theirs, too, for lots of good reasons. Fear of Muslim fundamentalism might be one conclusion. Fear of disease might be another. Alternatively, it could be argued that, lacking a clear signal about God's own word on the matter, homosexuality is like left-handedness: fine, as long as it is appreciated for its non-right-handed character, and not threatened, or threatening, for being such.

In reality, there is only one reason that Christians have judged homosexual behavior to be an offense to God, and it is the same reason that Christians judged stealing persons and enslaving them to be wrong and an offense to God: they took this as revealed by God himself, deferred to or confirmed by his Son, and ratified by the Holy Spirit. And how did they know this? Christian scripture, Old and New Testaments, was read in such a way that the literal sense was allowed to speak a word that cohered with the character of God himself. This was not always a simple matter, because Christian scripture contains different sections, different genres, different contexts, and, in the end, two different testaments. Difference has not been eradicated but belongs in the very nature of the thing. The fourfold character of the Gospels is itself a profound testimony to the providential ordering of Christian truth.

The question has always been fairly put: how to make sense of the whole of scripture, in the light of difference and proportionality. And this was not a literary problem for specialists only, but had to do with the gospel in its most basic sense: the bringing near by the blood of Christ those once far off, into the most intimate, forgiven, holy life imaginable, so that we have learned to call it salvation, justification by grace through faith, eternal life with God himself. The parts and the whole of scripture have to do with God himself and his eternal identity (the "immanent Trinity"). Christians do not worship

Jesus or his words, except in conjunction with the Father and the Holy Spirit. Christians do not worship Jehovah and his law, except in conjunction with the Son and the Holy Spirit. Christians do not worship the Holy Ghost, except as the Advocate who reveals that the Father and the Son are one and are truth in this sacrificial, obedient, and loving relationship. This theological conviction, expressed in creeds, is what drives the concern to hear the whole word of God across the two-testment Christian scripture.[6] It can be no small thing that Christians divided on so many other issues—because of the different weighting of portions of the canon or a different assessment of tradition, natural law, or the work of the Holy Spirit—have heard God's word clearly and distinctly on the matter of homosexual behavior. The plain sense of scripture on male and female difference, marriage, and sinful desire has been viewed as truly plain, in the most basic sense of the term. To point out that divorce or chattel slavery or other such departures from the plain sense of scripture have been condoned and justified by Christians is in fact to establish the general principle that God has a revealed identity and will and that one has a right to expect some conformity to this as essential to the Christian life. Only in this way can subsequent generations see that corrections were both needful and demanded, as consistent with God's very self and his revealed truth. Wilberforce did not mount arguments against slavery by appeal to new truth, or by dividing the persons of God, but by appeal to revealed truth—that is, that public, available, and plain truth rooted in scripture and in God's character as manifest there.

If this theological lens is indeed the way scripture has been viewed as God's lively and truthful word, it should follow as fully predictable that Lambeth produced the resolution on human sexuality that it did. What remains to be explained is how any other decision could have been reached and affirmed, as a statement of Anglican Christian faith in the late days of the second millennium. To address this, it will be helpful to take a glimpse at Anglican uses of scripture, especially as the remarkable statement has been made that a manifestly non-Anglican use of scripture was in evidence at Lambeth 1998—and resolutely so, one might add, in the light of the clarity of the decision, once the invocation of the Holy Spirit was made and the prayerful votes registered. What has happened in Anglicanism, especially in the West, that has turned off the plain sense of scripture or fogged the lines of communication that once were not fogged, such that two inherently contradictory views are now held to be the will of one God, Father, Son, and Holy Ghost?

If this question is answered fairly, then it will have the benefit of not producing yet another so-called defense of Christian teaching (as though God needed to be defended). Rather, it might serve to explain why two groups are talking past each other in about as resolute a manner as is possible.

THE OXFORD MOVEMENT AND SHIFTS IN ANGLICAN UNDERSTANDINGS OF SCRIPTURE AS REVELATION

The theological bearings of American Episcopalians have been shaped, if not calibrated, by attention to the English church, in its variety but also in its common features. From time to time, it is pointed out that American Episcopalians have no counterpart to a more robust English evangelical wing, and there is a measure of truth in this.[7] But still, all in all, seminary education, prayer book revision, or the general sense of theological convictions and trends does not take form in America in isolation but looks for identity vis-à-vis Anglicanism at large, especially as found in England. This is true as well with the assessment of the authority of scripture. Again, movements like Neo-Orthodoxy affected Britain and the United States differently, and German theological concerns penetrate our respective territories and ramify in different ways.

That being noted, it is fair to say that a watershed moment in Anglicanism was the Oxford Movement, and the effects of this movement spread quickly, and proudly, to American shores. Against an arid Deism or moralism, the Oxford Movement sought to inject new life into a Christianity become rationalistic or simply moribund. Appeal to the Church Fathers, so it was thought, meant that the movement was not content with continental Reformation categories, in certain parts or in the whole. Appeal to ritual and a high view of church and episcopate meant that this was a Catholic movement (the departure of Newman notwithstanding). As for scripture, it gives one pause to recall that Pusey was prepared to claim that the entire case for Christianity rested on the authenticity of the Book of Daniel and its attribution to him as author, against a growing German consensus (cf. Hävernick, Keil, and others).[8]

So it would be wrong to characterize the Oxford Movement, in its initial phase, as having a low view of scripture. A danger may have been sensed in overly individual interpretation, or a *sola scriptura* with no doctrine of the church, or in what was called "enthusiasm" or its opposite, "rationalism." But at the same time, Pusey was fighting bravely and with massive erudition to defend the authorship of Daniel because he was persuaded this was crucial to *any adequate account that the church had inherited of the authority of sacred scripture*. He had no other categories to work with. One either accepted a complex view, promoted by historical criticism, that half the book was written centuries after Daniel, in the Maccabean period (a view without grounding in prior catholic Christendom), or Daniel wrote the whole book. What is critical to note here is not the detail or persuasiveness of Pusey's defense but rather that he believed it critical to Christian believing that some substitute view of Daniel's authority—which he judged made out Daniel to be a fraud—was rejected, so that the view that had obtained in catholic Christendom, as he saw it, could be upheld and vindicated.[9]

Seen from this angle, it is astounding how quickly Pusey's concern was dropped or regarded as otiose by his own Anglo-Catholic successors. In *Lux Mundi*, in the next generation, Charles Gore labored to accommodate all the newest historical-critical trends, baptizing them by insisting science, not unscience, is the ally of Christianity; that the "idealized" dimension of the Old Testament is also important and had simply been underappreciated by historical critics; that, in any event, the New Testament is of a different character and can truly be trusted as a more firsthand sort of report; and that "our Lord" himself is the basis of our faith, not the Bible, and that when he spoke in any way inconsistent with the findings of "Old Testament science," he was accommodating himself as part and parcel of an incarnational religion. This constituted a form of "kenosis surrender" for his time and his followers of truths discovered in Gore's own day (even if for manifestly non-Christian ends) by historical-critical rationalism and objectivity. This is obviously an astonishing transformation of the doctrine of the incarnation, so that it might be squared with "scientific" finds in vogue at that time. Where Pusey was persuaded there was danger, Gore was persuaded there was promise.[10]

In retrospect, Gore may be forgiven for believing that this appeal to science and objective, historicist labor would bolster Christian mission and authenticity and win public approval. (In his own way, Jack Spong has worried along these same lines; e.g., Christianity will die if it does not get with it and persuade today's mocking Athenian through appeal to science and expert knowledge.) What Gore could not know was the extent to which the acids of new science would leave his "idealized" apology for the Old Testament looking quaint and hopeful, while pressing on to demolish his view of the New Testament and appeal to belief in "our Lord." If Gore could see what now remains of his appeal to the New Testament and "our Lord," he might realize that he was sacrificing the Old Testament as scripture on an altar of scientific optimism in order to produce an Old Testament of pre-"incarnational religion," which religion would in turn become the secure mooring for the faith Catholic.[11] It is questionable whether an entente cordiale between doctrine and historicism was either possible or desirable. Moreover, no one was talking about a smorgasbord of different theological menu options, where this vestige from tradition and that historical *novum* could be combined in an intellectually serious way.

If it were shown that "our Lord" was as elusive as the Jahwist, that "idealization" was not just confined to the Deuteronomist but was outstripped by the Gospel of John, that Babylonian and Assyrian documents confirmed a Great Flood actually better than Nag Hammadi tractates confirmed the identity of what Gore called "our Lord," then no last appeal to catholic faith as based in creeds would hold back the flood. These creeds would also be judged fraudulent efforts to press upon believers a view of Jesus and God indebted not to "historical Jesus" or an incarnational religion but to false Greek or Jewish categories, foisted on believers by an institutional church greedy for power and control. It is not a victory for Pusey, however, to say that Gore went too far. Neither knew quite how to retain a doctrine of scripture in the face of what are properly labeled "modern, scientific" challenges to Christian faith. This faith was once naturally rooted in what the Anglican Hans Frei called the uneclipsed biblical narrative, the form of Christian revelatory truth not fully amenable to science and historical reconstructions of truth behind Old, or New, Testament witness (Karl Barth had made a similar point in *Church Dogmatics* I.2.2). One can use the Methodist hymnal to reconstruct English church history, but one is not singing from it or treating it on its own terms of production or reception (not reading the Bible biblically, as Barth might put it). To dissect biblical narrative, Frei held, is to misunderstand its inner nerve and the special character of its means of communicating revelatory truth.[12]

By the time the next generation of Anglicans produced *Essays Catholic and Critical*, the mood was different still.[13] The essay therein on authority reveals a confidence now sufficient to chide readers about the importance of the "religious experience of Protestantism," which, it is generously conceded, "played a vital part in the life of the Church and the progress of mankind." Again, what is sobering is the degree to which *Essays Catholic and Critical* is oblivious to the fact that traditional doctrines of catholic Christianity (atonement, incarnation, resurrection, Holy Spirit, sacraments) cannot be built upon the "secure findings of historical science" about some truth behind the witness of scripture, available to experts working hard at it. There is insufficient foundation there for any true and lasting house of truth, even though promises to such and such objectivity were being made. Moreover, these doctrines cannot be based on a "religion of the incarnation" to the degree that they seek to be trinitarian in character. Trinitarian Christian faith requires a distinctive handling of Old and New Testament as canonical scripture, the dismantling of which *is the expressed aim of objective, critical retrieval*. Historical labor has demonstrated that what is elusive is exactly religion *qua* religion. The problem is that the writers of the New Testament did not inquire into the religion of the Old Testament, any more than "our Lord" did. This did not have to do with kenotic accommodation or some other condescension to human categories. It had to do with the actual character of God as revealed by the scriptures, according to which Jesus' life, death, and raising were calibrated and acknowledged as fulfilled.

Jesus is not depicted in the New Testament as interested in the religion of Israel, or Israel's thoughts about God, except to the degree he judged contemporary Jewish life an improper manifestation of the inner nerve of such a religious template (this being the constant prophetic critique from within Israel). Rather, Jesus spoke in the first instance of *the scriptures and of God's word of address therein and therefrom*—not of religious ideas or human responses to a divine Word not yet fully mature. To speak, as Paul does, of the "oracles of God entrusted to the Jews" is to reckon with scripture as a divine authority, not with an old religion in development toward a better new religion. Moreover, the earliest church catholic knew it was not the same thing as the "religion of the New Testament." If this were not so, the Jerusalem Council's kosher restrictions on Gentile converts, as reported in Acts 15, would remain to this day. The early church (like Jesus and the apostles) stood under a scriptural authority: the oracles of God, the scriptures, the law and the prophets, the "it is written." Unlike Jesus and the apostles depicted in the New Testament, the early church knew that scriptural authority to reside, for the church catholic, in a dual, two-testament witness to God, not to religion—either of (anachronistically termed) "Jews" accommodated to by God in the older religion of Israel or of new believers in an incarnational religion introduced by Jesus.

To fast-forward to the present, it is easy to understand how an "Affirming Catholic" movement has recently sought to bridge the gap that separates our late modern period from this first generation of Oxford Movement Anglo-Catholics.[14] There is, however, a decided irony in realizing that Newman's concept of doctrinal progress persuaded him to abandon Anglicanism and that a recent vestige in Anglo-Catholicism has created a movement of followers *Pusey would not be able to recognize as "catholic" in any sense but haberdashery and ritualism*. A defense of the authorship of Daniel might merit the now-ubiquitous charge of fundamentalism (ironically, from those very people who claim their Anglican identity is rooted in the Tractarian Movement and the catholicism of Pusey or Keble; this is clearly not the notion of doctrinal progress Newman had in mind).

It should also be stated, in fairness to them, that the authors of *Lux Mundi* and *Essays Catholic and Critical* did not intend their positions to be as open to the sort of radical change that has now come about. In theological terms, the atonement has been scaled down in a recent (ECUSA, 1979) prayer book revision, and in popular treatments is taken as a kind of tragedy, à la Girard—that is, why a scapegoat mechanism must finally be brought to an end.[15] The Tractarians would surely now shudder at modalistic expressions of the Trinity, like "Creator, Redeemer, Sanctifier," protected as they were by their knowledge of and affection for the Church Fathers. To worry about some of the moralistic excesses of the early church, as did Mortimer, could never find a counterpart in Affirming Catholic consideration of same-sex blessings. It is hard to see what view of episcopacy could be defended now as consistent with the Tractarian Movement—of late, a deteriorated office in the ECUSA, which one Lutheran colleague described as "150 Lone Rangers." When it comes to moral theology or ecclesiology, Kenneth Kirk and Charles Gore would be thrown out of an Affirming Catholic meeting as fundamentalists.

WHENCE THE JUSTIFICATION
FOR A NEW RELIGION FOR LIBERAL ANGLICANS?

Answer Number One: Jesus,
Martyr in the Cause of the Outcast

As long as a certain historical-critical confidence and ascendancy was in place, it was easy to see how a new position on sexual morality might be accommodated to Christian belief and practice. A survey of the early revisionary work will bear this out in quick fashion.[16]

First, one shows that the direct prohibition of "men laying men" in Leviticus is null and void by virtue of being in Leviticus. Christians are in no way taught by legislation from Leviticus, or else they would not eat meat and cheese together or wear different types of cloth at once or enjoy shrimp cocktail. Jesus dismissed Christians from the law. Usually, in the case of Leviticus, this view is registered strongly, if selectively.[17] In the ruling of the Council of Jerusalem on gentile Christian conduct in Acts 15—no *porneia*, no strangled meat, no meat with blood, no idolatry—these rules also are drawn directly from the Book of Leviticus, as conduct expected of sojourners within the house of Israel, which the early non-Jewish Christians were taken to be.[18] But *porneia* apparently does not extend to modern gay and lesbian physical relationships, as Acts might understand this, drawing on the laws of Leviticus to guide emerging Jewish Christian and Gentile Christian fellowship in Jesus Christ.

Second, passages that seem to view homosexuality as sinful are not primarily about that, if at all. The sin of Sodom was inhospitality. Why Lot's daughters got their father drunk to sleep with him, after escape from Sodom—that, too, presumably, was an act of inhospitality or an event unrelated to the sexual climate of Sodom.

Third, historical criticism seeks to show that the Greco-Roman context of Paul's condemnations or, if necessary, their unfortunate Jewishness points to special kinds of homosexual behaviors and phobias about them.

Fourth, Jesus does not address the topic, so on the theory of silence as probative, this means that modern homosexuals do not come up for discussion. The very notion of homosexuality as state of nature to which one is born is foreign to the world of the Bible and most intervening centuries.

This last bit of logic is now the most forceful of the lot. In modern homosexual behavior, we confront something that is truly new; that is, it may have
struggled for the status it now has in earlier days, and peeked through from
time to time, but only now are we able to truly grasp what we have when we
speak of "a homosexual" or "homosexuals" as a category. Indeed, as far as I
know, there is a certain consensus on this: that right now we are seeing something truly new and without actual precedent. Strict historical-critical logic has
worked: the Bible belongs, literally, to a bygone age, to religions of other peoples, including that of Paul, which we do not belong to now.

Now this shifts the burden away from a certain narrow historicism: what
was the Bible talking about when it mentioned this behavior and judged it to
be X or Y, given our ability to reconstruct an ancient historical world different than our own? To say we have a thing truly new is to raise a question about
how to assess it, given that no one knew it as we do, and the Bible was talking
about other things, or shadows not full forms. If we want to find theological
warrant for something not discussed in the Bible, how do we move forward?
Orthodox Jews, for example, worry about whether it is appropriate to wear a
Walkman in public, and because scripture does not address this, some appeal
to principles and the like must be adjudicated. Halakah respects the Bible's literal authority and works from it to confront the truly new or unanticipated
(life without a Temple, priesthood, etc.).

However, the analogy can be pushed only so far in the case of homosexual
conduct, for alongside negative prohibitions (even if inapposite) there are positive appraisals about the sanctity of Christian marriage: a lifelong, solemn
commitment of one man and one woman, no less holy for being dishonored
or tragically undone through sin or untimely death.

What is needed, then, is some marriage of the positive aims of true Christian living, as expressed in holy matrimony, and a behavior unforeseen in scripture about which good Christian people are seeking discernment. But how can
such a marriage of different yet proximate concerns be found? Is it enough to
note an absence here and a potential there and then conjoin the two? Especially as nonmarital sexual relating of any kind is inarguably not commended
in scripture or tradition? What is needed, then, is some sort of imitation of the
aim and goods of Christian marriage grafted on to a behavior that demands
fresh accounting from Christians and the world at large (including those
who wish not to restrict their sexual freedoms in such a way). So how can this
be done?

1. Abstraction: Jesus does not condemn people; he loves outcasts; he for-
    gives where the law condemned or the world misunderstood; this is what
    got him killed.

2. Jesus and his teaching must be taken on its own terms, in the sense that we know nothing about God before or after him that counts for Christian faith or teaching.
3. God is known primarily by what people generally experience as true to their own selves and identities: to speak of revealed truth about God, not generally available, would make no sense on this account of God; even Jesus is only a very special instance of this larger principle and counts as God only on these terms.

Still, all three of these fall short of a robust commendation of same-sex blessing of the sort now claimed as desirable. They could allow those engaged in homosexual behavior some room to consider their behaviors as demanding attention and acceptance, and indeed the space created could be filled with endless lobbying, study-grouping, liturgical proposing, changes in Christian education programming, and debate—exactly the sort of distraction from the mission of the church sinful men and women on both sides of a debate might enjoy. This concern is not alleviated by noting that many claim this to be the actual mission of the church—that is, engaging one another as an end unto itself, or gay liberation as Christian mission as such: a late modern crusades for gay rights—worthy of all the time and money we could throw at it as Christians.

This appeal to Jesus, then, as endorser of love and human acceptance has won a certain place of pride in recent defense of revision (so, Archbishop Peers of Canada places "hospitality" in priority over truth).[19] What cannot be shown, however, is that this appeal is consistent with the Jesus of Tractarian "incarnational religion." It is easier to see this Jesus as one whom the Tractarians and those after them worried about. They had no interest in a Jesus without conjunction with the God who raised him—that is, God as holy and righteous, who receives his Son's sacrifice to redeem the world and put it right with him, the holy and righteous Father. Although the incarnation theologians were selective about those aspects of the religion of Israel with which Jesus cohered, they at least knew this to be a matter for serious theological reflection. That is now largely gone in revisionist circles. "God" has no meaning as refracted through the scriptures of Israel, to whom Jesus and early church claim according fulfillment. Jesus' words, selectively chosen, are "God" in the traditional meaning of the term—namely, as that transcendent but revealed reality demanding our obedience and our wider communication to a world lacking knowledge of truth.

Answer Number Two: The Three-Legged Stool

At some point in the twentieth century, Anglican Christians became persuaded that they possessed a special divining rod for discerning Christian truth.

Indeed, it was raised to the status of Anglicanism's special signature as such, against the denominational distinctives of others. It so took hold in the last century, in the vacuum created by the loss of a serious, pre-Tractarian doctrine of scripture, that it succeeded in cutting a wide swath through ecclesial discussions before it won a major victory: claim to antiquity and venerable, across-the-ages authority; that is, it became just the sort of comprehensive, sufficiently vague, allegedly distinctive Anglican "principle" needed to do duty once it was no longer clear what Pusey had been worried about. This principle stood ready to accommodate Anglicans of every stripe, and indeed one might argue that it was the most lethal agent of obfuscation ever foisted upon Christian people, by virtue of its ability to confuse and forestall and shift and defer. The ultimate insult to history was to suggest that Richard Hooker was its progenitor.

"Scripture, reason, tradition" (and its various cousins) is a train able to stop at every station and always add one more carriage. There is practically nothing it cannot accommodate. We should probably not be surprised that an organic notion found in Hooker would be perverted by Western, consumerist Christians and turned into a sort of channel-changer, to find a stool leg to suit. How could homosexual behavior run this three-legged gauntlet? Is the scripture leg not clear? Would Hooker have regarded scripture as unclear on this matter? The answer is so obvious as to invite sheer puzzlement as to how anything so clear could have become unclear in the intervening centuries. This query into God's will would have been a real home-run ball for Hooker, where he got to touch all three bases and walk into home plate. In Hooker's universe, tradition would have been clear, and reason would have been even clearer. Hooker's natural law appeals are far closer to those of Calvin than of any post-Tractarian. Hooker's natural law was divine law, such as was described in scripture itself. It is precisely the same sort of appeal that Paul makes in Romans 1. Indeed, it is uncontroversial that until the nineteenth century, reason and natural law cohered and derived their status as Christian authority because of scripture's own revealed word about creation and God's sovereign design therein (prior to the technological manipulation of all things "natural"—scare quotes now being required).

The conclusion to be reached is that a vacuum was created after the failure of Anglicanism to retain a doctrine of scripture into the twentieth century, and the three-legged stool suddenly emerged as precisely the sort of comprehensive lens needed to accommodate varieties of Anglicans who had simply lost their way. Some could hear it as a very conservative principle, and did; others could see it as a channel-changer for an Anglican TV set inherently diverse and ambiguous. Indeed, it defined what Anglicanism is at its very center: a divinely given "right" to choose, and defer, and study, and then worship (in a

Eucharist). At least we should be fair and stop attributing such a view to Hooker.

The most tragic episode in Anglicanism's recourse to the stool is difficult to pinpoint, because the so-called principle is, in the nature of the thing, a study in ambiguity, as soon as it is removed from the environment in which it was originally deployed. Reformed catholicism of Hooker's day can be dragged only violently into the twentieth century. Legs would get sawed off, inevitably, and then used as clubs: some wielding one, and others another. It is hard to imagine a better way to mislead and confuse Christians seeking guidance and revelation from a scripture called holy, within a church called catholic, in a world that scripture tells us bears God's design and glory, however poorly perceived by sinful women and men, than by claiming a three-legged stool as a distinctive feature. This would wreak havoc, and indeed it has.

We should not be surprised that the stool is now in the attic. American Episcopalians and much Western Anglicanism inhabit a carriage the train added one day, when the stool seemed inefficient for adjudicating the moral high road claimed by revisionists. This new carriage is called either "experience" or, more ominously, "the Spirit."

Answer Number Three: Spirit, a "Taboo-Toppling, New Truth Revealer"

The language "taboo-toppling" is that of Marilyn Adams. In a recent volume, *Our Selves, Our Souls, and Bodies* (1996), she and other Anglicans appeal to the "Spirit" as the ground for Christian truth. The intellectual foundation for this move, if that is the right term, is argued to be found in two studies by Luke Johnson.[20] Chapter 9 treats this topic in more detail, so I will only summarize here. The seriousness of the matter should be apparent, when, for example, we hear the Bishop of Los Angeles address his diocese and claim an authority of "the Spirit" that was absent at Lambeth. So, the stool may be in the attic, but "the Spirit" is alive in the form of new truth. The Spirit must close the gap between a Bible become ancient religious resources, contain an appeal to dispersed authority that still needs to make decisions, and arc over to our present situation in Anglican Christianity as a carnal reality.

The argument must proceed along a bumpy road. Self-described gays are a new phenomenon. The church needs a word to speak. It does not have one in the scriptures. What it does have in the scriptures is an account of Gentiles becoming Christians by water baptism. Evidence of Spirit endowment is given in Acts, which shows that non-Jews can receive the Holy Spirit, and such is taken as sufficient, with confession of Jesus as Lord, for water to be brought. Baptism in the holy name takes place. Table fellowship, made difficult by virtue

62 Figured Out

of gentile habits and customs, is made possible by a decision to seek warrant in scripture for a new manner of coexistence. Acts 15 reports that four injunctions are laid on non-Jewish Christians (these are drawn from Leviticus). Moreover, the circumcision party's insistence that they be circumcised is adjudicated. Based on scriptural texts, this is regarded now, in Christ, as unnecessary. In time, in the subapostolic period, the injunctions of Acts 15 are modified further, as table fellowship gives way to the tragic "parting of the ways" of Jews and Gentiles. Kosher restrictions are no longer mandated, but idolatry and *porneia* can by no means be marks of Christian living. Justin and other early saints are martyred precisely for their insistence on keeping this way of life as what it means to be Christian, as such.

Now it might be difficult to recognize in this summary any ground for analogy with "gay Christianity," as others now claim so confidently. That is because the account given insists that the Holy Spirit is not about "new truths being received" but is about the Holy Spirit's chief and only business: pointing to the Lord as one with the Father, witnessing to him in the lives of those who confess his name, and convicting the world of sin (John 16:8ff.).

The fact that the church has for the first time two groups of people who consider themselves "homosexually oriented," in any way one might describe that, and that both claim Christian identities but disagree about what behavior is appropriate—that might suggest a situation analogous to Acts.[21] That is, the Council of Jerusalem sought to discern if this Holy Spirit endowment was consistent with God's word and, if so, what sort of conduct was appropriate. That was because the Holy Spirit was not reckoned to be different than Jesus or the Father who sent him. The Holy Spirit was the author of God's word, and one who is truth in conjunction with this word. So the apostles searched the scriptures and heard God saying ("it seemed good to us and to the Holy Spirit") that water baptism was all that was required of Gentiles in whom the Holy Spirit was working, in confession of Jesus as Lord, upon hearing the gospel of God's sending him to save sinful men and women. Repentance and new life were to flow from this gracious act of inclusion.

There is no evidence in scripture or tradition that the virtues associated with new life in Christ included homosexual activity. The Holy Spirit cannot contradict himself, in the nature of the thing. Truth cannot be its opposite. Peter's statement that he "remembered the word of the Lord" (Acts 11:16) before he baptized with water nicely integrates John's emphasis on the advocate bringing "to remembrance all that I have said" (John 14:26) and taking what is from Jesus and the Father and "declare it to you" (John 16:15). The Son is transparent to the Father, and his teaching is that of the Father (John 14:24). The Holy Spirit is the convicting agent of God's truth (John 16:8–11). John constantly emphasizes that certain truths about Jesus cannot be borne, or cannot be comprehended, during his pre-Easter life with the apostles. Only upon his ascension will the Holy Spirit come and open their eyes to how certain of his actions were in accordance with the scriptures or otherwise manifestations of the Father's sending him. To convert this understanding of veiling and unveiling into a doctrine of "new truth" *without any prior attestation* is surely to depart from scripture's presentation in Acts. It cannot be fairly concluded on the basis of scripture that the work of the Holy Spirit is to tell us something new that we simply had no way to comprehend before. This is manifestly to misread scripture and points to the wasteland that has become Anglicanism's regnant "doctrine of scripture" in the West. Acts 15 is a tribute to faith seeking understanding, by recourse to God's word, in order to comprehend God's present action. Gentiles were to be the recipients of God's special grace, flowing from and alongside his older covenants with his people. To pronounce the holy name over the one baptized was all that was required, and scripture could attest to this. No leap of imagination, no analogy, no Holy Spirit driven–search through the scriptures can turn up divine endorsement for same-sex intercourse, no matter how much it seeks to call itself Christian. Here the analogy fails and fails extraordinarily.

CONCLUSION

There is not space here to set forth a map of where Anglicans are headed or should be headed, in respect to scripture. I have written elsewhere on this, from a perspective not specifically Anglican. At the same time, I am mindful I have no "view from nowhere" and have heard scripture as a Christian within an Anglican Christian upbringing and formal seminary education, such as it has been.

It is surely a tragedy that modern Anglicans, many with very powerful positions, speak about an Anglican approach to scripture that is self-serving and without historical warrant. It goes no deeper than the late nineteenth century and is out of touch with Anglican Christian preaching and the history of Anglicanism prior to this time.

Lambeth Conference 1998 spoke a prophetic word, every bit as sharp as Isaiah's. God's word had actually shut ears and closed eyes in the days of that prophet (Isa. 6:10; 28–29). But a remnant preserved what he had said (8:16), and it was opened with fresh joy, currency, and truthful obedience, once a dark judgment had come upon an entire generation, their children, and their children's children (Isa. 40–48). The former things were seen for what they were by a generation mindful of God's mercy and his atoning, saving work for them. And through that lens and that gift of the Holy Spirit, new things were seen as well: the inclusion of the Gentiles by the sacrificial work of Israel and the Servant. This word of promise was found in the former things, but Israel could not yet know how God would accomplish his sovereign will.

In other words, the truth of what God was doing was not a departure from what he had done or said before, even as it had gone unheeded or was rebelliously rejected. God's truth through his word stands in accomplishing relationship to his prior words. This word cannot contradict what was said before but uses it as a basis for a fresh word to an obedient generation.

What is needed now is a "rule of faith" that refuses to divide the persons of the Holy Trinity in the name of setting portions of scripture off against themselves. Principles like *analogia fidei* or *sensus literalis*, deployed with great care under the rule of charity and love of God, have allowed countless generations of Christians to hear God's word in Old and New Testaments. At least from the time of Pusey's last gasp, Anglicans in the West have grappled with a coherent doctrine of scripture. Unsure of how to deal with historicism and science, they accepted a position that cut the Bible free from its own genre of sacred word in order to speak of religions of the past, of which we are the most enlightened, recent incarnation. Such a handling of scripture has all but destroyed this portion of Christ's body, with the bogeyman of fundamentalism constantly being paraded in as the chief enemy of Christian faith and life. We are witnessing a massive, self-confident, arrogant campaign to root out any understanding of the dynamic of scriptural authority, such as was available before what Hans Frei called "the eclipse of biblical narrative." It is the height of ignorance and intolerance to suggest that Anglican Christians at Lambeth who voted as they did, upon invocation of the Holy Spirit, having sought a word from the Lord in a scriptural legacy once regarded as our greatest joy and eternal touchstone, were reading scripture in a way that was un-Anglican. No, they were reading the scriptures, in the power of the Holy Spirit, in a way that would have been immediately recognized by Herbert, Donne, Andrewes, Hooker, Cranmer, Keble, and those saints nearer to our own day.

What is manifestly now true is that a generation of Anglicans has emerged, claiming authority of a Spirit, whose word is not just unamenable to, but in opposition to, the judgments of Reformed, Catholic, and Orthodox Christians around the world, as they worship God, the Father, the Son, and the Holy Spirit.

Can it be the case that the Holy Spirit speaks one clear word here, and its opposite there? Every time this debate has arisen in the church, as it did with Montanism or Zwinglianism, the answer was clear. No. Holy Spirit and God's Word cannot depart from one another. The same judgment was rendered at Lambeth 1998.

Concluding Unscientific Footnote

A principal concern at the beginning of a new century should focus on the First Person of the Trinity in Anglican theology. When one surveys the Church Fathers, so beloved of Tractarians, it is striking how the chief concern was, first, to coordinate the Son's relationship with the Father and, second, how to understand the Holy Ghost in relationship with them both. Language of "generation," "procession," and "spiration" came into service, as the mature catholic faith evolved, to account for distinctiveness and continuity within the Godhead, from Father, to Son, to Holy Spirit. At no point was it ever assumed that the church stood in possession of an incarnational religion—to use the language of the Tractarians—from which the claims of something precedent were to be adjudicated, as a self-contained religious system. This is a fatal mis-step within Anglican thought, and it is best seen in the mid-nineteenth century and thereafter, as discrete "New Testament" departments, ethics, and theology were thought to be representative of Christian theological reflection. Von Campenhausen's dictum is never more in need of recollection than today in Anglicanism. In the early church, the problem was not how to square faith in Christ with an Old Testament regarded as outmoded, but the reverse. How, in the light of a scripture everywhere regarded as authoritative and a privileged witness to God and his truth, could it be said that Jesus was in accordance and was one with the Father who sent him? To fail to see the proper direction of influence, captured theologically in the concept of "generation" from the Father to Son, is to believe that Acts 15 is crediting something to the Holy Spirit with no "procession," from anything, except the needs of human beings as these are communicated and request validation.

In sum, the problem is not just the severance of the Spirit from the persons of Jesus and the Father. Nor is it a romantic concern with, and isolation of, a "historical Jesus" or his words in an "incarnational religion." Rather, it is the most serious problem the early church faced, but from a new direction. We are facing in our late-modern West the insidious threat of gnosticism and its replacement religion of special knowledge, which haunted early Christianity for several centuries. Its low regard for Israel, election, revelation, matters carnal within Israel's scriptural legacy, creaturely goodness (male and female; animal; cosmic) and limit, and even the God of Israel himself as the Father of Jesus Christ—these are its hallmarks. It was not a simple Marcionism that dogged the church so long, because Marcion's extreme truncation of the biblical canon cut away most of the New Testament witness as well as the Old, and was judged early on as sub-Christian. Rather, it was the persistent drumbeat of a "religion of Jesus," in piety, special knowledge, spiritual endowment, and the like, and it ironically produced two opposite tendencies: moralism and licentiousness, because of its low regard for the God of Israel. We see the lethal combination of these two tendencies in the new religion of ECUSA, with its general indifference toward homosexuality as a carnal reality, seeing it instead as a "state of nature" endowed from before time, like a gnostic eternal type entering the sphere of flesh and form, and its shrill enforcement of codes of conduct, mandated by those appealing to new truths, not public or accessible until now.

When the church fails to account for the Old Testament as Christian scripture, what it is truly seeking is a dismissal of God the Father as relevant to Christian theology and daily life. The results are obvious in the American Episcopal Church. Lambeth Conference 1998 did not, however, let a local word become the last word but deferred to the legacy of prophets and apostles, Old and New Testament witnesses to the one God with whom we have to do: the Father, Son, and Holy Spirit. It will take a recovery of this theological lens before an Anglican doctrine of scripture recovers anything of the character it has had in its long Catholic and Reformed heritage. We do not need to go far to see the dynamic character of scriptural authority, but we will have to stop giving preference to new truths the Holy Spirit cannot and has not spoken, to this or that elite segment. We have the opportunity to revisit significant moments of our long Anglican Christian history and to build on these as the mission of Jesus Christ is solidified throughout the Anglican communion today. But no progress will ever be made unless the Holy Spirit teaches the church again how to hear God's voice through his word to Israel and the apostles. Nothing less deserves to be called an Anglican doctrine of scripture post-Lambeth.

Does Anglicanism have a doctrine of scripture after Lambeth? This chapter has been about tracing why, especially in the West, Anglican appeal to scripture has been so vague and confused in the past century and a half. The influx of historicism and its accommodation in Anglo-Catholicism was seen to be a fatal decision, with hindsight. Conservative evangelicals were left to defend the Bible's authority as best they could, but this often was nothing more than an effort to establish its *historical* character, before the very same judge and jury deemed relevant by Tractarians. Rationalist or scholastic defenses of scripture have been shown to be no true heirs of Luther, Calvin, and Augustine, but this seemed the only way to move forward with a doctrine of scripture worthy of the name. Much more could be said from a historical standpoint about the impoverishment within Anglican biblical-theological reflection, either on the side of Tractarians or the evangelical apologetic. Barth's complete nonreception at Oxford in the twenties should signal that ships were passing one another, and this is not mitigated when one considers evangelical resistance to Barth as well. Barth's robust Word of God theology placed scripture at the center in a way that neither Anglo-Catholics, with their high ecclesiology, nor evangelicals, with their rationalism and concern for facticity or secure intellectual moorings, could comprehend. Barth, of course, fared not much better in North America. It is beyond the scope of this chapter to chronicle why the major Barthian interpreters of our day (John Webster, Trevor Hart, Christina Baxter, Bruce McCormack, Neil McDonald) are a full generation away, but this does suggest that Barth was a stranger in Anglicanism whose importance has taken hindsight to appreciate more fully.

One subcurrent we have not been able to examine is the role of non-Anglican (Church of England) Christianity in the United Kingdom. Here, in figures such as Forsyth, Spurgeon, and Chambers, one sees enormously vigorous appeal to scripture, in theological writing, preaching, ascetics, and hymnody. Especially vibrant is the appeal to the Old Testament, to God's holiness, and especially to figural interpretation of passages across the testaments, linking that world with this one in a way no historicism or liturgical commemoration could. Here one could feel properly situated within the sovereign and providential world of God's eternal designing, as the Bible's frame of reference was honored for its distinctive place in God's economy, and yet was figurally linked to the life of the church centuries later.

Another subcurrent is the emergence of the novel in the United Kingdom and the United States and its enormous public success at creating a narrative world that could locate the imagination and transport and transform one's present place of standing. Where pulpit or biblical story once located the church and the individual in it, including a hopefully curious general public, within a plan called divine, providential, the novel has stepped forward and claimed this public space, especially in the United States and United Kingdom (less so, for interesting reasons, in Germany).

Hans Frei made an appeal to narrative theology as a way forward between, in the case of Anglicanism, anglo-Catholic credalism or ecclesialism without secure biblical foundation, on the one hand, and, on the other, conservative, rationalistic efforts to secure the faith from the side of science or empiricism or piety. He was surely onto something, and his debt to Barth is obvious and acknowledged. One missing link, not appreciated by Frei with his focus on continental theology, may well be the resistence, within Anglicanism, to typological reading after the rise of modernity in its Tractarian or evangelical forms. Still, as manifest in our hymns and our collects, this rich resource for understanding scripture's fit, fitness, and claim on us must be recovered. This is in part what we witnessed at Lambeth 1998. To label this "fundamentalism" must be called for what it is: a category error. It fails to understand what the true options for scriptural appropriation are: in this case, neither an appeal to church, special piety, nor scientific defense of the fall of Jericho, but a willingness to let the word of God speak across a two-testament Christian scripture with the same typological richness as has been preserved in our hymns. To hear people talk about fundamentalism would lead one to believe they had never sung a hymn from before the mid-nineteenth century!

What we learn from classical Anglicanism, and its Catholic forebears, in pulpit, poetry, hymnody, and theological reflection, or what we hear from outsiders who retained an interest in Old and New Testament presentation of the Triune God, and our fit life with him is not fundamentalism but is what Anglicans know to be their long-standing, "privileged access," doctrine of scripture. This must be recovered in councils in the West (it never left pockets of the laity), and scholars like Frei, Childs, Radner, Greene-McCreight, Young, and Yeago have pointed a way forward.

5

Scripture and Trinity

"The Virginia Report"

INTRODUCTION

In many ways, the struggle with globalization, and with the tension between diversity and uniformity in doctrine and practice, is widespread in the Christian churches. This essay deals with an Anglican form of this struggle, but it is assumed that Anglicanism's struggle is not without a wider relevance and purpose.

Because of the international character of the Anglican communion, certain problems become apparent when the various members of the Anglican family gather together. This happens formally every ten years at the Lambeth Conference, called by the Archbishop of Canterbury.

Decisions are often made to refer certain issues to committees for further study and for possible recommendations. The Virginia Report contains the deliberations of one such committee, which was charged with comprehending the challenges of diversity in the face of the Christian gospel. For convenience, an appendix to the chapter contains the Preface and Origins and Mandate of the Virginia Report. An Internet link shows where the report, which is not long, can be read in detail.

This chapter challenges several of the governing conceptions of the Virginia Report, especially concerning the role and authority of scripture and the appeal to the Trinity for models of diversity in the church.

From the Reformation Anglicans endeavoured to hold together people of different temperaments, convictions and insights: the puritans who wanted more radical reform and the conservatives who emphasized their continuity with the pre-reformation Church. Today, for example, evangelicals, catholics, liberals, and charismatics bring a diversity of insights and perspectives as

69

Anglicans struggle to respond to the contemporary challenges to faith, order and moral teaching. Bound up with these groupings are the differences which arise from a critical study of the Bible, particular cultural contexts, different schools of philosophical thought and scientific theory. ("The Virginia Report," 31)

The Virginia Report (TVR) correctly notes that at the time of the Anglican Reformation, it became necessary for the church to contain several diverse groupings. The diversity, however, is not sufficiently explained. Far more misleading is the effort to draw an analogy between the diversity of sixteenth-century Anglicanism and the diversity of modern Anglicans, which the report judges is "bound up with" the rise of modern historical-critical methods.

The reason for concern is wide-ranging. First, historical-critical methods were introduced to Anglican Christianity only in the nineteenth century—that is, several centuries after the Reformation, during which long period of time whatever theological or ecclesial diversity existed had nothing to do with a modern diversity occasioned by historical-critical methods.[1] Second, these critical methods were met, initially, with extreme resistance.[2] So it would be quite wrong to view the diversity occasioned by critical method as a natural evolution from a kindred sort of diversity from the sixteenth century. Third, as scholars of intellectual history have noted, the change wrought by the Enlightenment and the rise of critical methods is virtually epochal. This renders any description of continuity (intellectual, ecclesial, exegetical) impossible. The Virginia Report analogizes two periods of time (the diversity of Reformation Anglicanism; the diversity of modernity) in the space of several sentences. The analogy is false and intellectually misleading.

The present chapter begins with this root problem for a reason. There was a diversity at the time of the Reformation, and it had to do, fundamentally, with the role of the Bible in the light of the continental Reformation and its attendant handling of sacred texts, within a changed climate of ecclesiology, authority, and exegesis. What was at stake was the perspicuity of Holy Scripture. Could the scriptures speak a direct, inspired word to the individual and the church? Or was it necessary for the scriptures to be handled from within an ecclesial framework wherein the work of the Holy Spirit, in sacrament, preaching, and teaching, was already attested and certified as present (and in other places, as absent) by the Roman church's teaching authority?[3] When TVR speaks about continuity and discontinuity with the pre-Reformation church as that which parses diversity in the period of the Anglican Reformation, presumably it has this sort of diversity in view.

The irony is that scripture plays a role, as perspicuous testimony to God's self, will, and purpose, in this document *only in the manner that occasioned the*

Reformation itself; that is, scripture has become but a small piece of furniture in a room whose architecture, decoration, and inhabitants have already been determined. This is true of scripture itself, and it spills into the way the document handles the Trinity in its opening chapters. In both cases, a prior, second-order metaphysic displaces the actual sentences and paragraphs of holy scripture, in such a crafted and self-contained way that the scriptures' plain sense is obscured, in precisely the manner the Reformers argued had been the fault of medieval scholasticism and/or Roman appeals to tradition alongside (or inclusive of) the canon of holy scripture.

It would be churlish to point out what TVR has not done, if its authors could only reply that they had an altogether different agenda before them. But this is precisely what is at issue. We learn as much from the decisions that have been made in this report as from those we judge to be preferable, which we can only sketch out here. Nothing less is at issue than the relationship between the doctrine of God (the Triune God, to use the language of TVR) and the holy scriptures. This report makes high theological claims for the church on the basis of a doctrine of God and the Trinity, and it does so within the context of a discussion of unity and diversity in the communion. Within this context, the exact character of the relationship between the authority of holy scripture and the person of the Godhead is never worked out but only assumed.

However, given the frank admission that Anglican diversity is itself derivative of different attitudes toward modern critical (post-eighteenth-century) approaches to the Bible, how could we hope that a doctrine of God, based on a scriptural witness to him said to be generating diversity, might be immune from the same engines of diversity and disagreement noted as alive among modern Anglican Christians? As it stands, there is every reason to suspect that the very diversity the report notes, and which is the subject of its analysis, will be projected onto God himself (see the quote later in the section "The Trinity, *Koinonia*, and *Ecclesia Anglicana*"). This is true because of the report's failure to relate its statements about God to an adequate doctrine of holy scripture, on the one hand, and because there is a tendency to valorize diversity as a good unto itself and to conflate such diversity with traditional doctrines of the Trinity that are under modern examination and popularization.

The first part of this analysis will focus on the problematical use of scripture in TVR. The second part will briefly examine the use made by the authors of recent trinitarian theological literature, often with a decided drop in the exchange rate as this literature is brought to bear on modern Anglican problems in ecclesiology.

ON HOLY SCRIPTURE: THE LOGIC
OF THE FORM OF THE REPORT

Speech-act theory has taught us that communication occurs in locutions (the words on the page; the words spoken), illocution (the intention of the author or speaker), and perlocution (the goal or longer-range concern to persuade and convince).[4] In grammatical terms, the analogy is: the words, sentences, and paragraphs or chapters of written or spoken discourse. So, in understanding TVR's use of scripture, we must attend not only to what it says but also to how what it says fits into the logic of its total speech act.

The actual treatment of scripture as an authority for Anglican Christianity comes only in chapter 3 of TVR.[5] Scripture, we must assume, undergirds or informs what is said in the first chapters about the Trinity and *koinonia*, but the fact that this is not stated as a matter of formal principle (as in chapter 3) is surely relevant. Lacking is explicit and extended exegetical defense for statements such as Christian baptism is "into the life of the Triune God" (p. 23), (2) the Holy Spirit "lift(s) the community into the very life of God" (p. 26), Christians as "participants in the divine nature" (p. 29), or (3) "God invites his people to enjoy diversity" (p. 30). What we have is an abstracted appeal to the prayer of Jesus in John 17, which is of course a prayer and not a template confirmable by observing the present life of the church, which life is marked by empirical division, human sin and rebellion, and oppression in the world.

The more worrisome example of scriptures' attenuation comes in the chapter where it is explicitly referenced ("Belonging Together in the Anglican Communion"). The perlocutionary act of this chapter is reasonably clear: we have an acknowledgment of (varieties of) diversity present in the communion, with theological reflections on this, concern for the limits of this, with special attention to the office of bishop.

Why, it might reasonably be asked, is it more critical at this point than earlier to speak about the authority of scripture? Why hold up, at this juncture, the 1988 statement from Lambeth:

> *Anglicans affirm the sovereign authority of the Holy Scriptures as the medium through which God by the Spirit communicates his word to the Church. . . . The Scriptures are the "uniquely inspired witness to divine revelation," and "the primary norm for Christian faith and life." (p. 32)*

This 1988 Lambeth statement is, it should be underscored, full of promise. Upon it should be built all that precedes regarding *koinonia*, the Triune God, diversity, and the like. This is so because matters so central as the Trinity, the doctrine of the church, the work of the Holy Spirit at Pentecost, the character of baptism, the gifting by the Holy Spirit in the church, the office of bishop, and the nature of unity (in the Godhead and in the body of Christ) are not peripheral issues (*adiaphora*) but are intimately tied up with the plain-sense presentation of "the uniquely inspired witness to divine revelation."

However, the 1988 Lambeth statement is not linked to this particular concern—namely, defense of the statements regarding the Trinity and the church as derived from "the sovereign authority of the Holy Scriptures" bound up, as such authority is, with the character and will of the Living God who gives himself to be known through them. Rather, appeal is made to scripture so as to make two things clear.

First, scripture is said to function in a special way for Anglicans, and this requires its authority to be coordinated with what is called "reason" and "tradition" (these being, "since the seventeenth century," "fundamental to the Anglican way of living and responding to diversity," pp. 32, 33). Second, by introducing a considerably robust understanding of scripture in the 1988 Lambeth document, the way is then clear to correlate this with a very different, diffuse, complex understanding of authority and then to claim that it constitutes an Anglican distinctive. What is then to be required, is that this Anglican distinctive (so claimed) become the governing authority; that is, by enclosing the 1988 Lambeth statement on the authority of scripture within the authority of an Anglican distinctive, scripture becomes, not one of three authorities, nor even (as with Hooker) the prime norm, but a piece of a larger principle, which now has the right to be labeled "tradition" on the logic of its own conceptuality. With this, we are fully back to the issue joined at the Reformation. Can scripture be said to have an authority that rises out of the church, on the one hand, and that addresses the church competently, clearly, and uniquely, on the other?

The Lambeth 1988 statement clearly says, "Yes." Richard Hooker, like his Anglican contemporaries, also would have said, "Yes." So, in fact, we read in *Laws of Ecclesiastical Polity*:

> *What Scripture doth plainly deliver, to that the first place both of credit and obedience is due; the next whereunto, is what any man can necessarily conclude by force of Reason; after this, the voice of the church succeedeth.* (vol. 5, p. 8)

But this report is telling us that scripture is part of an interpretative "Anglican distinctive" and that scripture's existence and unique capacity is to be understood only from the standpoint of a *tradition* of "Anglican distinctives" (which itself must be defended as true to Hooker, as well as the ensuing centuries). To then try to relate this "Anglican Tradition," as chapter 3 does, to a diversity brought about by the rise of historical-critical methods (fully unanticipated by and without genuine intellectual analogy for, the seventeenth-century doctors of the Anglican church) is misleading and inaccurate.

Two problems require further attention. The authority of Scripture is bound up with its subject matter: God in Christ. The authority of the Bible within Anglicanism is not in the first instance a matter of getting one's hermeneutical or material principle in place (e.g., a "scripture, tradition, reason" hermeneutic) and claiming for this something distinctive. Why would Anglican Christians wish to be "distinctive" from other Christians when it comes to the authority of scripture, particularly in a report in which lavish and optimistic claims are made for the empirical church *simpliciter*?

But there is a deeper problem, and it surfaces in the presentation of chapters 1 and 2. Their statements about the life of God, wherein Jesus has ascended to enjoy a certain particular life with the Father and the Spirit, is conflated with the life of the church. Baptism becomes a sort of ecclesial ascension. Missing is any sense of the scriptural logic of Nicaea, "And He shall come again with glory to judge the quick and the dead, whose kingdom shall have no end." That is, missing is some urgent dis-analogy between the life of the church on earth and the life of God *in se*. The immanent and the economic life of God have been conflated (in a manner John Zizioulas has decried),[6] but then to this has been added a doctrine of the church, and individual believers, who by baptism become participants in the divine nature, empirically and presently, on analogy with the Son's present and empirical (so we hold by faith) life with the Father and the Holy Spirit.

I say this with all respect to the drafters of the report. But what is at issue is decidedly not an Anglican principle of authority, said to be a "distinctive" and urged upon the present church as somehow consistent with Richard Hooker. What is at stake is an adequate doctrine of God. This includes, as fundamental to any even attenuated appeal to scripture, how this God makes himself known through the witness of the apostles and prophets, reliably and sufficiently. It stands to reason that a document that has not worked this out formally may well feel free to put its explicit theology forward in chapters 1 and 2, with very high-sounding claims for the relationship between the church on earth and the Triune God, his "diversity" and our own, and then, only secondarily, introduce an account of the role of scripture for making this God known, which immediately is enclosed in something argued to be an Anglican distinctive. Yet this is precisely what is at issue in Anglican Christianity, in any day: the unique authority of the holy scriptures as bound up with the trustworthy and holy God who inspires the words, sentences, and paragraphs (the mind, the scope, the "whole story") of the two-testament canon of holy scripture.[7] This is why the 1988 Lambeth statement speaks of the "uniquely inspired witness to divine revelation." The Bible is the only means by which the economic life of God can be known and then correlated, theologically, with statements having to do with God unto himself, in his trinitarian immanence.

"TRADITION" AND "REASON" AND THE LOGIC OF THEIR INTRODUCTION IN TVR

It would be possible to engage in an extended critique of the definitions provided for "tradition" and "reason" in TVR. Indeed, it is arguable that such critique would be helpful and clarifying.

But also at issue is the logic of their introduction in a document involving instruments of unity in the Anglican communion and their relationship one to another.

Several criticisms can be conveniently filed by title. First, Hooker spoke of the primary authority of the scriptures, before the reason of the individual, and before the voice of the church, and he did not refer to tradition in any way that imitates or anticipates what is said here by TVR about tradition (more on this later). Second, it is clear that for Hooker, authority is graded. Only when the scriptures are silent or unclear do secondary authorities X or Y come into play. Third, one suspects that his interest in the individual is not primarily to do with an investment in reason as such, and certainly not in reason as Hume or Locke meant this (an objective rationality riveted to unaided human reason, universal natural truths, and the like). Rather, he believed that the scriptures can be apprehended in their truthfulness by individual men and women and obeyed, reasonably. The church does not bestow an authority on scripture that it cannot exercise on its own, by God's own sovereign deployment, for the edification of sinful human beings grasped by the power of the gospel of Jesus Christ; that is, the emphasis of Hooker is not on establishing three individual authorities, less still on establishing a "distinctive." Rather, he is setting the primary authority of scripture within a context of a proper understanding of the relationship between the authority of the church and the individual Christian.

In TVR, this subtle ecology has been disturbed. "The voice of the church" (which has meaningfulness where scripture has not said everything, for Hooker, as in vestments, frequency of communion, etc.) has become tradition in TVR and has been ranged before reason. More of concern, however, is that tradition is said to be something going on in scripture itself.

Now this is true enough, as historical criticism has sought to show, most deftly, perhaps, in the work of Gerhard von Rad and "tradition-history." But this tradition-history is not what sixteenth-century Anglicans meant by "the voice of the church."[8] Moreover, recent canonical approaches are at pains to demonstrate that at some juncture it is meaningful to speak of tradition having become scripturalized and stabilized, with an authority over ensuing generations (see Zech. 1:6; Isa. 55:11). In the New Testament, reference to "the law and the prophets" is reference to scripture, which is different than (not to mention, set over against) traditions (Mark 7:3ff.). The Virginia Report makes tradition into a principle of dynamic interpretation, at work first within and behind the stable scriptural word and then, on direct analogy and by extension, in the church. On this reading, tradition is not just found in the Bible, *it is the Bible*, and in this sense, a distinction between scripture and the history of its interpretation is destroyed. Augustine, on the one side, and the scriptural witness he regarded as authoritative, on the other (in a way he did not accept for himself or his own thoughts), have been effectively leveled, thus producing one continuous, dynamic tradition-process. The "mind of God has constantly to be discerned afresh" (p. 33), we are told. There is no stable deposit of faith ("the primary norm for Christian life," so Lambeth 1988) unless one differentiates it from a process of discernment, *which must be directed toward an apprehension of its plain sense*, to which "both credit and obedience are due" (in the language of Hooker).

We return to the point, introduced by TVR itself, regarding the Anglican Reformation and its diverse groupings. The Reformation was contesting the very way of thinking about the authority and perspicuity of holy scripture TVR is setting forth and attributing to Hooker. Hooker could well have agreed that "the mind of the Church carried by worship, teaching, and the Spirit-filled life" (p. 32) had a certain reality and weight of consideration. But he would never have regarded scripture as capable of conflation with tradition.

Then TVR goes on to define "reason" as the capacity to symbolize. Hooker believed in reason in the sense that Aquinas or Calvin believed in reason: as a moral earnest, whereby God had ordered creation toward certain ends, such that grace and nature could speak to one another when God so urged. In TVR, it is as difficult to disentangle reason from tradition as tradition from scripture, in that all three are parts of one dynamic, natural process of "interpreting afresh" (p. 32) and exercising "common sense" (p. 32).

It must now be asked what the logic of this section on scripture is, given the thrust of the entire document, which has to do with diversity in the Anglican communion and instruments of unity. The answer is given on page 33:

> *The characteristic Anglican way of living with a constant dynamic interplay of Scripture, tradition and reason means that the mind of God has constantly to be discerned afresh, not only in every age, but in each and every context. . . . In order to keep the Anglican Communion living as a dynamic community of faith, exploring and making relevant the understanding of faith, struc-*

tures for taking counsel and deciding are an essential part of the life of the Communion.

In other words, the discussion of scripture (enclosed within an alleged Anglican distinctive) has essentially to do with leading into an accounting of diversity in the communion, wherein the mind of God is constantly being discerned, in different contexts and cultures, and in ways that require difference and diversity in the nature of the undertaking. In other words, the point of discussing scripture at this juncture is to open it to tradition processes and the differences produced by reason in culturally different contexts. The point of discussing scripture at all is to the degree that it serves to illustrate a reality in the church the report knows about and seeks to find confirmation for. Once that is done, we are back to strategies for getting along and making things relevant within the constraints and realities of a worldwide communion. To attribute this sort of rationality or horizon of concern to Hooker and a unique Anglican distinctiveness is a misreading of historical fact (as the report later suggests when it points to problems of universalizing an Elizabethan Anglican ecclesiology; see p. 49).

THE TRINITY, *KOINONIA*, AND *ECCLESIA ANGLICANA*

Through the power of the Holy Spirit we are drawn into a divine fellowship of love and unity. Further, it is because the Holy Trinity is a unique unity of purpose, and at the same time a diversity of ways of being and function, that the Church is called to express diversity in its own life, a diversity held together in God's unity and love. (p. 26)

Even surrounded as this last sentence is by less severe extrapolation of scriptural statements into theological high notes, it is still unmistakably loud. The church's empirical diversity (however one might wish to describe that) is held to be a derivative of something going on in God's own self, and indeed its very expression is willed or necessitated by the ontological reality of God as God.

Here is a place where second-order reflection has simply become detached from the sentences and paragraphs of scripture, instancing exactly what I have argued earlier is the danger of failing to correlate theological talk with an account of scripture's living authority for the church.

If one were to try to connect this *theologumenon* to its closest potential biblical match, where would one go? First Corinthians 12 speaks of varieties of gifts, services, and workings, but the clear rhetorical force of the statement is to do with God's unitary and singular purpose. It is a conviction about such a unitary purpose that drives the later church to speak of *perichoresis*—that is, the total overlap among the persons of the Trinity when it comes to the thought and will and activity of any single member. At this point, it must simply be insisted that there is no adequate human analogy for such talk.[9] It must also be insisted that the report has turned human analogies for the church (in some eschatologically realized form) into direct theological talk about God himself. It is here that the caution of Zizioulas (otherwise problematical) becomes relevant. The immanent Trinity is a transcendent and free reality, for which human analogies will fail. This is so, moreover, because the economic Trinity has been revealed—not in what we might imagine the greatest human example of diversity might be, in the body of Christ, but in the sentences and paragraphs of sacred scripture, sufficiently and reliably, because this Triune God therein makes himself known.

What is said about diversity in the church and its correlatability with scriptural revelation about God holds true as well for much else that is said about the church on earth. We have noted several problems in this regard in previous sections.

In much recent work on the Trinity, the discussions have focused on several key matters that fail to appear in TVR. When, for example, James Torrance speaks about the Trinity and the church, he does so from the governing perspective of the sole priesthood of Christ, who is Lord and High Priest, without analogy in the church on earth.[10] When Zizioulas speaks of participation in the life of God, one cannot imagine more concern for the absolute transcendence of the Father.[11] When Hart explores the Trinity and pluralism, or when he carefully assesses the contributions of Moltmann, Barth, and Rahner within a similar climate of concerns, he rightly cautions:

> At the heart of the difficulty of trinitarian reflection lies the truth that there is no created *vestigium* with which to compare or illuminate this paradoxical *Dreieinigkeit* (three-in-one-ness). Neither the three persons of social analogies nor the one person in self-revelation will suffice. We are dealing with a permanent antinomy rather than a dialectic to be resolved in a higher synthesis, and we must therefore continue to speak and think on two distinct levels: now referring to the mutual interpenetration in which Father, Son, and Spirit can be named together as he, and now of them severally in their unique hypostatic distinction in which they may legitimately be set alongside and even over against one another.[12]

The point at issue is only in part the careful sorting out of a Moltmann-Barth distinction over person and being. Hart's larger point, applied to the language of TVR, would be that human language becomes inadequate unless it is explicating something given to it, from outside the natural analogies of human expression, and that something is the gospel of Jesus Christ. One cannot "speak up" the Trinity through human ingenuity; one can only seek to comprehend and then articulate what the scriptures uniquely declare in the gospel.

A yet greater caution would apply to analogies for the church. As Barth would insist, the Trinity is a gift to the language of the church's life. It cannot be read off religions or nature. But because this is so, the church has a greater responsibility to steward this language appropriately, which would rule out any conflation of what it means to say that God is three and one, and the church's diversity models something in God. Diversity can just as easily be a matter of human pride and sinful resistance to the truth of the triune life. The logic of 1 Corinthians 12 is running in the opposite direction to that of TVR, I fear.

CONCLUSION

What must be remembered is that the church of which TVR speaks is not self-evidently Anglican Christianity, on its best three-in-one day. The church of Jesus Christ is, since the Reformation most famously, a divided reality, seeking to see unity beyond those divisions, which seeing and which living is a gift of God the Holy Spirit himself.

This conforms to the reality that the life of God, as the obedient and loving life of the Father, the Son, and the Holy Spirit, is not the life of the church, but involves the present work of Christ, God's bringing all things unto subjection unto him, and "Then comes the end, when he hands over the kingdom to God" (1 Cor. 15:24).

At the moment the gospel reveals the depths to which God has gone to redeem a fallen humanity, in the sending of his only Son, we see the inappropriateness of forming analogies for the church's diversity that are said to be appropriate to the eternal life of God himself. The Virginia Report never speaks of "the urgent dis-analogy," and so, too, it does not speak of the church as displaying a diversity that could, quite really, put itself outside the life of God. Not surprisingly, failure to give serious expression to this dis-analogy means failure to define the terms by which the church might need to place itself under discipline, when those in its blessed midst perceive, tragically, that the life of God in Christ has been forfeited and one of the many idols of human engineering put in its place. That the New Testament speaks frequently and soberly of this reality is conspicuous by its absence in TVR.

6

Bait and Switch

Rite I in American Book of Common Prayer Revision

In this chapter, you will hear a biblical scholar who rejects the choice between "fundamentalism," on the one hand, and "the advance of biblical criticism" (by Anglicans and like-minded moderns), on the other. These are Hobson's choices. For the Church Fathers, medieval church, Reformers, and other cadre theologians, the literal sense of scripture is neither a *sensus historicus* (historical sense) nor a *sensus fundamentalis*. The church reads the final form of Christian scripture as canon, the parts informing the whole, the whole informing the parts, according to a rule of faith.

I will look at the canonical shape of the classic eucharistic tradition (pre-1979) and its deconstruction in Rite I revision. This will entail a series of formal observations. The theological thesis I will defend is as follows: The removal of Augustinian notes, combined with a rearrangement of the canonical shape of the classic tradition, did not produce participatory, incarnational rewards. (That would have been an exciting and salutory outcome.) Rather, removal and rearrangement rendered the Augustinianism so carefully presented by Cranmer a torso and left us with a vague, vestigial Augustinianism and a yet vaguer theology of participation and incarnation. Indeed, with proper adaptation, the classic tradition holds far more potential to achieve an incarnational and participatory goal than its Rite I replacement.

INTRODUCTION

I want to avoid two extremes. I will defend full retention of the classic Book of Common Prayer (BCP) worship tradition. It should take its rightful place alongside modern revisions of the Rite II type (as the 1662 rite does with

authorized services in England and Scotland, e.g.). I will do so not on the basis
of some misguided nostalgia: "Those were the days." Instead, I will argue,
retention of pre-1979 Common Prayer worship guards against a more virulent form of nostalgia: the historicism of liturgical experts, who correct the
classic BCP in the name of what really happened long, long ago, in ancient
liturgy (e.g., Hippolytus).

I trace this liturgical historicism to the influence of biblical studies, with its
quest for origins and theories of development, in the name of finding Q or the
Jahwist or what, after three quests, is still referred to as "historical Jesus."
These atavistic efforts have "eclipsed the biblical narrative" (to use the phrase
of Hans Frei). This view of biblical studies was popularized at the approach of
the nineteenth century in Anglicanism (in the rocky transition from Pusey to
Gore), and it has become the stock-in-trade of theological education in this
century. Little wonder liturgical studies worked with similar instincts. (Sadly,
time will not allow showing how Catholic and Anglican versions of this litur-
giology were influencing one another, but against very different backgrounds,
e.g., the Council of Trent and a classic Anglican Common Prayer tradition.
Concern to correct a rigid or specious Tridentine mass should have been irrelevant to Anglicans, working against the backdrop of a rich Common Prayer
legacy stretching from 1549 into the twentieth century.)

The second extreme I wish to avoid is 1928 BCP idolatry. I will argue that Rite
I is a "bait and switch"; that is, it was created to persuade us that the classic tradition was still on offer, thus allowing American Episcopalians to dismiss the prior
tradition altogether. The instinct to tinker and back-correct, manifest in Rite II
worship, was misplaced and destructive in Rite I revision. Here I will defend what
in biblical studies is called the "canonical shape" or final form of the classic
eucharistic tradition, in four areas: (1) the location of the Gloria as unrelated to
Kyrie, (2) the placement of the Kyrie before the collect as a response to God's
holy law, (3) the Confession as the connective tissue joining Word and sacrament,
and, related to this, (4) the classic tradition's resistance to dividing eucharistic worship into two sections, "The Word" and "The Holy Communion."

If I can avoid these two extremes, I will come away unscathed as (1) defend-
ing the classic eucharistic tradition and yet as (2) no antediluvian in my preference for it as making appropriate use of ancient tradition *on its own terms*,
without the corrections of "liturgical experts."

MODERN HISTORICISM, THE BIBLE, AND LITURGICAL STUDIES

Liturgical revision in North America has adopted the varied instincts of historicism, especially as these have taken form in modern biblical studies since

the nineteenth century. It is not necessary to show a one-to-one correlation between the historicism of biblical studies and of liturgical studies because we are talking more generally about a shared history of ideas, one in which both disciplines have taken form. I think it is patent, however, that biblical studies was the first place where more trenchant historicism had its effects.[1] Because most modern liturgiologists are trained theologians who attended seminary and learned about Q and JEDP, it should not be surprising that when they worked on liturgical renewal they brought to the task instincts borrowed from the study of scripture and the wider intellectual *Zeitgeist*.

What is historicism in biblical studies?

1. The belief that the presentation of scripture must be recast through attention to origins and a theory of development. So, for example, the literary-theological movement from Genesis to Deuteronomy is deconstructed and replaced by a theory of the development of Israel's cult from free-wheeling (J/E), to restricting (D), to rigid and parochial (P). The various pieces that together make up the literary presentation of the Pentateuch are rearranged according to a theory of their proper (original) order.

2. The belief that changes from this to that episode in the development of NT or OT religion are corrections or modifications, made for functional reasons. Luke disagrees with Mark over Gentiles and thus writes to correct an incomplete theological legacy. Past traditions exhibit their pastness in terms of their need for modification, seen with the hindsight of the theory. Things get better or things deteriorate, according to some standard imposed by the model of development.

3. There is no special character to the way the literature has matured and seasoned that would disqualify an interrogation into what is believed to be "the true state of things." Here adverbs are deployed. What did Jesus *actually* say (before Matthew got ahold of it)? What *really* happened at the Reed Sea? Gadamer and others have succeeded in showing the problems with such an understanding of history and facticity, and biblical scholars are well aware of the hermeneutical problem with such a view of objective facts. Adjustments that attend to the formal character of the literature, in biblical studies, could be instructive for liturgical revisors, but sadly there is no evidence that this is so or that it will be so in the near future. (See my concluding remarks.)

How did this historicism affect liturgical study?

1. The appeal was made to ancient traditions insufficiently represented, so it was contended, in the seasoned and matured product of Common Prayer worship from 1549 to 1979. The final form, or canonical shape, of the Book of Common Prayer was corrected by recourse to Hippolytus and other "original witnesses." The very notion that this mature liturgical form is amenable to correction in the name of antiquity ("what really happened in the early church") is consistent with historicism as applied

to the canonical form of the Pentateuch or the fourfold Gospel record. So, for example, there is nothing meaningful in Luke-Acts being separated in the final form of the NT by the Gospel of John, or the placement of Deuteronomy in the Pentateuch. The final form, as arranged, is not cooked and delightfully seasoned but raw and requiring further manipulation and reheating in the microwave. The most virulent form of manipulation comes in the name of historical accuracy: that is, what *really* happened in the early church.

2.   Liturgical renewal offers a teaching example of what biblical scholars call redaction-criticism. In the recent history of liturgical renewal, we have the "before" and "after" pictures in our possession. When we fail to hear "that our sinful bodies may be made clean by his body" or "and there is no health in us" or "and take this Holy Communion to your comfort and make your humble confession," the erasures of redactors leave their telltale smudge marks.

3.   In the ECUSA, a novel thing occurred, in some ways outstripping the discordance alleged by Wellhausen to exist between the theology of J and the theology of P (multiple altars, no priesthood; single altar, priests/levites) or between James and Galatians, to use an NT example. The prior tradition, represented in this analogy by J, was simply banished from use. Therefore, P did not have to contend with J and sit uneasily alongside its variant view of the cult, now enshrined in the scriptural deposit. Instead, J was banished altogether. Its existence and meaningfulness would be restricted to the purview of historians, archivists, and the liturgiologists (who know both the prehistory and the ongoing place of pre-1979 worship in other parts of the communion).

4.   The banishment of the prior history was, shrewdly, soft-pedaled. Rite I, we were told, has maintained the continuity with pre-79 liturgy. This was a brilliant ploy. It was not having one's cake and not eating it either. The 1928 BCP is eliminated from use and is said at the same time to never have been banished. But is Rite I truly representative of 1928, 1662, and 1549 worship, with just the latest hemline?

In three distinct ways, it is not. Here I signal my indebtedness to the discipline of canonical reading of the scriptures. Canonical approaches take the findings of form-criticism and apply them to the final form, or shape, or canonical shape of the scriptures. This is a three-dimensional approach, and so goes beyond the two-dimensionality of form, source, or redaction analysis popularized in modern biblical studies and, I argue here, infecting modern liturgical study.

What is the canonical shape of the classic, pre-79 Rite I communion services? To reflect on the 1979 BCP is to see what has been lost in this canonical "former thing," remembered not (Isa. 43:18).

First, there is the transposition of the Gloria. It has been removed from its location at the close of the worship as a postcommunion hymn and placed next to the penitential Kyrie. Why does one move so abruptly from "Lord, have mercy" to a hymn of praise, except as a consequence of transfers and displacement within a mature canonical shape? The concern here is not with some pure defense of where the Gloria belongs, by appeal to antiquity. (Cranmer made his own decisions here.) The concern is with the consequences of rearrangement of a "former thing," in this case leading to a juxtaposition of Kyrie and Gloria. (Incidentally, I can still hear the upbeat tune to which we were meant to sing the Kyrie in the years of zebra and green books in ECUSA. This could have been the point: to erase the penitential or prayerful appeal of the Kyrie so as to get it to line up with and not be discordant with a hymn of praise.)

Second is the intention of the Kyrie's location. The Kyrie was once a response to the hearing of the holy and life-giving law of God. The Ten Commandments are that gracious and holy will of God to which Lutherans said, "Lord have mercy," the Reformed said, "Incline our hearts to keep this law," and Anglicans said both. A Kyrie with only a summary of the law, followed then immediately by a Gloria, is a disruption of major proportion in the canonical shape of pre-79 Anglican worship. The Kyrie threatens to become an existential grunt: a generic or pagan announcement that God is to be feared—not a response to the God who revealed his gracious will at Sinai in the Ten Commandments and on the NT Mount, from his Son.

Moreover, the retention of the Decalogue served another very important purpose. The Decalogue gives God the capacity to speak in the assembly, through the agency of the minister, at the very opening of the worship, *in his own first-person voice*. "I am the LORD thy God who brought thee out of the land of Egypt." This "I" and this "me" meant we were confronting the God with whom we have to do, the "I am" toward which Jesus' own correlative *ego eimi* is directed. A "dial tone" was established, early on, personalizing and making absolutely clear that our worship is of the Father, through the Son, by the Holy Spirit. "Lord, have mercy upon us, and incline our hearts to keep this law" is personal speech to a personal Lord who has a will and an integrity for which the only proper adjective is and remains "jealous."

Third, the Confession of pre-79 worship included "draw near with faith and take this holy sacrament" because it was a Confession integrated with examination of conscience prior to receiving the sacrament. The shape of the liturgy (to use Dom Dix's term)[2] of pre-79 Anglicanism had Confession after sermon and hearing of Decalogue, Psalms, and lessons, and before prayers and communion.

In the present shape, a division has been introduced between Word and sacrament that is meant to give each its proper due but that leaves unexplained how they are formally related. The sharpness of the division is exacerbated when this time is used for announcements, drawn out peace exchanges, anthems, and so on—all good and proper in their own right, but serving in this location as a sort of time-out or intermission between two halves once held

together by the Confession, which looked back to word and forward to sacrament at the same time.

And, finally, what of the Exhortation? It was only confusion of intention
that kept the liturgiologists from placing it in an appendix with other "historical documents"—that archive of past pieties made uncouth by time's march
toward new truth (what C. S. Lewis called the "chronological arrogance"
that earmarks modernity). The Exhortation can now sound only abrupt or
cruel, given the excision of Augustinian statements from the pre-79 tradition,
the Decalogue, and a Confession from sinful and then forgiven lips about
approaching to receive the sacrament.

The sole rationale for detaching the present ECUSA Common Prayer worship from its prior history, the classic tradition, was given by liturgists in the
creation of a eucharistic rite. In this, the contrast with other sections of the
Anglican communion is stark (the United Kingdom, e.g.).

The burden is therefore on those who created (or reheated the leftovers in
order to serve up) this rite to demonstrate how it preserves the classic tradition. Given the seasoned, canonical shape of the classic communion rite, my
judgment is that the classic tradition was the atoning sacrifice put forward by
liturgists, giving life to a new and different rite I service, with a claim on Anglican Christians in ECUSA. It fails to preserve the classic tradition, however,
and it is difficult to know how much has been lost and what the effect of this
loss has been.

The only way to gauge this is to use an ancient rite (1662), as we did on the
275th anniversary of Prince George Parish, in Georgetown, South Carolina,
and watch the effect and hear the response. Many said, "I felt like I took communion for the first time in a very long time." That reaction had nothing to
do with itchy ears or nostalgia. It had to do with the address of God's gracious
Word and Self, in the classic eucharistic rite, breaking open hearts to receive
the most intimate sharing of himself, in the real presence of his Son.

CONCLUSION

A recent development in the history of ideas is what I would call the "vis-
à-vis" trend. Many suppose that X can simply supplant Y. However, there is a
formal difference to be noted. X operates as a vis-à-vis and requires the memory (fading) of Y to gather its logic. New liturgies are corrections of older "primary sources," but it is questionable how much they can stand on their own
and do the sort of teaching and instruction that was the remit of older rites.
Once the memory of the older rites is extinguished, the torso character of the
replacements becomes less obvious.

In biblical studies, the vis-à-vis of historical criticism operated to challenge the literary-theological assumptions of the final form or canonical shape of the scriptures. It presented a challenge and positively taught generations of students to read texts closely enough to see the problems for which the critical reconstruction was a solution. Today, however, there is so little sense of the primary source itself that the vis-à-vis can proceed fully autonomously, with no such (allegedly positive) challenge. The critical reconstruction becomes a matter of memorization, where once the scriptures themselves asked for that. But when the vis-à-vis stands alone, it becomes a displacement, and the loss of a primary source knowledge is complete.

The second trend is the atavistic trend. What we need to know is something lost to our time. Nag Hammadi, Qumran, Q, "the Yawist," and "the lost ark" are all signs of this intellectual trend. There is a golden age, a magic bullet, a stone that turns all to gold, and it is in the grafitti rubbed out by time's cruel march of power and self-interest. Recover that grafitti and you will know that women were once Catholic bishops, gays were abbots and had same-sex rites of blessing, and, to complete the picture, worship was conducted in a special way, sadly not preserved by the legacy before us.

One need not accept that sin and self-interest are "chronologically challenged" in order to believe that what we have received in the tradition (otherwise said by ECUSA Anglicans to be a leg of equal length on a three-legged stool) is quite more than obfuscation of some "shard" lost in time's cruel march. The search for a clue from a lost age that will set all things right is its own form of sinful idolatry.

In teaching scripture, the atavism trend gave "expert status" to professors who had been to Qumran Cave 12 or to Hebraists who alone could verify sources J and P. Sadly, however, it snuffed out genuine curiosity in all but the more aggressive students and unleveled the level playing field the Bible has always insisted is its primary place of hearing and study.

The third trend can be seen in the example of Bible revision, in which the donkey and slave of the Tenth Commandment almost got changed to refugee and domestic animal. (Why would coveting "the right thing" not still be a coveting offensive to God?) This is the deconstructive instinct, nurtured in part out of suspicion of or laziness toward the objectivism of trends one and two in this chapter. Suddenly, the text of scripture (or liturgy) is simply a matter of our needs, our day, our language, and so forth. It is forgotten, as was pointed out in this example, that "slave" and "donkey" actually connect to a scriptural text, and through that to genuine Israelites, real people, and not cyber images open to endless morphing and remorphing. The deconstructive acids have worked their final magic when liturgy becomes experiments in self-worship, what the scriptures now displaced called without delight but with sorrow and realism, "idolatry."

These three trends are interrelated, and they use each other's respective weaknesses as their food source. Could it not be hoped that a return to primary sources, with fresh eyes and ears—even ones made so by the amnesia of a long Manasseh-like age—would rejuvenate a new generation in worship of the Father, the Son, and the Holy Spirit? Let us take our hope from the example of Josiah and his generation, "all the people, from the least to the greatest" (2 Kgs. 23:2). Reattachment to the classic tradition would signal not nostalgia for a lost day but an assertion of the conviction that God is and has been watching over this part of his body, in ECUSA, even through seasons of famine and doubt and blatant idolatry.

Part Three

Two Testaments,
One Scripture, One God

7

Booked Up

Ending John and Ending Jesus

How are we to discuss the scandal of particularity that lies at the base of Christian claims? Does Easter faith require some form of defensible empirical evidence, which we adduce on analogy with the first witnesses? Does such faith oblige historians, more broadly, to establish the claims of the fourfold Gospel witness by demonstrating the reliability of these Gospels; that is, can they be shown to point to a Jesus who said this, did that, and had such and such a consciousness of his mission, a demonstration without which Christian faith is vulnerable, if not misleading and vain? At issue are the philosophical categories of knowing: through a positivity gained using Troelsch's "almighty analogy"? Or is there an alternative to this quest for "reality" to which the Gospels are said to point, to be encountered in the category of "testimony" or "witness"?

The alternative way of reading the fourfold Gospel accounts here put forward is not one more thing to learn in a New Testament introductory class, after redaction criticism. Rather, it suggests an altogether different understanding of the form and purpose of a fourfold record and will demand from NT scholars who cannot operate outside the lines of what C. Stephen Evans has called "methodological naturalism"[1] a genuine defense of the Streeter and kindred approaches,[2] which in the larger history of ideas have been in place for but a brief moment.

INTRODUCTION

The idiom is familiar. You call the restaurant for a 7:30 seating, and the response is, "We're booked up." The problem is, there is no more room. The "book" is what registers the seatings. When there is no room, "booked up" is the answer. The opposite response is not "booked down," but "How many in your party, please?"

There is another sort of idiom in the Bible, and it pertains to books as well. Yet its meaning is not necessarily so terse and clear. This chapter is an effort to understand the force of John 21:25, "if every one of [the many things that Jesus did] were written down, I suppose that the world itself could not contain the books that would be written." What does this line actually mean? I suspect a reigning possibility is "We better stop somewhere in chronicling what Jesus did, because to keep at it would mean to produce more books than the world could hold." Or, to modify the previous idiom, when it comes to Jesus, he is never "booked up"; that is, there is always room for more, and the books that have been written never by definition register all possible seatings. The negative implications of "booked up" do not apply when Jesus is the subject matter. Indeed, that is the point. Still, it is a very odd image, of the world not able to hold all the books that could be written. One senses at least a possible irony lurking here, and in that sense the comparison with the "booked up" idiom is at once false and yet also intriguing.

A more quotidian possibility is that the final line is registering its awareness that other accounts of Jesus exist. In this, it resembles the opening line of Luke, which speaks of the fact that "many have undertaken to set down an orderly account of the events" based upon reports of "eyewitnesses and servants of the word." Luke knows about these and decides to give his own "orderly account."

In Luke's case, the reference to other accounts does not necessarily direct us to, say, Mark and Matthew as rival accountings, and the entire mechanism of historical-critical endeavor has been released toward another interpretation of this line and of Luke's relationship to Matthew and Mark. Because of its final position and because of its existence outside the synoptic triad, however, John may have a different force when it comes to the final line. The "many things that Jesus did" find expression in the preceding Gospel accounts of Matthew, Mark, and Luke and could find expression in many additional books, should they be written; indeed, the world could not contain all the books that could be written.

In other words, John's placement in the canon (probably enhanced by the consciousness of critical judgments favoring John's later date vis-à-vis the synoptics) as the final Gospel account means that its final line could be coordinated with prior Gospel accounts. That John 21 seems supplementary, that a perfectly good ending appears to be provided in chapter 20, and that in that chapter's final line we have reference to "many other signs . . . not written in this book" all support the conclusion that John 21, with its final reference to "other things that Jesus did," may be editorially composed with an awareness that other Gospels exist and that John's Gospel is appropriately in the fourth position.

DAVID TROBISCH

In a reformatted English version of his Heidelberg dissertation, David Trobisch has sought to investigate signs of "canonical shaping" in the formation of the New Testament canon. That first work paid attention to the Pauline letter collection of Romans, 1 and 2 Corinthians, Galatians, and Ephesians.[3] Trobisch argues that Paul edited these letters himself, de-occasionalized them so that they would function beyond their original purpose, arranged them into a collection, and literally "signed off on them." By observing letter-writing conventions in antiquity, Trobisch knew that scribes were responsible for composing through dictation, and the composer would then reread, edit, add final notations that pertained to more specific matters, and then testify to the letter's having been his own. "See what large letters I make when I am writing in my own hand!" (Gal. 6:11) means what it says. Paul is signing off with letters unlike the tiny script of trained scribes, and we know thereby that he is the author.

In a public lecture at Yale in 1997, Trobisch signaled what would be several of his findings when he turned to look beyond the letters of Paul to the Gospels and the larger New Testament canon itself. The subject of his lecture was the Gospel collection and John's conclusion. The argument can be summarized without difficulty.

Trobisch is in essence a text-critic. He studies New Testament manuscripts. In a major manuscript, he noted a peculiarity at the end of John. The final verse has been written over something, and it can be reconstructed without difficulty. Below verse 25, one sees two words that scribes overwrote to set down the now rather lengthy notation about many things Jesus did and many books and the world. They had first written "according to John" (*kata johannen*).

Scribes formed a professional class. They took dictation. They knew when they were approaching the end of their task (a universal intuition), and Trobisch examined enough ancient writing to say how this was so. Works such as John ended in certain relatively fixed ways. The narrative draws to a close. Then we have reference to the author. Then there is a final, antique "jacket blurb" endorsement for readers, commending the author and his work. This is exactly what we have in the penultimate verse of John, "This is the disciple who is testifying to these things and has written them, and we know that his testimony is true." In other words, some plural entity ("we") is identifying the author of the work as the disciple whom Jesus loved, mentioned in the preceding verses, and insisting that what he has to say can be trusted. And why not, because he has this obviously close relationship to the subject matter of his work, Jesus Christ?

At this point, the scribes sensed the natural end of the letter and so wrote what scribes were trained to write when books came to an end, "*kata johannen*," or "here ends John." But another verse was still to be heard, and so they wrote over what they had written, and their ultimate verse became penultimate. They "stopped for a break" before it was appropriate to do so and overwrote their mistake (which Trobisch, without scolding, has identified).

So where did this verse come from? Not ostensibly from the "we" of verse 24—that is, those who were endorsing what they testified to be the beloved disciple's composition. This verse is aware of the theme found at John 20:30, concerning "many other signs . . . not written in this book," but speaks here with reference not to the context of John's Gospel itself but to the entire Gospel collection. This is, in general terms, Trobisch's thesis; that is, the ultimate verse of John is the ultimate verse of a Gospel collection of Matthew, Mark, Luke, and John. It is saying that many other things have been written down, and such a process could go on indefinitely. The scribes overwrote their concluding rubric because they were right about the force of verse 24 but wrong about the force of verse 25 and its conclusion to the entire fourfold Gospel collection. John is not a single Gospel only but a Gospel in a distinct literary position vis-à-vis the three preceding Gospels (and, as Trobisch argued, intentionally separating Luke and Acts).[4]

WHAT IS THE FORCE OF JOHN 21:25?

Now it could be argued that this final verse means to say something more explicitly about the character of John's relationship to the prior record, and here again the difference with Luke's notice is clear. By signaling his awareness of "many other things that Jesus did," John wishes us to see his account as without any sort of priority. The frank acknowledgment that his record is but one of many serves to tell the reader not to focus on his alone, or his especially.

Another further nuance has been adduced, however. Because John 16 speaks of a Spirit of truth who will come and lead the disciples into all truth, it has been argued that John is committed to an understanding of truth that is in its very essence always being augmented and, indeed, must be. Reference to the many other things that Jesus did signals that books could forever be written down and, indeed, might well need to be written, because the dynamic character of the historical Jesus is by definition incapable of written constraining. Any gospel account is, because of the nature of Jesus, provisional and incomplete. Jesus could never be "booked up," and that is what makes him Jesus!

A FRESH LOOK

Thus far, we have seen that the interpretation of John 21:25 is capable of opposite renderings, and this is so even when the fascinating work of Trobisch is brought into play. Either the force of the verse is to signal John's provisional and essentially supplemental word, over against what else has been said; or the need for continual augmenting, filling up the world with books being no bad thing; or the verse is an ironic commentary on what will happen if people seek to record all that Jesus did.

The emphasis of verse 24 is manifestly on the truthfulness of what has been written and its connection to one trustworthy to speak. To account for the verse, it is necessary to broaden the inquiry in several ways. What is the force of chapter 21, and why does it now speak a final word, when one appears to be provided in chapter 20? Are there any other signs of canonical shaping in the New Testament that could help us through comparison here? Because the verse seems to have a degree of independence, as well as dependence, can we be helped by determining whether there might be an intratextual connection somewhere else in the canon?

I have in mind the conclusion of the Book of Ecclesiastes. The difficulty will be with showing the probability of intentionality, for the conclusion to Qoheleth is a distinct warning about quantifying wisdom. The theme of "many books" is demonstrably cautionary in the case of Qoheleth. As wisdom has its beginning (the "fear of the LORD"), it also reaches a limit. Can John be saying something like this about Jesus? The implication of such a reading for modern Jesus quests is enormous. Are they filling the world with books, that being in the case of Jesus no good thing but indeed a false trail, a manifest ignoring of John's final word and John's role in the Gospel collection, in respect of what is now called "historical" or "earthly" Jesus?

JOHN 21

The interpretation of John 21 turns on the proper determination of its denouement, or final point. John 21 is manifestly supplemental and appears to be meant to be taken this way. I will argue that it has been composed by the same hand responsible for the penultimate verse, and the final verse serves the function Trobisch has more generally suggested, with reference to a larger Gospel collection. More precision, however, will be sought in determining the final verse's theological intention.

We have an obvious conclusion in chapter 20's finale. Many signs that Jesus did have not been written down. These are written not for the purpose of comprehensive chronicling but to produce belief. Heard in the context of the preceding Thomas encounter, with its repetition of the belief theme (vv 24, 27, 28, 29), the point is actually fairly clear. The record as here presented can produce belief sufficient for having "life in his [Jesus'] name" (20:31). There is no suggestion that such a life is bounded by not having "the Thomas experience," and there is every evidence to suggest that apostolic proximity can indeed produce nothing but confusion. This is a running theme in John (2:22; 6:66ff.; 12:16ff.; 14:8ff.; 16:12ff.; 16:31). Holy Spirit and scripture (2:22; 12:16; 20:6) illumine Jesus because they point to him, and so, too, to this record, with their aid.

If we had the reference to quantity in 20:30–31 only, it would be hard to conclude that more signs would be helpful, much less necessary, for belief that gives life in Jesus. The ones that have been written, in the record of John that precedes (there is no allusion to the synoptics here), are fully competent to produce belief. Conversely, there is no suggestion that the believer would be better served by more signs. Nor would proximity to Jesus itself be preferable, for "blessed are those who have not seen and *yet have come to believe*" (emphasis in the text! 20:29). When the next verse speaks of the adequacy of what has been written to ensure that people "come to believe," it cannot be said that more signs would augment this in some way.

John 21 begins as a fishing story, but the main thrust of the story is not on the need for another resurrection appearance (any more than "more" signs would be helpful). The focus is on Peter and the beloved disciple. The more specific focus is on their death, especially the order of their death. Peter will die following Jesus (vv 18–19). Will the beloved disciple die, too, or will Jesus return before he dies? "If it is my will that he remain until I come, what is that to you? Follow me!" (v 22). The author wishes to make clear that Jesus made no promises that he would return before the beloved disciple died, even though a rumor to this effect spread. Rather, Jesus exhorted Peter not to worry whether he would die first, before the beloved disciple. Speculation about Jesus' return clearly lies behind the account, and whether Jesus said anything more specific about this to his disciples. The record is clarified by quoting Jesus' own words, twice for effect.

When the beloved disciple is commended as the truthful author of this Gospel account in 21:24, it does not sound like chapter 21 is from his own hand. On the surface, it is difficult to determine whether the "we" of 21:24 know whether the beloved disciple is still alive or not. In sum, chapter 21, lacking the final verse, falls into the category of commendation of the beloved disciple, the author of this Gospel, with clarification that he could well die before

Jesus' return, as would Peter. Indeed, the very fact that the account wants to put to rest the idea that the beloved disciple "would not die" suggests he has died, as has therefore Peter. This is fully consistent with what the "we" recall of Jesus' own words.

If this is true, is the emphasis on the unimpeachable character of his testimony in verse 24 also intended to set aside a rumor that he would not die, which others traced back to himself? That is, the trustworthy character of the record of the beloved disciple could have been questioned if he had made some claim about the Lord returning before he died but after Peter had died. That allegation, if alive, is here put to rest, and the Gospel's truthfulness in general is at the same time testified to.

REVELATION 22 AND CANONICAL SHAPING

An obvious place where a New Testament writing is closed off, with implications for such closing clearly stipulated, is the Revelation to John.

The vision John has received is endorsed as true, as in the manner of John 21:24, but here by an angel (22:6). A parenthesis follows, with speech from Jesus, blessing those who keep the words of the book, not unlike the blessing of John 20:29. Then John testifies to his vision, is warned against worshiping the angel who delivered it, and told not to seal the vision (22:8–11). Jesus then speaks directly, as at once the Alpha and Omega (22:12–13) and the descendant of David (22:16) and the Spirit (22:17). There then follows a solemn warning about adding or subtracting from what precedes in the account (22:18–19). This is an explicit example of canonical shaping insofar as it intends to recognize the literary form and speak about it as a finished product in a finished form—a form under discussion as inviolable and sacrosanct, deviation from which is eternal death. Then we have a reiteration of Jesus' promise of his coming soon with a response (22:20), and a final benediction for the saints (22:21), who will presumably read and attend to this revelation still open until Christ comes.

What can this conclusion teach us, if anything, about the conclusion under discussion in John? On the face of it, there is no sign of literary affiliation. Yet they share at least one common concern and could have been read as intended to inform one another on the basis of this. Both John and Revelation are obviously concerned with the return of Christ.

It is clarified by the angel that the vision John has seen is not to be sealed. Why not? Because the coming of the Lord is not so imminent as to make consultation of the vision by others unnecessary. "Do not seal up the words of the prophecy of this book, for the time is near" (22:10) means near enough for choices to be made that will be reckoned accordingly; "let the evildoer still do evil, and the filthy still be filthy, and the righteous still do right, and the holy still be holy" (22:11). Still, Jesus is coming soon, 22:12 insists (echoing 22:7), and there will be an accounting, "to repay according to everyone's work." The one who keeps the words of the prophecy will, like the one who believes in Jesus through the testimony of the beloved disciple, be blessed (Rev. 22:7; John 20:29).

Here Revelation continues with a theme stated less prominently than in John. Revelation 22:18–19 constitutes a dire warning about adding or subtracting from what has been written down in the book of this prophecy. And with that dire warning, we get yet a third insistence that Jesus is coming soon.

The Gospel of John ends with a similar concern about the return of Jesus, insisting that Jesus did not say that the beloved disciple would witness his return, even after Peter had been martyred, thus stipulating the time fairly closely. Nor did the beloved disciple say this himself, because his testimony is true and to be trusted over any rumors flying around not grounded in Jesus' own words as recorded.

It is at this juncture in John that the final verse, with its mention of many books being written, now draws that Gospel to a close. Revelation closes with a warning about not adding or subtracting from the book, and the point is clear. Can the same things be said, however, about John's final verse?

ECCLESIASTES 12:9–14

There are a number of obvious formal parallels between the ending of John and the ending of Qoheleth. First, the book would appear to conclude at 12:8 with the motto, "Vanity of vanities, says the teacher [or, Qoheleth]; all is vanity." The inclusio with 1:2 is obvious. Is the Hebrew word (*kohelet*) a proper name, an office, or both? If a name, it also can be an office, and "collector, assembler, preacher, teacher" are all possibilities; that is, the name is not a name without further ado (like "John") but opens onto the world of vocation, not unlike "beloved disciple."

And of course the end of the book proper is not its canonical end, as is also true of John 20–21. Ecclesiastes 12:9–10 functions in the same way as John 21:24, as a commendation by a third party of the author of the book. Indeed, it can be said of this author (*kohelet*) as of the beloved disciple, that "he wrote words of truth plainly" (12:10; John 21:24, "his testimony is true"). Then we have a more general statement about wisdom, running from verses 11–12 to 13–14, in two parallel statements. As with John 21:25 in the account given previously, many have argued that the "epilogist" at work here in these last verses is commenting on wisdom, not just in the Book of Ecclesiastes but in general and as this finds its place in the canonical writings (e.g., Proverbs, Job, and so forth); that is, the final verses of Ecclesiastes are written with a canonical shaping function, to coordinate different writings and self-consciously to speak about how one is to hear them. Wisdom has a beginning (in "the fear of the LORD"). It also has an end: "The end of the matter; all has been heard. Fear God and keep his commandments" (Eccl. 12:13).

It has been argued that this epilogue refers to a specific canonical arrangement, in which Ecclesiastes follows Proverbs and stipulates the limit of a certain sort of wisdom reflection, as found in the sentences or sayings of proverbial wisdom (so 12:11–12, "The sayings of the wise are like goads. . . . Of anything beyond these . . . beware"). These are limited to the literature of the canon. Reference to the commandments (v 13) is likewise delimiting. Wisdom is to be understood in correlation with divine revelation in law and subordinate to it.

ENDING JOHN AND JESUS

If the editor of John 21 composed the final chapter with Qoheleth in mind, we have a clear answer to the question of how we are meant to understand the force of the final verse. Indeed, this same force can be identified at the close of the other canonical writing associated with John: the Book of Revelation. The force of the final verse is, first of all, limiting or, to use the language of Qoheleth, "Of making many books there is no end, and much study is a weariness of the flesh" (Eccles. 12:12). Or, as it might be restated, "all has been said about Jesus. The end of the matter. Fear God and keep the commandments of Jesus." "If you love me, you will keep my commandments," as Jesus puts it in the Fourth Gospel.

A second force is that the final verse of John is the final verse of the present Gospel collection. Acknowledgment is given of the many things about Jesus already on record. John's is not the fourth in a random series. John's could not just as easily be first. John's Gospel is positioned with an awareness that accounts of the earthly Jesus precede, and none follows the same order. John is, in other words, aware of the potential for a quest of the historical Jesus as a quest for some distillate below the record that exists in its present fourfold form. It rules out, in other words, an appeal to fifth and sixth Gospels if such an appeal is grounded in the need for more to be said. It also rules out a retrieval of an earthly Jesus below or behind the accounts given, as though revenge on the fourfoldness of the account was a requirement if justice be done to accurate retrieval of the "true Jesus." John reckons that proximity to earthly

Jesus neither adds nor detracts from the task of identifying him as he truly is. This task is not a human endeavor but involves being given eyes to see by the Advocate and by the scriptures (of Israel) that bear witness to Christ.

A third force is that it could be said that such a reading of John is accurate, in respect to the possibility of his anticipating a quest of "the historical Jesus," but that John is not to be followed; that is, even if John is making such a claim about historical inquiry, he is wrong and ought not be seen as a constraining force on how one regards the earthly Jesus, standing outside the canon's witness.

This would, in other words, be a true force of the last line of John, but not one that should be followed by the modern interpreter.

But this is where the second force must be considered seriously: what if John is not just constraining possible quests for reasons of historiography and a conservative estimate of how portraits of Jesus are to be available for properly instructing Christian belief. What if the concern of his Gospel—what has been called its perlocutionary force—is to do with the theology of history itself? That is, John is considering whether historiography reaches its aporia in Jesus Christ. The literary record to Jesus available in the fourfold Gospel record, with John's own testimony in the signal fourth position, cannot be seen from any angle apart from the one it imparts, in exactly that form. There is no access to Jesus to be called "historical" that seeks to interpret the real Jesus in any form but the one given. Any effort to get below or behind the record encounters a different kind of difficulty referred to in John.

Historical proximity, if that is what we should call it, actually breaks apart the very form of the testimony required for comprehension in the first place. To get behind the Gospel record would be to ignore the pivotal role of Israel's scriptures in showing who Jesus is, on the one hand (see John 19:35–37). On the other hand, to get behind the literary record of the "we" who broker to us the Gospel is to enter a realm where Jesus can be veiled to eyes that lack *in the very quest meant to find him as a historical datum* that very strange gift: the testimony of the Holy Spirit at work through the testimony of the fourfold Gospel witness. It is a truism that *the Holy Spirit's sending is a function of the Gospels having reached the form in which we now find the record to Jesus the Advocate intends to work with.*

In other words, John has in mind a twofold illumination of a sufficient canonical record, a record whose literary limits and form he deems fully competent to compel belief and give life. The chief form of illumination is the sending of the Advocate, but in addition to this, John reckons the witness of Israel's scriptures also essential in testifying to who Jesus is for those who seek him truly. Insofar as quests for something called a historical Jesus must stand outside these parameters, in order to do their work, they will fail to comprehend Jesus on the terms the Gospels insist are nonnegotiable for encountering him. This encounter deserves to be called historical, because the fourfold apostolic witness to Jesus is witness to reality and truth. The burden remains with those who seek something else under the label of historical questing to clarify how their use of the term "historical" can be correlated with the parameters for comprehending Jesus set by the record to him.

To conclude: "booked up" is, I fear, the consequence of ignoring the plain sense of John 21:25. The late-modern world is being filled to the full with books about "the real Jesus." Serious and expensive debates are being arranged for maximalist and minimalist opponents concerning "historical Jesus," and *Time* magazine reports the results for the general interested public. But I wonder if the saying from Mark Twain is not pertinent, "it is not the things I don't know about Jesus which bother me, but the things I do." In the spirit of Kierkegaard, Twain sensed that the problem of Gospel truth and obedience resides in the will, and not in the mind's eager and earnest desire to have the best information, so that faith may follow. In this, probably against his better judgment, Twain heard the final line of the Gospel collection rightly. In this, he sat closer to Qoheleth than he may have realized (though they are kindred spirits). Indeed, it is the argument of this chapter that he sat closer still to the real Jesus, which the Gospels really and effectively place before us day after day, precisely through the medium of a fourfold, uncollated, and at times divergent account. One does not get the real Jesus by resolving this medium in the name of uncovering the true state of affairs. That this has been called "historical" is only begging the question.[5]

8

Of Mortal Appearance

Earthly Jesus and Isaiah
as a Type of Christian Scripture

"Of these and such like words written by the prophets, O Trypho,"
said I, "some have refererence to the first Advent of Christ, in
which he appeared as inglorious, obscure, and of mortal appearance: but others had reference to His second advent, when He shall
appear in glory and above the clouds."
                                    —Justin Martyr, *Dialogue with Trypho*

INTRODUCTION

This chapter comes in two parts.[1] In the first part, a distinction is drawn between
the earthly and risen Jesus, on the one hand, and the "Jesus of History" and the
"Christ of Faith," on the other. Only the former pairing was intelligible to the
early church. This was a consequence of an assumed "collapse of earthly Jesus
with apostolic witness about him" (see later). This discussion is meant to set
the groundwork for the second part, where I focus on the figure or type, "former and latter things," and its significance within the Book of Isaiah. Ambrose
sent Augustine to Isaiah to hear the gospel of Jesus Christ. In so doing, he witnessed to the capacity of "earthly and risen Jesus" to be fully communicated by
a book of prophecy from within Israel's bosom. This is consistent with the perspective of the Church Fathers. They likewise operated from the scriptures of
Israel, prior to the formation of the New Testament. They argued that the perspective of two advents, one glorious, one in suffering, found in Israel's witness, was the key to comprehending earthly Jesus and returning Jesus and to
the confession that earthly Jesus had theological significance: not for who he

was or what he thought as a figure of the past, as historical Jesus, but as one and the same promised, incarnate, and returning one.

The second part of the chapter shows how Isaiah, within the Old Testament witness, can itself reveal what in time becomes the mature two-testament witness to Jesus Christ of Christian scripture. This serves to illustrate that the perspective of Justin, Eusebius, Tertullian, and Ambrose, to name but a few, is built on a solid foundation and does not involve simply working from the New Testament back into the Old and finding things there that simply were not there. It was important that Jesus was who God said he was and would be, and that reference to some inherited, public witness could validate this; the same concern is voiced in Isaiah 40–48: namely, that what has occurred in Israel and in the world at large has already been shared with God's people. The gospel of earthly Jesus and risen Lord is found in Isaiah, *in nuce*. Isaiah saw a horizon of salvation in which the former things are providentially instituted in biblical Israel. Something goes wrong within Israel, and a new providential design is set forth: complete judgment of Israel brings forth something new. A remnant of survivors becomes the focus of hope and promise, and then in a dramatic extension—built on the foundation of former things but incapable of being fully seen on the basis of them—an individual prophet becomes Israel, in suffering and in death. In this way, nations are brought into the compass of the one LORD's dealings with his creation, as had been promised in former Isaiah chapters and reasserted in Isaiah 40–48. The new does not eclipse the old but serves as a validation of its word, even as new things are set into motion. Part of the new thing is the raising up of servant followers of the servant, Israel, and their portion with him in suffering and righteous obedience. Israel and the nations are riven, as the work of God is brought to its dramatic conclusion.

The thrust of the second part is to show that, already in Isaiah, it was crucial that the work of the servant find its relationship to what had gone before ("the former things") and to what God had in store for all creation, even to the end of time. In its temporal, literary, and theological organization, the Book of Isaiah is a *type of Christian scripture*, Old and New Testaments. The theological significance of earthly Jesus is not to be sought in Jesus' thinking, teaching, or sense of who he was (the "new thing"), as this can be reconstructed historically, but in who he was ("the former thing"), given the record of God's ways with Israel: both promised Lord, suffering servant, and the one who would return in judgment. This is precisely what it means to use the language of "accordance" to speak of Jesus' death and rising in 1 Corinthians 15 and in credal confession in the body of Christ, the church. Accordance with the scriptures is the means by which the earthly Jesus is comprehended and located within the plans of God for all time, formerly and latterly.[2]

EARTHLY JESUS AND THE OLD TESTAMENT

The theological significance of the earthly Jesus is a topic that interests me enormously. About ten years ago, I was researching a small book on preaching in Advent.[3] As may be known, in some parts of early Christendom, Advent was not the first but the *last* season of the church year. This is still reflected in the lectionary readings that have come over into present systems. Lessons from the Old Testament and New Testament speak of messianic exaltation of a sort not experienced in the Gospel record of Jesus' earthly life, death, resurrection, and ascension. Lessons from Isaiah are not read to point ahead to earthly Jesus but to the Messiah of Israel and the nations, coming in glory to bring down the curtain of time. Only when the liturgical year became more cyclically oriented did these eschatological passages serve to introduce the Christmas and incarnational aspects of Christian faith. Christian messianism involved an adjustment of the eschatological scenario, so "the full number of the Gentiles" might come in (Rom. 11:25)—an adjustment obscured when Advent is too closely connected with Christmas.

Cyril of Jerusalem is representative of many early Christian thinkers when he enjoined the church not to look back to the Jesus of the Gospels, who in his earthly pilgrimage was mistreated and crucified, not revered and worshiped. For Cyril, the Gospel record showed humanity where it had failed to honor Jesus, and this debit could not be canceled on account of what the record might also reveal about a "historical Jesus." This bears only slight resemblance to the late-modern verdict of scholars who see in Mark the birth of the anti-hero genre par excellence.[4] That is, what we are meant to see in Mark is the refusal to believe and the failure to accept even a risen Lord. This serves to warn against self-justification, against belief that proximity to earthly Jesus was an advantage, against idolatry of past heros, and against conflating the mighty Savior with commensurate belief and conviction in his Way.

Now on the face of it, this need not mean that the earthly Jesus presented in the Gospels serves no ongoing purpose in the life of Christian faith and living. But it does serve as a warning that reflection on earthly Jesus uncoordinated with reflection on the Jesus of Hebrews, at the Father's right hand; or apart from the exalted Messiah of Israel, for which we have only first-fruit verification in earthly Jesus; or apart from scriptural (what we call Old Testament) clues given in 1 Corinthians 15 as to how submission to Christ was taking place in the present time of waiting—that reflection on earthly Jesus apart from such realities would have been viewed by Cyril and the early church as truncated, a torso Jesus only.

My own sense of things is that earthly Jesus emerged as a narrated figure in Gospel form under two pressures, and that these should be borne in mind. First, it is clear in the Church Fathers, up to and including Irenaeus, that Jesus' *teaching* and *teaching about Jesus* is what the church recalls; that is, before the NT takes written scriptural form, the Church Fathers have access through apostolic memory and testimony to a Jesus who taught them and continues to teach through the apostolic recollection and transmission.[5] Earthly Jesus is not a figure to whom pilgrimage is made by collapsing the then and the now, imaginatively or really. He is not a character to be disclosed by what we would now call historical labor. "No one knows his buried place to this day," Deuteronomy insists (Deut. 34:6). This is meant to ward off reverence of the man Moses as past figure.

Moses lives on, all the same, in what he has left, *Torah*. This did not decrease but transformed interest in Moses as *bios*, for successive generations, in assessing the prophetic office and him as the abiding template for it.[6] In Deuteronomy, Moses speaks to a new generation and to every generation to come, poised on the banks of the Promised Land of God's life with faithful Israel and ecclesia. He is the beginning of a line of servant successors like him.

A fortiori, earthly Jesus is teacher, his words live on, and *he is himself instruction*, in an abiding way, but an assessment of who he was as implied by the phrase "the historical Jesus" is nowhere so paramount a concern in the early church. Figuring out who Jesus thought he was (so N. T. Wright, see later) or what sort of classification he should be given (sage, cynic, charismatic) suitable to the times in which he lived could only sever earthly Jesus from the testimony of Israel's scriptures to him on one hand, and who he was at present and would be, *based on the record of those same scriptures*, on the other. What Jesus taught is consistent with what the church confesses him to be, then and now. Here we see the tightest possible connection—unseverable—of earthly Jesus and apostolic witness, not unlike Joshua's recitation of Mosaic testimony and his own "burning bush encounter" (5:13–15) on the other side of the Jordan.

What changes things is the disappearance of the apostolic circle, already fraught with meaning in the writing of Irenaeus (who is usually classified with the Apostolic Fathers of the second century because of his association with Polycarp).[7] With no living testimony, with no ongoing, providential collapse of earthly Jesus and apostolic word, the genre Gospel as written *bios* emerges. Through this medium, Jesus will be available to future generations, empowered by God the Holy Spirit (John 14:15–30). The implications of this for interest in earthly Jesus, as we mean it here, are relatively unchanged, however. Cyril has the written record, but it is a tragic record, and the eyes of faith seek coordination of this Jesus so presented with eschatological hope, this itself to be found in the record of First Advent promise. This is an obvious deduc-

tion to be drawn, based on the plain sense of much of the Gospels and Epis-
tles, which also emphasize this dimension, and so it is not a theological pressure without exegetical warrant.

But now we come to the second and much more far-reaching factor and the
one that will be the focus of my chapter. The second pressure upon the development of the Gospel genre, with its presentation of earthly Jesus, involves
the formation of the Christian canon in larger terms. Both in the ante-Nicene
Fathers and in Paul, earthly Jesus is promised in the scriptures of Israel. It is
not enough to say that the scriptures of Israel looked for a messiah; they
patently did and do. It is not enough to say that the messiah they looked for is
the messiah who will come in glory, for a glorified messiah is how the scriptures of Israel depict him. To speak of accordance with the scriptures meant
that *earthly Jesus* was who the scriptures of Israel pointed to, and this in a dual
and seemingly incompatible role. The scriptures show him to be both executed
and glorified. Earthly Jesus was and is glorifed Jesus, exalted Messiah of Israel
according to Isaiah and the prophets. Justin puts it this way to his interlocu-
tor, "therefore Scripture compels you to admit that two advents of Christ were
predicted to take place,— one in which he would appear suffering, and dishonored, and without comeliness; but the other in which He would come glorious and the Judge of all."[8] Without the witness of the scriptures, the two
advents of Christ would of necessity come apart, producing a historical Jesus
whose failure to bring down the curtain of time meant only that this act was
not what he was ever meant to do. This means earthly Jesus as presented by
the Gospel accounts was misguided, wrongly presented, or some combination
of the two.

Here one sees the logic of early New Testament confession and its necessity. First Corinthians 15 relates in brief compass twice that events happened,
"in accordance with the scriptures." The associations are made with death and
burial, on the one hand, and raised by the Lord of Israel, on the other. This
raising of earthly Jesus caused a mystery for which the scriptures provided Paul
an answer: where did earthly Jesus go, what is he now doing, and how is his
death and raising related to anyone else? Scripture said to Paul, he went to
the Father, he is bringing all things into submission to the Father, and in Adam
all died, but in Christ all are made alive and are a part of this great time of
submission.[9]

Justin makes it abundantly clear that earthly Jesus is sufficiently and fully
available from Israel's scriptures, in his dialogue with Trypho. He needs no
New Testament, which lies still on the horizon, but is satisfied that the
prophets said all we need to know.[10] Earthly Jesus is messiah en route to final
exaltation to the degree to which what is remembered about him in the witness of the apostles is consistent with the Word of God as spoken beforehand

to Israel in the scriptures. Trypho is happy to say that Jesus is a superior prophet, even the best of all, but he is a creation of the One God, blessed be he.[11] Justin argues that Jesus is Messiah and God, and he does this on the basis of the selfsame record, Israel's holy "oracles of God." Still in the third century, Eusebius maintains the same stance, using only the Old Testament scripture to ground the church's christological confession, prompting the editor to explain what he calls this "strange use of the Old Testament" for such an "essential Christian doctrine."[12]

When the New Testament emerged in the form we know it now, the Gospels in genre are essentially about what Justin was about in his dialogue with Trypho: sustained argument with the larger purpose of showing that Jesus is who the scriptures of Israel had in mind. He is who the One God promised. At God's name, at Jesus' name, every knee shall bow, an exegetical move which reveals later *homoousia* logic.[13] It will not do to conjecture about the genre of Gospel apart from an assessment of this argument for accordance with scripture and its centrality to the Gospel form.

Sadly, however, the emergence of the New Testament caused a problem for subsequent reflection on Jesus. That is my thesis in this chapter. The creation of a twofold scriptural canon was and is a distinctly Christian development, with far-reaching consequences for how we think about Jesus.[14] So long as there was one scripture and an apostolic witness—obvious in the New Testament and arguably still the case for Irenaeus, who speaks of the church hearing on the sabbath readings from "prophets and apostles"[15]—then Jesus was a figure of the past who lived on in apostolic testimony, and through the inscripted Word of God. In Romans 3:2, Paul refers to this scripture as the oracles of God entrusted to the Jews. This is the more decisive testimony for Justin in the second century and Eusebius in the third, because these oracles contained the solution to the great mystery of how Jesus was an earthly figure, whose execution was providentially ordered before all time, and also how this earthly Jesus was in his execution the fully exalted Messiah, who would return to demonstrate that he was the promised, glorified Lord, as the prophets had said. The ultimate mystery, and its resolution, were fully resident in the scriptures: the executed one was the One to come in glory as Israel's promised Lord and savior, at whose name all creation would bow down, without any allowable space between Isaiah's first word and Philippians's accorded word. The holy name, *adonai/kyrios*, and the name of Jesus are conflated in mature Christian confession. In formal terms, this is the same situation for the way two testaments achieve scriptural stature. Consequently, 2 Timothy's remark that all scripture is inspired by God (2 Tim. 3:16)—even when the quote means the scriptures of Israel only—can only with difficulty be heard in such a way.[16]

I have argued elsewhere that the emergence of a "New Testament"—both the term itself and the fact of a second written scriptural deposit—is comprehensible only when we come to terms with how the scriptures of Israel came into being, functioned as the living word of God, and finally described Jesus and anticipated the mature confession about him, as seen in Justin's brilliant defense.[17] But the existence of a twofold canon, Old Testament and New Testament, potentially blurs the role of Israel's scriptures in christological work, and this is all the more true under the pressures of historicism. It looks like the New Testament is about Jesus, and so it is. Before long, we talk about a "historical Jesus," a figure behind the record about him, a substance or *res* toward which each Gospel and NT witness incompletely points. Seeing the theological problem with historicism, especially of the virulent late-modern variety, we may now wish to speak instead of "earthly Jesus." At least this provides room to maneuver, and one can understand heuristically how "earthly Jesus" and "historical Jesus" are not the same conceptual reality. "Earthly Jesus" need not be a product of historical reconstruction, only derivatively and historically compatible, if at all, with risen Jesus, bringing into submission Jesus, high priest in heavenly intercession Jesus, exalted judge come again Jesus. To speak of "earthly Jesus" at least holds open the possibility of some coordination of Jesus in the various presentations of him from promise to final eschatological revelation, without introducing language on the other side of Lessing's ugly ditch: Jesus of history, Christ of faith.

But does this go far enough? My concern is that "earthly Jesus" and promised, inscripted Jesus, or exalted and returned Jesus will be artificially circumscribed within sections of the canon where that is unnecessary and misleading. Most will assume that "earthly Jesus" is a more theological version of historical Jesus, but gone in both cases will be reflection on how the Old Testament remains an abiding theological witness, with a horizon that leads into but also leads beyond New Testament reflection.[18] The Old Testament provides the clue as to how Christology can and must relate the earthly son of a carpenter with the One through whom all things (including wood) were made, who will return in glory to judge the world. Put another way, the existence of a twofold canon sets before the Christian reader, now at considerable temporal distance from Jesus' mortal appearance, the live option of understanding the canon's constitutively twofold character as *developmental*. The New Testament becomes more instrumental, instead of differently instrumental, in comprehending the theological significance of earthly Jesus. The subject matter of the New Testament is God in Jesus Christ, at the level of plain-sense presentation, but the temptation is to consider Jesus in an earthly mode divorced from a larger welter of theological convictions concerning his advents. For these, the Old Testament is essential in establishing christological claims coherent against a backdrop of all time and God's sovereign purposes in Israel and in the world at large. This chapter is dedicated to showing why a consideration of earthly Jesus apart from the Old Testament is fragmentary and a category error.

CAN ISAIAH HELP?

Thus far I have been slightly disobedient in my assignment. Rather than address the topic of the earthly Jesus, I am complicating matters by reintroducing a perspective in which we do not have a twofold canon. Instead, a single scripture functioned to present earthly Jesus to Christian faith, when properly understood in accordance with what the church was coming to know of its Lord from the apostolic memory of Jesus and his teaching. I am purposefully placing my discussion within the constraints imposed by von Campenhausen's helpful reminder. It was not the Old Testament that required coordination with Jesus, but Jesus demanded an appraisal that could find full assent only in accordance with the scriptural witness, everywhere judged to be the inspired word of God.[19] Luke captures this perspective well at two key moments: "If they do not listen to Moses and the prophets, neither will they be convinced even if someone rises from the dead" (16:31) and "Then beginning with Moses and all the prophets, [Jesus] interpreted to them the things about himself in all the scriptures" (24:27).

In a recent work dedicated to an assessment of the effect of Isaiah 53 on earthly Jesus, N. T. Wright complains that most of the essays did not ask how Jesus' contemporaries might have heard Isaiah 53 and the Book of Isaiah.[20] Instead, they proceeded backward from NT to OT, isolating individual Isaiah texts, in Hebrew or daughter translations, which seem to have influenced NT formulation, as we can detect that through close reading of NT texts.[21] Or, equally wrongly, a heavily theological discussion has been rekindled, especially by Germans, which is doctrinally conditioned and anachronistic and has introduced a sort of category error into what should be an essentially historical question, which the colloquium narrowed down to: Did Jesus interpret God's will for Israel, and therefore for himself and his disciples, in terms of the Suffering Servant of Isaiah 52:13–53:12?[22] Finally, to complicate this last point, Wright complains that Isaiah is frequently read through a historical-critical lens—precisely the same one judged appropriate and essential to handling the New Testament—wrongly preoccupied with questions of no essential connection to NT refraction of Isaiah's plain sense.[23] A reconstruction is offered by Isaiah scholars of great historical ingenuity and careful labor that could not have been on the horizon for readers of Isaiah searching for insight into the man from Nazareth.

In the remainder of this chapter, I want to take Wright's first and last points seriously and attempt a reconstruction of how Isaiah may have been heard in the period of earthly Jesus. I wish to show that Ambrose was correct and representative when he sent Augustine to Isaiah to hear the gospel of Jesus Christ.[24] Finally, I wish to show that the distinction between doctrine and historical reconstruction is apt, but that the former is far more closely tied to the sort of close-reading model of exegesis Wright seems to be implying for the Old Testament's hearing in the New. Why this does not extend to the New's hearing in the light of the Old or in subsequent theological reflection—especially in what he worries is an anachronistic, doctrinally imposing formulation of the problem—is far from clear, especially when what is being held up as critical for theological construction is a strictly historical frame of reference: what did historical Jesus think he was doing? Christian theology grounded in the mind of Jesus or our reconstruction of what he thought he was doing is surely a truncating of the larger theological task: a description of how God was in Christ and how God is in Christ and how God will be in Christ.[25] These are interconnected dimensions of Christian theology that cannot be pulled apart in the name of imagining who Jesus thought he was and how he thought that, however significant such questions may be in an otherwise curious enterprise called "Historical Jesus Research."

ISAIAH AS A TYPE OF CHRISTIAN SCRIPTURE

In sources as temporally, culturally, and religiously diverse as Qumran, the New Testament, Justin, Clement, and Eusebius—to give but a sample from the Church Fathers—it is clear that Isaiah was interpreted as a canonical whole, passages from very diverse sections compared and used to illuminate others, across all sixty-six chapters.

At the same time, in the ensuing history of interpretation, long before the Enlightenment, a key index in the book as a whole was the distinction between two epochs: a former time and a latter time. It was not necessary to work out how one individual prophet was responsible for such an epochal portrayal, spanning centuries. If forced to give an accounting, theories of prophetic clairvoyance or other such rationalizations could be and were adduced. Still, concern with the subjectivism inherent in the notion of authorial voice is largely to the side in the history of interpretation. To say that the book as a whole was inspired by God and that his word did not return empty but accomplished what God intended over a wide compass of time—this bundle of convictions was far more central to the constraints of proper interpretation of Isaiah than the modern question, Who wrote this or that portion of Isaiah, when and where?[26]

The refrain "former and latter things" appears in a variety of forms in Isaiah 40–48. Not until the final refrain at 48:6 is the emphasis on radical novelty, of a sort that cannot be even typologically present in a former time ("created now, not long ago, before today you have never heard of them"). The intelligibility of the final refrain depends upon its being in a series in which, previously, Israel was enjoined to pay attention to things established long ago by God. The problem addressed by this series is amnesia and doubt about God's sovereignty, called into question by Israel's judgment and Zion's destruction. The appeal to the former things is intended to show that God was not caught off guard by, but planned what has happened. Moreover, the nations are challenged to bring forth similar ancient testimony and evidence from their gods and cannot. The former-latter motif serves the dual purpose of comforting and exhorting God's people and of rebuking the gods and nations who have asserted YHWH's impotence and no-godness.

So, when the final refrains insist that God is about to do a new thing, such a notion is comprehensible only after God has established his supreme and unique control over time. From this vantage point, he can then speak of things yet to come and expect a hearing from a people once without ears that now has been revived. In other words, "remember the former things" and "remember not the former things" are not incompatible notions but depend upon each other and a certain sequencing for their intelligibility. Here the caution about attention to the larger context is fully on target, as against proof texting or passage isolation.[27]

It has been argued that the notion of two distant epochs coordinated by the mysterious will of one holy god is not an invention of the mind at work in chapters 40–48 but existed in germ form in Isaiah 1–39.[28] A former time of judgment and a surviving remnant only, followed by a latter time of glorious and international salvation, belongs to the explicit statement of 9:1 and the larger shape and logic of 6:1–9:7. The mind at work in Isaiah 40ff. understands Israel to be in the latter time, and the nations, too. From this operating perspective, new things or latter things can be contrasted with former things, with an insistence that the holy One of Israel has coordinated this, and no one else; indeed, "I, I am the LORD" can virtually be glossed "Who declared it of old? Was it not I, I the LORD?" (45:21) in these nine chapters (40–48).

Debate continues to swirl over the precise referent for "former things." An older climate in which Isaiah 40–55 was strictly separate from 1–39 was forced to posit prophecies now lost to us that had been issued by Deutero-Isaiah to contemporary challengers, probably concerning the call of Cyrus by

YHWH.[29] Moving Isaiah 40–66 into editorial coordination with 1–39 has meant a rejection of this sort of argument from (historical!) silence, but there is still disagreement over whether "former things" refer to prophecies within the Book of Isaiah narrowly considered or any long-standing, indigenous Israelite confession appropriate to thwart the challenges of no-gods. In my recent commentary, I tend toward the latter view, but it should be emphasized that both choices only came into play once a narrowly historicist view of Isaiah 40–55 and its independence was rejected.[30]

The conclusion to be drawn from this is that although the Book of Isaiah was read as a unified witness at the time of earthly Jesus, it also spoke of a distinction between two eras: one past and gone, which contained the seeds of promise and plan, and one coordinated with it, but only after a period of judgment had passed, by divinely given insight. In this sense, chapters 40–48 could be taken by any plain-sense reading as displaying the transition from a time of former things, including judgment but also promise, to a time of new things, calibrated beforehand, but also giving rise to something truly new. It is this dialectic that reveals the Book of Isaiah to be a type of Christian scripture. The New is dependent upon the Old for its logic, its sense of fulfillment, its vis-à-vis authority, and its radicality. The Old requires the New's authority of Newness and finality to complete its own picture of God's final ways with creation—this is precisely the burden of Justin's argument with Trypho—and yet it is in the Old that the promises and the hope and the judgment become ingredients in a much larger plan of former-latter sovereignty.

Chapters 40–48 also give witness, not just to the dawning of a new day, but of the substance of that newness. Israel is presented as God's servant before the heavenly council and set out on a mission involving God's work among the nations (42:1–9).[31] Israel's vindication and release from deafness within and national rebuke without are not ends unto themselves but entail God's plan for the whole cosmos. Still, even this plan, one could argue, was not all that new, uncreated until now. Chapters 40–48 know that Israel has a role and has had a role among the nations. Isaiah 1–39 know this as well, as 2:1–5 makes abundantly clear. So it could not be said, strictly speaking, that God's use of Israel as light to the nations has no history of former utterance, such as is implied at 48:6–7. The truly new thing is suggested at 48:12–16 and made the clear burden of 49:1–6.

This is established beyond doubt when one attends to the structure of the next section of text, chapters 49–53. The notion of radical newness stated so clearly in chapter 48 finds its counterpart in the frame of this section, in 49:1–7 and 53:1–12. One of the most trying interpretive cruxes in this section of Isaiah is found at 49:3. There is no good textual evidence for a gloss "Israel" in the verse, though such a move is urged by commentators seeking (1) conformity of author and perspective across a series of "servant songs" and (2) a specific servant over against a more generic, Israel-servant reading.

Recently, Hugh Williamson and his students have suggested a subtle solution to the problem of 49:3, which came into play once one paid attention, not to a series of servant songs as such, but to the flow of the chapters as they are now set forth. The argument is that the Israel commissioned to be servant in 40–48 fails in this capacity; God commissions the individual prophetic figure responsible for the proclamation of this material to be what he had commissioned Israel to be: "you are my servant, you are the Israel in whom I will be glorified," is how one might paraphrase the force of 49:3. The individual becomes Israel as God had intended in 40–48.[32]

I have argued for a variation of this reading, which stresses a shift from Israel to individual servant without an evaluation of whether Israel was a failure in 40–48.[33] In addition, I have argued a critical piece of the reconstruction offered involves chapter 48, where the radical new thing motif is introduced. The first occurrence of individual "I" speech thus far, where God and "I" have always been the same, is found at 48:16, "and now the LORD God has sent me and his spirit." This intimate use of the divine name, the tetragrammaton and the gloss for it combined (YHWH *adny*), appears in prominent form four times in the third servant poem, where the "I" describes his individual affliction at the hands of enemies (50:4–11). In chapter 48, the "I" of the prophet emerges from the secret council of God and announces his presence. The new thing is that this "I" is to be Israel (49:1–7) and as such will be light to the nations, and in this way Israel will find vindication before the nations, and the nations will come to the light of knowledge of YHWH.

I confess to coming late to the work of Tom Wright on this topic, working as he does with the latter things record of the New Testament.[34] I was pleased to see areas of convergence, though it strikes me that what he has done is historicize the mental state of Jesus, in a particularly provocative and not unappealing way, through an enormous act of imaginative speculation that deserves to be called a tour de force. It is Jeremias versus Bultmann, but with Jesus' mental and existential state standing in where once all we had was concern for the facticity and ongoing theological importance of the pre-Easter Jesus for the post-Easter church.

What we see in chapters 49–53 of Isaiah is the servant as Israel (49:1–7), suffering at the hands of his own people and likely the nations, seeing God's vindication and God's real presence in his affliction (50:4–11), and dying an ignominious death. The climax of this section is the final, unique servant tribute (52:13–53:12). I can only summarize my conclusions here. I believe the servant dies. Against Whybray, his suffering is more than shared, innocent affliction, alike in kind and in significance to any general Israelite suffering;

rather, his suffering and death, however typical, come to signify an offering for sin for those making confession in the tribute.[35] Moreover, these servants of the servant believe the nations will come to enlightenment and confession because of the work of the servant, so that their own confession stands as surety for what nations and kings will come to understand. Insofar as the servant is Israel, his death is a sign of Israel's own bearing of judgment unto death in exile; insofar as the servant is himself, his death is an offering for Israel; insofar as the servant is Israel, light to the nations, his suffering and death are not forlorn episodes but belong to the way the nations come to the light of truth.

The final chapters of Isaiah (54–66) form a fitting conclusion and again provide the profile that allows us to see in the Book of Isaiah a type of Christian scripture, Old and New Testaments, former and latter testimonies, providentially linked, yet different. From chapter 54 to 66, the servant is replaced by servants. They share in the servant's affliction, for the sake of God's righteousness.[36] They are the seed of the servant, which was to prosper. God's judgment in the latter days involves a cleaving of Israel into righteous servants and wicked, idolotrous, falsely religious, oppressive counterparts, within the household of Israel. At the same time, the righteous servants of the servant are joined by the nations, and together, as Zion is restored, they take part in God's intended bounty. The joining of the nations to Israel entails their witnessing God's judgment, on his own people and over all creation. A new creation awaits unfolding, where the curses of Eden are gone, where old age is nothing but the start of life, and where no labor pains afflict God's people. Zion's painless birthing of new citizens is emblematic of the new life promised for all God's servants, offspring of Zion. Zion sees seed, and in this way the promises associated with the servant's vindication are made good. Yet the servant must witness these from afar, as did Moses the promised land.

Here, perhaps, one can see the character of type and antitype come into play, which differentiates Isaiah and Christian scripture, strictly speaking. We have noted the important parallels: former, latter things; Israel, servant, becomes an individual servant as Israel; suffering and death as the means of extension, bringing atonement for Israel and recognition for the nations; the servants carry on in the manner of the servant, as the nations come to witness God's final judgment, together with citizens as Zion. Note, too, as have so many recent scholars, how closely the final chapters of latter Isaiah resemble those of former Isaiah. So, too, the closing of the Christian canon offers not so much a fresh vision as a recycling of Isaiah's older vision under a new set of constraints and hopes, as first advent and second advent merge on the horizon of YHWH's final intention and former-latter sovereignty over his world.

Where there is space between the type and antitype involves especially the role of the servant and his final vindication. We see this promised in the final suffering servant tribute unmistakably, indeed, to the degree that some wonder about resurrection or assumption, and rightly so, of the servant; especially if, as has been argued, Daniel 12 offers the first exegesis of Isaiah 52:13, taking the *yaskil* of "prosper" to mean give wisdom, even new life after martyrdom. But within the compass of Isaiah, no individual servant returns to "see seed." Zion and Israel see seed, but here a transfer has occurred that has unlocked the original connection between an individual atoning servant and God's promises specifically to him—not Israel or Zion.

In the New Testament, that gap is closed. Earthly Jesus steps into a void every bit as courageously and confidently as the servant of Isaiah, for the servant was sure of his vindication by God. But we must take the servants' confession that in the servant's death an eschatological promise has opened up and been fulfilled. The servant does not tell us that. Neither does he promise his return in glory; rather, others see into this reality God is intending, and he never himself appears in fulfillment of the promises made about him.

Neither is it clear that the servant's atoning work takes the same character for Israel as for the nations. One could say that this is true as well in the New Testament confession, but not to the same degree and certainly not as a developed theological credendum (see Romans 9–11 for the different work of Israel and the Gentiles in God's one act of salvation in Jesus Christ). Nor is it clear that the nations become Israelites or the Israelites generic worshipers, but both retain their identity in God's judgment and division of them both into the righteous and the wicked. One can, however, read Acts 15 in the same way, for the type and antitype are compatible there.

Did the New Testament read Isaiah as do modern historical-critical readers? No. Is this decisive for understanding the theological significance of the earthly Jesus? Yes. Is this significance a matter of Jesus' perception of his mission, as this is revealed in the scriptures of Israel? Yes. Does Jesus' comprehension of his own mission provide the essential clue and starting point for theological reflection? No. To say this is to confuse the authority of God's word held in trust in Israel with the New Testament's according confirmation of it, whether in the reconstructed thought and world of Jesus or in its plain sense statement of the gospel of Jesus Christ. The latter does not exhaust the former, but confirms and elaborates it, forcing its historical sense to enclose a horizon prepared for, but as yet not fully brought into focus, resident in the *sensus literalis* of the oracles entrusted to the Jews. Even here, the clue as to the relationship of Old and New Testament scripture, as God's word, is provided for within the Book of Isaiah, a type of Christian scripture.

9

Dispirited

Scripture as Rule of Faith and Recent Misuse of the
Council of Jerusalem: Text, Spirit, and Word to Culture

The decision reached by the council of Jerusalem in Acts 15 is a witness, within New Testament scripture, of how "the faith once delivered" was creatively guiding and constraining the early Christian community on a matter of great concern. For this reason, it has been taken as paradigmatic for the church's confrontation with another matter of great concern. I agree, and seek to show how this is so.

INTRODUCTION

In the same-sex blessing debate, two opposing positions have emerged. One is that the Bible condemns same-sex behaviors; the other is that it does not, because what we have today is not a behavior, but a state of nature, called in John Spong's *koinonia* statement a "morally neutral" state of nature. In the first position, it is granted that a specific sort of behavior is condemned by scripture, but this behavior entails a form of power abuse. Such behavior is distinguishable from a theoretically virtuous, monogamous (*sic*), blessable relationship, which contains the same physical acts but with appropriate "spiritual"—indeed, Christian—intentions of love. In the second case, appeal is made to a morally neutral condition, one that has no actual known appearance in late antiquity and is certainly absent within the cultures of a yet earlier period. As Foucault has pointed out, the nominal form "homosexual," as distinct from the behaviors associated with it, is a modern distinctive, emerging in nineteenth-century English jurisprudence.

In both cases, then, a behavior or a state is said to exist today that was not foreseen by scripture. Fresh moral judgment within the Christian church is therefore called for, and, if it is possible, this would ideally include appeal to a scripture that knows nothing of it.

In one popular recent treatment, *Our Selves, Our Souls, and Bodies*, this new frame of reference is presupposed.[1] Not content with saying we lack warrants from scripture or tradition for how to adjudicate same-sex behaviors, several contributors to the volume speak of "the Spirit's" endorsement of same-sex blessings. Appeals to tradition to defend homosexual conduct need not detain us here, as the burden of proof is enormous and requires convoluted—indeed, perverse—assessments of male relationships within the Trinity: an ironic late-modern deployment of gender marking, requiring literalism and radicalism in equal measure, both foreign to the Patristic and medieval worlds of Christian reflection on the Trinity.[2]

Scripture, by contrast, is said to provide analogies and exegetical resources for our late-modern confrontation with this cultural *novum*. The Spirit's illumination, active within the NT period, remains active now. Hence the three integers in the subtitle of this chapter: text, spirit, word to culture. Not content to argue from general moral theory, civil rights, or scientific evidence pro or con regarding predispositions (increasingly unreliable in moral argument), specifically Christian writers claim specifically Christian theological warrant and scriptural resources for a positive, spiritual evaluation of same-sex behavior or states of nature. One can see here a hope that such warrant might trump the ongoing scientific debate about genes, states, nature-nurture, and the moral ambiguities that result from conclusions given on these matters.

A thesis of this chapter is that a single source can be found for these late-modern arguments; that is, a popular, quasi-scholarly reading of Acts 15 has served wittingly or unwittingly to generate a whole school of thought in favor of a "Spirit endorsement" of same-sex behaviors. We could inquire here whether such a use of Acts 15 was inevitable, given the pressure to produce a "Christian" and "biblical" and "Spirit" endorsement for same-sex blessing. Stated counterfactually, if no scriptural warrant were needed to adjudicate the moral character of same-sex life, if one could have been content to appeal to a new word for a new day, unprecedented because of the unprecedented character of a new behavior in late-modern culture, then no analogy from scripture would have been required or sought. Rather, a real vision from God or the appearance in dramatic manifestation of glossolalia among same-sex practitioners would have sufficed.

That is, not an analogy alone but *a direct counterpart itself to Peter's vision or a similar form of Azuzu Street/Toronto/Brownsville spirit outpouring* would have been in evidence across all general (Christian) expressions of same-sex life and behavior. Distinctions would then have emerged among those who engage in same-sex life and eroticism, in direct proportion to that which distinguished those gentile Christians upon whom the Spirit came down before and after baptism in the name of Jesus and those Gentiles who mocked Paul at Athens. To the best of my knowledge, no such manifestation has occurred. "Gay Pentecostals" evangelizing the bath-house—we would surely have seen the headlines by now. Same-sex practioners in late modernity have never argued for a spirit demarcation characteristic of late antiquity, as the gospel of Jesus Christ cut a massive swath through the Mediterranean basin and beyond, dividing what had been a gentile world into Christian and non-Christian, Jewish Christian and Jewish.

But the purpose of this chapter is to take the culture, scripture, spirit argument seriously long enough to show it to be false and misleading: a distortion in the spiritualistic, virtually New Age conclusions it reaches for Christians. The source of the argument for Acts 15 as foundational for decision making in the church is a book of the same title by Luke Johnson.[3] Marilyn Adams is representative of a recent wave of same-sex blessings and approval when she says,

> Happily but not surprisingly, the New Testament offers us a model for negotiating institutional crises in the power of the Spirit. In this paper I take my cue from Acts 10–15, the story of how the church dealt with the shocking surprise of Gentile conversions in her earliest years. (129)

Adams goes on to speak of the "taboo" of Jewish belief, which is challenged in Acts by "experience" (130), with the result of an "institution" learning "from the Spirit" and changing its "policies," because the "Spirit's taboo-toppling was the key to the spread of the gospel."[4]

To summarize, then, one could well inquire about visions or tongues in late-modern same-sex advocacy on the basis of Acts 1–15: visions from enlightened proponents, tongues, or other obvious "Spirit manifestation" among those engaging in the behavior. Failing this, we must ask how far the analogy can be stretched that credits to spirit and scripture the selfsame character and authority within the earliest Jewish Christian and gentile Church, attested in Acts, and in late-modern Western culture. Parenthetically, scripture is no anachronism within the narrative structure of Luke-Acts; indeed, by this is meant the scriptures of Israel, en route to the status "Old Testament," from which the New Testament finds its proper declension, these two testaments together constituting Christian scripture. Israel's scriptures, we shall see, are decisive for determining God's word regarding the life of his Son among those manifesting his spirit, inside and outside the household of Israel. Our conclusion will be that scripture offers a word to the church on same-sex behavior, in late antiquity and late modernity, whatever differences between these two contexts may be alleged, and that Acts 15 offers a fine example of how God's word to Israel and in Jesus his Son provided guidance and indeed divine judgment on the gentile mission and can today offer both on same-sex life and practice.

MAIN ARGUMENT

Two challenges must be met in this presentation. First, the argumentation of Luke Johnson must be set forth in as fair and economical a fashion as possible. Because his view is now fairly representative, he can be used only as a "for instance," and attention to his position is not intended as an attack on him alone. My own view is that the pressure to produce such a reading as he has produced is enormous, and so it would have emerged in due course anyway.

The second challenge is to tackle a bundle of interrelated topics in summary fashion, given the constraints of time. A full treatment cannot be attempted here.

The relevant topics are five:

1. The Holy Spirit in Luke-Acts
2. The structure of Acts, namely, is the counsel at Jersualem a pivotal episode, or does the dramatic movement of Acts suggest a different emphasis?
3. Gentile conversion: what does that mean?
4. The four prohibitions in Acts 15: where do they come from?
5. Biblicism and theological reading of Christian scripture (the Western text)

LUKE JOHNSON'S TREATMENT

In his book *The Nature of Doctrine*, George Lindbeck contrasts modes of religious discourse.[5] One he terms "experiential-expressive," by which is meant that the words of scripture describe or thematize a prior religious feeling, truth, or disposition: scripture contains the accidents of a deeper and more universal substance. Modern post-Kantian appeal to religious experience is perhaps best exemplified by Schleiermacher and his disciples.

Luke Johnson operates fully in the experiential-expressive mode. He dedicates his 1983 *Decision Making in the Church* to "the students at Yale Divinity School who taught me"—a dedication later explained as entailing the reading of these students' "by no means self-indulgent spiritual journals" (96), including those in which "committed, sincere and intelligent believers have discovered that their lifelong struggle against a homosexual orientation has been in effect a rejection of the way God has created them" (96). He then says, in 1983, that we need "a narrative of experience" (97). He says not all religious experiences are "encounters with the true God" (99). "We can, as individuals, mistake the movements of the Spirit" (99). Therefore, the way we know the Spirit to be at work is by its fruits. These fruits are described in the NT, and they include rejection of works of the flesh, above all *porneia*, but we are not to suppose that these fruits are wrong because scripture says so but only because the church knows this as truer than "unreflected Scripture citations," which presumably state only by accident a truth that is truer because it is experientially substantive in the life of Christian faith, and only secondarily so in scriptural attestation.

Perhaps the best illustration of Johnson's experiential-expressive insistence is found in his curious reading of Acts 15:16–18. James says that the manifestation of the Holy Spirit agrees with the prophets' words, found in Israel's scriptures (cited is a LXX rendering of Amos 9:6–18, whose Hebrew rendering was likely known by the Jerusalem church).[6] Johnson's take on this is: "He (James) does not say, 'This agrees with the prophets,' but, 'the prophets agree with this.'" Johnson here exemplifies—on the basis of a heretofore unrecognized syntax marker—the experiential-expressive instinct in its representative arc: scripture is not consulted for divine guidance but for correlation with what has bubbled up in the realm of experience in the community, in this instance, "agreeing with the prophets."

In the face of this, let us turn to the topics listed previously. Nothing I shall say here has not been covered in previous scholarship, though the times call out for a reconsideration of what has been said in the light of late-modern culture's challenges.

THE HOLY SPIRIT IN LUKE-ACTS

Johnson, Marilyn Adams, and others speak of a fresh word from the Spirit on the matter of same-sex life and practice, on the basis of Acts 15.

How does Luke-Acts describe the work of the Holy Spirit?

1. The Holy Spirit inspired the visions of pious Israelites, like Zechariah (1:67), to speak of Christ before the incarnation.
2. The Holy Spirit overshadows Mary, and Jesus is so conceived.
3. The Holy Spirit descends upon Jesus in bodily form at his baptism by John.
4. The Holy Spirit works to embolden and comfort Jesus prior to his crucifixion and resurrection.

In Luke, the Holy Spirit is at work within the old Israel and within Jesus.

At the conclusion of Luke, the Holy Spirit is promised by Jesus for his disciples (24:49), though Jesus speaks only of "what my Father has promised" and of being "clothed with power from on high." The gap separating Luke's final statement and the manifestation of the Spirit in Acts is filled by a Johannine stipulation and clarification. What is promised from the Father is the Advocate (chapter 14), the Holy Spirit sent by the Father.

This Spirit comes on the conditions of obedience to God's commandments (14:15) and adds nothing to what original witnesses have heard from and beheld in the Son. The Advocate is recapitulator, teacher of judgment (16:8) and sin and righteousness (16:9–11). He is the Spirit of truth, according to John. He teaches nothing new and, because he is one with the Father and the Son, is about a revelation properly understood as confirmation of the apostolic testimony, beyond that immediate circle, in boldness and in truth.

In Acts, this intervening depiction from John is confirmed. The Holy Spirit is boldness and power, is an endowment preceded by repentance and judgment, and is a recapitulation for those who witnessed the resurrection and a fresh attestation for those, such as Stephen, who know of Christ by means of the Father's direct gift of the Spirit.

THE STRUCTURE OF LUKE-ACTS

According to Luke Johnson, Acts 15 is the key dramatic episode in the theological movement of Acts. For his argument to work best, a dramatic decision in the church regarding an unprecedented event would provide a useful analogy for the church's present confrontation with gay life.

Two forces are operative throughout these first fifteen chapters: the outpouring of the Holy Spirit and the use of scripture to defend, support, and interpret what is happening by his dramatic hand. Cited are Ps. 69:25; 109:8; Joel 2:28–32; Ps. 16:8–11; 132:11; 16:10; 118:22; 2:1–2; Amos 5:25–27; Isa. 66:1–2; 53:7–8; Ps. 89:20; 1 Sam. 13:14; Ps. 2:7; Isa. 55:3; Ps. 16:10; Isa. 49:6; and, in chapter 15, Amos 9:11–12. The density, range, and length of citations mark these chapters as concerned with scriptural accordance, and virtually no episode in the life of the church prior to Acts 15 goes without according comment and scriptural refraction.

Not suprisingly, Acts 15, too, is about adjudicating a matter confronting the church on the basis of scripture. But Johnson's pivotal episode notion requires Acts 15 to be the beginning of a new day: from here on out, gentile converts are not required to become Jews in order to become Christians. An unprecedented occurrence—Gentiles accepting an unprecedented LORD and Messiah without becoming Jews—is taken to be analogous to the church's confrontation with a new behavior today, even one reckoned to be religiously virtuous. Lying behind the pivotal decision is, however, a long process:

> The decision is not made all at once. It is not made by the entire church from the beginning. It is not made on the basis of a priori principles and practices. Even the Scripture and the words of Jesus are reread. . . . The experience of diverse people and the narrative of those experiences . . . *provide the primary theological data.*[7]

The pivotal character of Acts 15 is its bringing to a head all the prior experiences with their raw value as primary theological data. No wonder, then, that Amos 9 is said to agree with these experiences. Once experience is granted priority, it is only a vestigial notion of scriptural authority to say that the scriptures are in any way determinative in the "decision-making process." Ironically, it is an odd sort of literalism *cum* proof text mentality that would suggest the church was searching around in its scriptural legacy to see if it could find something to agree with what was going on. The density, scope, and range of citations suggest otherwise. As in 1 Corinthians 15, the scriptures are God's word to Israel, which, in the light of the eschatological event of the resurrection of Israel's Messiah, are used to direct the church's new life and mission—and that includes a life and mission beyond carnal Israel and Torah observance of old. Here the narrative flow of Acts 1–15 is fully consistent with and, indeed, illustrative of Luke 24:27, "Then beginning with Moses and all the prophets, [Jesus] interpreted to them the things about himself in all the scriptures." Where Jesus leaves off, the Holy Spirit takes over in Acts. This finds expression in the narrative citation of Israel's scriptures to interpret the Holy Spirit's bold work in the church post-Pentecost, with a new territorial horizon.

In order to properly assess how and if Acts 15 is pivotal, we must now turn to our third topic.

GENTILE CONVERSION

What exactly does this phrase mean? Not content with the radical notion that the nations can become Christians through the work of the Holy Spirit independent of circumcision, Johnson goes yet further: "[Peter] says that Jewish believers will be saved by the grace of the Lord Jesus, *just as the Gentiles* (15:11). The implication of this reversal is that Peter has come to learn from his experience of God's work among the Gentiles the basis for his *own* salvation. . . . Can it be that Peter and the Jewish Christians needed the conversion of Cornelius more than Cornelius did?"[8]

Johnson obviously means here to be rhetorically provocative, and allowance should be made for that and for the truth about the gospel's power his statement captures. Granting that, one still sees clearly that Peter's Christian life and authority as apostle turn in some measure on his capacity to properly interpret the raw theological data of experience: in this case, urging his decision to set aside food laws, whose necessary adherence is a derivative of circumcision and proselytization for Gentiles, in order to have fellowship within the household of Israel. His vision and its wondrous conjunction with a delegation from Cornelius, narrated with superb (one is tempted to say, scriptural—namely, Old Testament—narrative) power, conspire in the providence of God to place Peter in the midst of a gentile assembly, in the house of Cornelius, where, preaching the word of God concerning Jesus Christ, the Holy Spirit comes down upon his uncircumcised listeners. His Jewish Christian associates ("circumcised believers") are astounded that tongues are manifested among those uncircumcised, but their acknowledged, selfsame reception of the Holy Spirit levels the playing field. Water is brought, and they are baptized in the name of Jesus Christ.

In the narrative flow of Acts 1–15, what does it mean exactly to call Cornelius "the first Gentile convert"? To answer this question is to revisit Johnson's notion of Acts 15 as pivotal.

Of course, the so-called gentile mission does not begin after Acts 15, nor does it even begin with Cornelius. Because of the persecution in Jerusalem and because of the geographical implications of the gospel and the Pentecost event, an expansion into the table of nations (Genesis 10) occurs almost instantaneously. Stated differently, the movement of the nations to Jersualem at Pentecost is the inverse of the gospel's movement into the nations shortly thereafter. The prophecy of Joel used to interpret the Pentecost event had, however, spoken of "all flesh" as the target of the Holy Spirit's claim (Acts 2:17–21). "Everyone who calls on the name of the Lord will be saved"—so Israel's scriptures insist.

After the stoning of Stephen, the expansion begins. Philip goes to Samaria (8:5). The word is received. Peter and John are dispatched, they pray that the Holy Spirit might come upon those baptized, they lay hands on them, and the Spirit comes down. They preach throughout Samaria.

An Ethiopian eunuch is baptized by Philip on the wilderness road to Gaza. In one fell swoop, Isaiah 56 is filled to overflowing as a foreigner and eunuch, who has become joined to Israel, is brought by baptism into the fellowship of Jesus' death and new life. That he is reading Isaiah and returning from worship in Jersualem suggests he is no ordinary gentilic pagan. To ask if he is circumcised might be the question the narrative *means* to beg.

After the conversion of Saul, our narrator informs us that "the church throughout Judea, Galilee, and Samaria had peace and was built up" (9:31).

Joppa, Lydda, Caesarea, and Antioch, and synagogue preaching, become the rule and not the exception. Peter finds accommodation in the region where he raised Tabitha, with a tanner. Here he has his vision. A tanner works with hides and so is by definition a threat to Jewish food restrictions. The narrator does not explain or interpret this. Before his vision, we are only told that Peter "became hungry and wanted something to eat" (10:10). "While it was being prepared," the narrator states, "he fell into a trance." Food taken to be unclean, Peter is commanded to kill and eat. Meanwhile, Cornelius is praying to God, holy angels are visiting him, and he is a God-fearer and almsgiver, respected by "the whole Jewish nation." Different from the Ethiopian but like him in his devotion to the one God of Israel, it cannot be supposed that Cornelius is a typical Gentile in the sense that you and I once were, before we became Christians.

Peter is forced to defend his actions in not requiring circumcision of the baptized in Acts 11. It has been argued in another place that "circumcised believers" need not *only* refer to Jewish Christians. It must suffice here to merely lodge the suggestion that circumcision, required of full proselytes to Judaism, may have been required of, or thought suitable for, non-Jews baptized into the name of Jesus and receiving the Holy Spirit. We have no good way to determine if all "circumcised believers" were therefore of the household of Israel. What Acts 11 does report is that such believers accepted Peter's explanation and indeed praised God (11:18). The circumcised believers conclude, in a phrase unhelpful for Johnson's experiential logic, "Then God has given even to the Gentiles the repentance that leads to life" (v 18).

There is one further thing to note in this important chapter. Peter has a vision. He uses it to defend his actions at Caesarea, in the house of Cornelius where the Holy Spirit came down as he preached. The vision explains his decision to associate with these Gentiles, but without the delegation and the angelic word to a devout God-fearer, Cornelius, Peter would not have had complete and specific marching orders.

But note what he says to the "circumcised believers" about the moment he decided to baptize those who received the Holy Spirit. "I remembered the word of the Lord, how he had said, 'John baptized with water, but you will be baptized with the Holy Spirit'" (Acts 10:16). He then reasons, "If then God gave them the same gift that he gave us when we believed in the Lord Jesus Christ, who was I that I could hinder God?"

It is the thesis of this chapter that here the narrator gives intentional expression to the doctrine of the Holy Spirit as it is found in John 16:13–15: "When the Spirit of truth comes, he will guide you into all the truth; for he will not speak on his own, but will speak whatever he hears. . . . All that the Father has is mine. For this reason I said that [the Spirit of truth] will take what is mine and declare it to you." Acts 11:16 provides attestation that the Holy Spirit, fully at work in Peter, has brought to mind what was the Lord's own word (Acts 1:5), which was itself verified by the Father as the Holy Spirit descended upon Jesus at his baptism (Luke 3:22). We need look no further for a doctrine of the Holy Spirit than here. One might well ask if a vision without this accompanying word of the Lord, without scriptural attestation from the prophets ("All the prophets testify about him," Acts 10:43), and without a providential conjunction in the person of Cornelius, "well spoken of by the whole Jewish nation," could be a misleading and demonic vision, given by a spirit hostile to the Spirit of truth. The conjunction of scripture, remembered word of the Lord, and the Holy Spirit is essential if experiential data are to mean anything. Acts knows full well of false and misleading spirits and deceitful appeals to experience or prophetic endowment (Acts 5:1–6; 8:9–24; 12:20–23: 13:4–12).

To summarize: No, Cornelius is not the first Gentile to be converted. The terms used are oversimplified and potentially misleading. They are representative of a form of Christian theological amnesia regarding the various ways in which synagogue and, indeed, temple worship had included the non-Jew, both in late antiquity as a reality and in the scriptures of Israel as a divine word to Israel regarding the nations. They are typical because the problems confronting Christianity changed once Judaism was birthed as an ongoing, differentiated, scripturally derived phenomenon, an extension of but also a new form of the various Judaisms existing at the time of Jesus of Nazareth and the church of Acts 1–15.

It would therefore be a form of biblicism to adopt the plain sense of Acts as immediately probative for the Christianity that emerged over time, as its Jewish roots, in messiah, scriptural word, worship, and table fellowship took distinctive form, in the vis-à-vis brought about by God's eschatological act in Jesus.

The charge of biblicism is oblique in the case of Johnson's process reading, because he is a complex combination of literalistic reader deriving loose analogies above and apart from the letter. We will investigate in our final section how another form of biblicism might emerge, with a different conclusion than Johnson's about the force of Acts 15 for Christian decision making, but one also theologically and hermeneutically unsatisfactory.

THE FOUR PROHIBITIONS OF ACTS 15:
WHERE DO THEY COME FROM?

Right away, let me signal my indebtedness to Richard Bauckham and commend his painstaking analysis of this topic in "James and the Gentiles (Acts

15:13–21)."[9] Read him as a correction on my own summary here and, for the purposes of this chapter, as a supplement with close exegetical concerns. In this chapter, I want to push beyond these to attend to theology and hermeneutics as well, which will be the subject of my final section of this chapter.

By now, it should be clear that the so-called Council of Jerusalem does not invent without prior missionary realities a doctrine regarding gentile Christians. Various non-Jewish Christian communities are thriving, under the threefold pressure of scripture, preached and remembered word concerning Jesus, and the bold manifestation of the Holy Spirit. What happens is that a certain segment of Jewish Christianity objects to the willingness to dispense with circumcision for those who are Christians; indeed, final salvation is held to be connected with this key initiatory rite (15:1). It could be that the objection has to do not with failure to become Jewish in some full sense (there is no mention of food laws, e.g.) but failure to observe the restrictions set forth in God's covenant with Noah and all flesh, long before Sinai. (Galatians, as is well known, goes a different way; here we are interested in the narrative logic of Acts itself, in which Peter is credited with the first Gentile mission [Acts 15:7, compare 8:14; 10:34ff.]).

Peter, Barnabas, and Paul all rehearse before the assembly what had been true for some time: the Holy Spirit's cleansing the hearts (15:9) of non-Jewish Christians, neither preceded by nor followed up with circumcision, in the manner of God's covenant with Noah. This is important because it is commonly held that the rabbis regarded Noahic restrictions to be applied to the righteous among the nations; they might apply here as well—quite apart from the question of "becoming Jewish."

Bauckham has shown that lying behind what looks like an ad hoc appeal to scripture (of the sort Johnson literalistically assumes) in Acts 15:16–18, there is a legacy of exegetical practice that explains why here, among all other possible texts—one thinks immediately of Isaiah—Amos 9:11–12 was selected for divine guidance. "The dwelling of David" had become a phrase pointing to the church and its apostolic pillars. "The Gentiles over whom my name is called," based on a sophisticated scriptural (OT) intertextuality, has become a direct reference to Christian baptism, apart from any previous rites of proselytization—including those from the scriptures of Genesis dealing with the nations. An eschatological promise, for a time beyond the days of Noah, has now come to pass. And yet this promise claims great antiquity, "Thus says the LORD, who has been making these things known from long ago" (Acts 15:17–18).

In so doing, however, Moses is not set aside. Far from it. "For in every city," James concludes, "for generations past, Moses has had those who proclaim him, for he has been read aloud every sabbath in the synagogues"—not just to

Jews, but to proselytes. This concluding remark is meant to ground the prior four prohibitions, against *porneia*, meat undrained of blood, idolatry, and blood itself (an obvious Noahic detail), laid upon Christians uncircumcised in the flesh. That these are not Noahic restrictions has been pointed out; their location, in the order given and in specificity, is Leviticus 17–18, part of the "Moses proclaimed in every city." The prohibitions apply not to the sojourner as a general category (as Bauckham shows) but to the sojourner *in the midst of Israel*.

At this point, we should note in passing that Johnson, for all his utilization of the letter of Acts 15 on which to ground his process hermeneutic, passes up the chance to have one of these restrictions—unrelated to dietary matters—continuing in its binding character, thereby deploying a common Christian distinction between moral and ritual law as this would emerge in time, under the influence of a two-testament presentation. The one obvious perduring category, "sexual immorality" (*porneia*), cannot be expected to comprehend something like "homosexual orientation" in late modernity, though exactly why, except by virtue of process logic with massive philosophical ramifications, is unclear. Exactly at the moment when a process was at work of discerning how Moses might apply to Gentiles in Christ, Johnson excludes the discernment where it most obviously applies.

Johnson concludes that the dietary restrictions were, in essence, functionally derived by James, so that Christians and Jews could have table fellowship (including the Lord's Supper). The role of Leviticus 17–18 and the laws for the sojourner, noted by many commentators, is not even mentioned by Johnson in his treatment.

BIBLICISM AND THEOLOGICAL
READING OF CHRISTIAN SCRIPTURE

In the Western text of Acts, we see already a change in the four prohibitions. The situation of James, the Lord's brother, and those for whom Israel's scriptures were *sola scriptura*, will in time come to an end. A New Testament will emerge and stand alongside the Old, deriving its genre as scripture and its authority as written word from the Old Testament and the claims of 2 Timothy 3:15. "All scripture" will come in time, naturally enough, to mean both New and Old Testament, while for James and his fellow apostolic leaders, there is one Spirit, one Lord, one baptism, and one scripture, whose word, in Christ, commands gentile Christians not to be circumcised but to be as the sojourner in Israel's midst—a grand image. In Christ Jesus, by claim of the Holy Spirit, Gentiles once without God in the world are brought into fellowship with the people of his promise, as God's blessing promised in Abraham's

seed is fulfilled in his Son. Being in Israel's midst means hearing God's word
to Israel, under the influence of the Holy Spirit. Cornelius threw himself at
Peter's feet, and so, too, the early church threw itself before God's word, having, like Cornelius, been brought near in Christ.

The late-modern, virtually all-gentile Christian church does not stand
beside James and Cornelius. Here Luke Johnson is right, but not by the logic
of his process-experience model. If we are looking for a dynamic by which to
comprehend the movement out of the providential moment of that first generation, we have one tailor-made in the way the four prohibitions changed
under the pressure of tragic separation from the emerging Judaism.

Murder, idolatry, *porneia*, and doing to neighbor as self become the prohibitions or rule of Christian life, as one scripture gives way to two testaments,
and new theological forces emerge from new exegetical parameters. There is
no process by which, given these new parameters, we can draw a line from prohibitions against *porneia* to blessing same-sex relationships, any more than the
Christian community has the freedom to endorse idolatry or murder. That has
been the consistent teaching of the church, East and West, because it is the
word of the Lord, the word of scripture, and the word of the Holy Spirit, one
with the Father and the Son.

When the Jewish-Christian matrix is replaced, Judaism is birthed alongside
a unique Christian development: retention of the scriptures of Israel as God's
word to Gentiles in Christ and the formation of what would come to be called
the New Testament. The relationship between these two is not developmental, in some simple chronological sense, but involves the subject matter:
Father, Son, and Holy Spirit, the Lord of Israel and the heavens and the earth.
James and the early Christian community knew that in Christ we were seeing
the first-fruits of a final consummation. Far from driving it away from the
scriptures of Israel, Jesus provided the clue to their interpetation and gave simple access to those once far off. Israel was something of a loner in antiquity on
the matter of *porneia*, and her failures in this regard—in religious expression
no less than in carnal expression—testify to the holiness of God, not of his people. The early church never regarded this as an "example of pre-modern ignorance" but, in Christ, as a glimpse at life eternal, a mirror of the fidelity and
holy obedience among of the persons of the Trinity themselves.

It is time to shift the discussion away from scripture's plain word to pastoral
care. In that sense, appeal to experience is right: as indicating where God's
Holy Spirit and Word are to judge, heal, inspire, and renew, for those of us
brought near by his sacrifice for our sakes.

10

Handing Over the Name

Christian Reflection
on the Divine Name YHWH

In this chapter, I investigate what it means for Christians to have possession of an Old Testament scripture in which the Name of God is central to its highest theological claims.[1] Yet that name is not sounded in either the New Testament or common Christian practice. Instead, it is referenced by means of various conventions.

I offer this chapter in tribute to Professor Jenson, who has labored to speak of the name of the God of Israel as he who "raised Israel from the dead."[2] This effort at equivalence with Christian claims—namely, that God is he who "raised Jesus from the dead"—goes a long way toward highlighting for Christians the delicate matter of identity in speaking of God's person. God's identity in Christ must be situated in relationship to God's identity with and to Israel.

THE PROBLEM: CONVENTIONS

The LORD

The most widely adopted convention for speaking of the God of Israel by name is based on the translation practice in place when the scriptures were prepared for Greek speakers, and it is the one we are most familiar with. The named God of Israel is referred to as "the LORD" (*kyrios*). That the earliest renderings also preserve other conventions need not bother us here.[3] It should remind us, however, that the situation was fluid from the very beginning, and the production of a major, large-scale translation meant that the inherited fluidity was being constrained and interpreted through the very nature of the undertaking. The Hebrew text of the Old Testament was likely already evidencing similar conventions within its own field of expression (see the use of *adonay* before YHWH in Isaiah 50:3–9, for example). I will say more about that in due course.

Even to speak aloud the convention "the LORD" points to a fundamental problem. It is impossible to differentiate, in public speech, between a common use of the English word "lord" or even "the Lord" and this very specific convention (LORD), whereby a personal name has been glossed, out of reverence, fear of misuse, or other such probable explanations. Capitalization in the convention (LORD) cannot be orally reproduced.[4]

This situation can be helpfully illustrated with a modern example. When celebrating the twenty-fifth anniversary of the (then illegal) ordination of women in the Episcopal Church, the worshipers were not to have to hear the phrase "the Lord" in their praying, because it was patently a male-oriented, oppressive term. The logic of the complaint is by now familiar and, in certain circles, unimpeachable.

But at just what is the umbrage directed? At a metaphor ("lord"), at a person who is called that in scriptural texts (Jesus "my Lord"), at the naming practice itself (by disciples, the church, etc.), or at the convention here under discussion, whereby Israel's properly named God is referred to, for dense historical reasons, the LORD? Ironically, an act intended to guard a personal name, with corollary—indeed, massive—implications for what it means to address Jesus this way, has at the end of our era been heard as an act of oppression. The most charitable thing to say is that those who feel oppressed have forgotten, if they ever knew, that the practice of referring to God's personal name by this convention coincided with the joy and bracing confession of seeing in Jesus of Nazareth the very face of God, the LORD, the maker of heaven and earth.[5]

What this illustrates, however, is the far more banal problem of asking a convention to carry the weight of its own clarification, which it patently does not. Moreover, there is no good way to speak the convention aloud and stipulate thereby that the God who raised Jesus from the dead is intended (the LORD), and not the raised One himself (e.g., "my Lord and my God"). Traditionally, context has been relied on to provide the clarification and, added to this, a certain basic knowledge of Christian or Jewish faith, but these are the two things precisely under negotiation at present. It is probably no coincidence that repudiation of the name of God under the cover of liberating us from oppression in reality means detaching Jesus as Lord from convictions about the One who raised him, the LORD. Instead of the Named One (YHWH), the Philadelphia worshipers invoked a god they called "Sophia." Here we have a strange turnabout. A common Greek word for wisdom is meant to stand as a personal name, allegedly because it points to a deity or a deifiable Hebrew reality, which, of course, has no personal name in the manner that Israel's God does. This is a perfect inversion of the state of affairs proclaimed by the Old Testament and Christian theology. A personal name has become a Greek concept has become a deity invoked to offset the offense of "lordliness." "They know not what they do," one might generously infer, but that is far from clear.

The "Yahweh" Convention

I have written in other places about the problem of actually presenting us with what purports to be a true or proximate vocalization of the personal name of God.[6] But I want to go over more of that ground here. Parenthetically, I saw a livery service at a major airport in the United States called "Yahweh's Transportation Service," or something to this effect. I doubt scholars responsible for this learned production of the name would have anticipated the success of their efforts along these lines.

Although it is not possible to police motivations, it is possible to conjecture about the reasons for this modern practice having taken such hold.

First, there was the recognition that an older practice of calling God "Jehovah" and meaning thereby to state his personal name was based on a mistake (I use the term with caution); that is, the vowels supplied for the name were drawn from its ancient gloss (e, o, a from *'adonay)* and not from the name proper. This conflation produced a perfectly presentable, suitably sonorous name for God, Jehovah, and it gives one pause to consider how many people, how many hymns, and how much praying went on under the influence of the King James Bible's rendering. Indeed, simply in the realm of linguistic aesthetics (not to mention livery service advertising), I think one could make the argument that the name Jehovah is in fact a decent rival for "Yahweh." In the light of the Philadelphia example, we ought not forget that knowledge and custom are two different things and spin on different orbits. The custom of speaking of Yahweh instead of Jehovah is now largely independent of any knowledge of the reasons that we have these two alternatives in the first place.

Second, and related to this ethos of "scholarly correction," was the conviction that we actually stood in a better position to vocalize the name properly than we had before, based on our knowledge of Hebrew, cognate languages, and other matters. This confidence was part and parcel of a general mood of enthusiasm ushered in with the rise of historical criticism, among its manifold practitioners. A quick look at Frank Cross's *Canaanite Myth and Hebrew Epic* will show a confident discussion of the divine name with arguments for the vocalization adopted based on internal and comparative linguistic investigations.[7]

Third, it was thought to somehow de-Christianize the Old Testament if we could speak the name of God unsullied by later conventions, and this was judged a good thing. The hunt for origins and the atavism that hovered all around encouraged us to "get at the true picture of things" without later contaminations or missteps. The Jerusalem Bible adopted the convention of referring to the personal name Yahweh directly, not as Jehovah or through a glossing convention, and many popular lectionaries and preaching aids went along with this, too. Far from being a scholarly move only, all church people could hope that with the proper name available for pronunciation, we would be getting a truer picture, would be capturing the God of the Old Testament on his/God's own terms, would be standing alongside Moses and Miriam, not just Paul or Peter or later churchly practices, and so forth.[8]

A fourth version of this comes with specific ecumenical concern. At a conference on prayer I recently attended, one prominent New Testament scholar defended his use of "Yahweh" in his writing and in his speaking, quite passionately, as connected with his sensitivity for honoring the "Jewish context" of Jesus. Because most people do not understand the function of the convention "the LORD" and its connection to a personal name, it was argued that the use of "Yahweh" will remedy that and will assure that the historicality of the New Testament remains in the forefront. It does not matter, in the logic of this concern, whether the historical context of the New Testament was actually more familiar with a convention (*kyrios*) than with an alleged vocalization ("Yahweh"). Reproducing the vocalization in our day will jog us into a more historically oriented mode, and release, it is hoped, the historical character of the New Testament in a theologically appropriate way. Using the name Yahweh, in other words, serves the purpose of putting us on notice that God has a personal name, and that putting on notice is the critical thing, indeed, it may be supposed, more so than the actual name itself. Therein, to my mind, lies a major part of the problem. Are we honoring the name by vocalizing it or honoring historical contextualization as theologically necessary?

At this juncture, it would be appropriate to suggest what is wrong with these several rationales for vocalizing God's personal name as "Yahweh."

First, the scholarly production of the name is just that; that is, it does not belong to any genuine history of usage in the life of the church or in the wider culture in the manner recent scholars mean. Indeed, that is its appeal! As a scholarly finding, in other words, it turns on special knowledge, which is, in turn, open to debate and scrutiny only within a fairly circumscribed realm. What if, for example, someone were to argue that the proper vocalization of the name of God was "Yehweh"? In practical terms, would a new Bible version have to appear with all references to God's personal name spelled this way?

Would the precise inflection have to be policed? Who would be in a position to judge which vocalization was accurate?

Let us be clear. In a matter as important as God's name, it would certainly be possible (and, indeed, it has happened) that scholars would produce a different, equally precise vocalization. Why would "Yahweh" remain in currency? For all sorts of reasons that have nothing whatsoever to do with scholarship, which shows that "Yahweh" is not in a position to lay claim to any scholarly lock on accuracy, *but has simply become its own kind of convention*. That has to do with the fact that the Old Testament has not chosen to preserve for us one precise vocalization but, in the form we have it, has left that precision hidden and therefore lost to the ages. What does it mean, then, to recover or discover the vocalization? It is nothing more than the reassertion of a convention under the guise of learning and accuracy.

Second, it is helpful to be clear about what we are doing when we purport to be pronouncing the name of God, "Yahweh." I suspect the practice of saying "Jehovah" is different at this point, because in reproducing this name in Bibles there was not the same attendant confidence about recovering or discovering the "real" name. The reproduction of the name was innocent and genuinely naïve and likely had something more to do with respect than learning. The return to primary sources meant that the name was there for translation on the terms it appeared to wish to be rendered, and in this, translators of the Hebrew into a daughter tongue were keeping company with other translators, not doing them one better.

The desire for sympathetic participation in the life of Israel, or with some New Testament version of it, can only with difficulty be squared with the practice of actually speaking the word "Yahweh" and meaning thereby "the personal God of Israel who raised Jesus from the dead." "Yahweh" is, after all, a transliteration extruding into the daughter translation. It does not exist with any possible cognation in the English language, except, of course, as an exception, as a "marked word," in the same way "Moshe" or *fatwa* are marked.

The effects of this on sympathetic participation are twofold and massive. First, the word will of necessity be "foreign," and that runs counter in the nature of the thing to wonted intimacy and participation. How much personal prayer addressed to Yahweh actually takes place? Second, and this is far more critical, we are told that the name, when it is explained to us in Exodus 3, has something to do with the verb "to be" (*hyh*). God's personal name conveys something about him personally, and that something entails being or becoming. Stated differently, those who spoke the name of God heard therein a reference to God being or becoming something, and that resonance existed within the framework of the Hebrew language. It cannot, by definition, exist in another language. Moreover, the name of God is related to a specific act of being or becoming, riveted to Israel's own historical experience and memory, and that is God's *being who he would dramatically and really be,* in deliverance from Egypt and revelation at Sinai, acts which are themselves demonstrations that YHWH is Lord, the maker of heaven and earth.[9]

It is simply false to believe that pronouncing the phoneme *yahweh* in English will produce anything like the same sets of associations and identifications that are said by the account of participants in those events to have been in place, when God revealed his name and said something crucial about it and about himself, at the same time. "Then you shall know that I am the Lord" is the way YHWH puts it through his various servants, Moses, Ezekiel, and Isaiah the latter.

YHWH and Kindred Conventions

Here we confront the opposite problem as with the convention, "the Lord." Certain conventions for handling the divine name work only in texts, not in speech, and indeed their rationale is thereby disclosed. By leaving the vowels out, a signal is sent that pronunciation and signification are different things. Saying aloud "the Lord" can lead to the Philadelphia confusion mentioned previously, whereas adopting the convention of vowelless signing solves the problem but at the cost of leaving unresolved what we are meant to say. W. F. Albright is said to have argued that whenever an obscurity in Hebrew declared itself in the text, the wisest translation practice was to simply indicate by dots an ellipsis and leave the text untranslated. This is an example of how the phrase "merely academic" is not a compliment. Ellipsis invites us to defer to a mother text, but silence in speech is still silence and not genuine communication of the sort most seek when they wait to hear the Bible's word.

In any event, this sort of textualized convention is restricted in the nature of the thing and does not move us very far along in how to handle the problem of the divine name. What it does suggest, just the same, is that many conventions have their home in quite specific settings. The practice of referring to God's name as "the name" (*hashem*) or with a substitute acclamation, "the Eternal" (*ha'olam*), went on within circles that knew full well that God has a personal name, and they were not offering thereby new substitutes or learned corrections but were ranging their practice alongside the Bible's own interior logic.[10]

This is particularly true in the case of *hashem,* "the Name." Throughout the Psalms, for example, we are bidden to praise God's name. God's name is worthy of honor, we are told, and that statement is made and can be made without the tetragrammaton ever appearing, though usually a parallelism asserts this. In other words, in the Psalms it is the reverence held for Israel's God, known by reference to his revealed name and self, which leads to the practice of holding up the name while not mentioning it as such. "Bless the LORD, O my soul, and all that is within me, bless his holy name" will become in time, "Bless the Name, O my soul."

Barth once said that all Christian theology is commentary on the phrase YHWH-*kyrios*. The practical problem remains of how to speak of the God of Israel by his personal name.[11]

New Testament

It cannot be our task here to sort out the various social and historical reasons for the Name's withdrawal from the sort of general speech and use we see throughout the Old Testament.[12] One thing that is clear is that the New Testament presents no exception to this picture and, if anything, confirms it. At most, we see allusions to the divine name or evocations of it. The "I am" statements of Jesus in John's Gospel and his statement that "before Abraham was, I am" appear to direct us to the "I am who I will be" divine (first-person) explanation for the name, as this is found in Exodus 3:14. John is both insistent that the Father is greater and that Jesus and the Father are one, and the "I am" statements assert through the simple force of their declaration what later theologians sought in the term "of one substance" (*homoousia*) to describe the relationship between Jesus and the LORD, the God of Israel, maker of heaven and earth.[13]

Otherwise, what we find throughout the New Testament is not the personal name but conventions for referring to YHWH or attributions that point to him. Again, there is not space here to demonstrate all of these, but two can be filed by title (a third I will look at in detail later in this chapter). "The God who made the world and everything in it, he who is Lord of heaven and earth" is Paul's language in Athens before his non-Jewish audience (Acts 17:24). "The Lord of heaven and earth" is doubtless an unambiguous reference to YHWH that should not be thought of as Paul's effort at genericizing deity on behalf of his audience; indeed, it is more likely that here Paul uses a formal convention already well established in his own Jewish context. The only referent he intends by this is YHWH, making Paul's use of the phrase before those who worship other gods, including an unknown one, confessional by its mere utterance.

Second, in the Book of Revelation, alongside the very high Christology associated with the Lamb, the Son of God, we hear in the opening chapter a self-declaration that could otherwise appear in the Old Testament without further ado. Isaiah 44 and Exodus 3 (and doubtless other texts) combine to announce in a new spirit of inspiration, "'I am the Alpha and the Omega,' says the Lord God, who is and who was and who is to come, the Almighty" (Rev. 1:8).

In both cases, reference to YHWH by specific attribution or convention stands on its own, and we must wait to see how christological statements are correlated with it. Here is Christian theology at its most basic and crucial form, as commentary on the divine name YHWH-*kyrios*.

Holy Trinity One God

In the last decades, there has been a trinitarian revival of sorts. Moltmann's *Crucified God* (English translation, 1972)[14] was an effort to detach discussion of God in Christ from a conceptual framework overly indebted to metaphysics and Hegelianism. This meant greater attention to the literal sense of the New Testament and especially the passionate and nonpropositional character of its depiction, which never fit well in certain metaphysical discussions. The language "crucified God" was selected to drive home the outlandish potential of Christian God-talk. This also obliged Moltmann to be clear about God-talk with respect to God the Father, because the crucified God was God the Son. At this point, it was not clear he had escaped the gravity pull of previous metaphysical systems, and I shall have more to say about this in constructive proposals to follow.[15]

Alongside this, there has been a wider effort to speak in more personal terms about the Trinity. Here again, the blame is assigned to a metaphysics more interested in substance or being, and coherency, than in personal language true to God's personal character. Sometimes the appeal has nothing to do with scripture's *sensus literalis*, or defense of its specific, personal language over against philosophical systems. Who would not want a personal deity, dancing and celebrating, within one's own self?

But the problem is with simply introducing yet another, friendlier or more participatory trinitarian conception, without any genuine anchorage in Christian scripture as a whole, Old Testament and New Testament. Swapping philosophical systems is not what Paul was about at Athens, at any rate.

One can see how a special burden is here carried by the Name in the Old Testament and in Christian theology. Is it not the self-revelation of God, in his name, that stands at the very center of the Old Testament? It is hard to imagine a more personal form of disclosure. It is the word "God" that opens itself to abstraction and depersonalizing manipulation. The word "God" (*'elohim*) in the Old Testament carries with it this and other problematics, including the capacity for natural existence within polytheism, idolatry, and syncretism. The sentence "I am the LORD your God" is a dense confession, combining two things: the personal and the sovereign. This rules out any genericizing or universalizing from anthropological insight and rules in jealousy as the decisive complement to holiness and righteousness in God's personal character.[16] He will be as he is quite truly, in the disclosure of himself to a people he loves and holds accountable for that love, with jealousy and holiness. It is this solemn disclosure that grounds the personal character of God and shows his name to be the critical lens on himself, without which history reveals nothing and "acts of God" make no sense at all except as conjuring tricks of the wise or crafty.

THE NAME IN THE OLD TESTAMENT

I have at other places sought to establish the centrality of God's personal name for any theological account of the Old Testament theologically. In this, I am following where others have led the way (e.g., Zimmerli). I will only summarize and abridge here, because I am concerned to return to the question of trinitarian talk and the practical need for personal language about the God of Israel, the LORD, maker of heaven and earth.[17]

In the revelation of the name in the Book of Exodus, several things are going on at once. Only narrative is in a position to carry the weight of establishing theological truth when so much is at stake and when the issues are so complicated. Propositions or religious experientialism fall short.[18]

First, there is the revelation of God's name to Moses. Moses asks to know God's name because he does not know it and assumes when he appears before the people of Israel, commissioned by him for them, they will know the name and will expect him to know it as well. How else could they verify that the God of Israel, and not someone else, had sent him? God reveals his name to Moses in response to his request.

Second, however, the revelation of the name gathers to itself a set of other concerns, over and above validating Moses, should such an inquiry arise from the people of Israel. Before the solemn declaration of God's name, hints are given that God's name will involve the verb "to be" or "to become." The phrase "say to the Israelites, 'I AM has sent me to you'" (Exod. 3:14) harks back to the response of God to Moses at verse 12 about his own adequacy ("I will be with you") before the formal explanation is given at verse 14.

Third, this explanation of God's name is meant to say something to Moses and to the Israelites who otherwise know the name, as well as to the reader, and the full import of this is not shared until Exodus 6. At this juncture, Moses has joined the Israelites and has himself been joined by Aaron. An audience with Pharaoh has, as God indicated it would, demonstrated Pharaoh's resistance. Exodus 6 then explains to a complaining Moses that the resistance is part of God's design, that a protracted encounter will eventually mean a dramatic deliverance, and that "you shall know that I am the LORD your God, who has freed you from the burdens of the Egyptians" (Exod. 6:7). Knowing the name is one thing, and knowing God as he means to be known is another thing, and this latter knowledge will come after trial and testing, so that all the world may know as well that the LORD is God.[19]

The cruciality of the name is also underscored in the context of sin and forfeit, in the affair of the golden calf. How Moses is assured that God will accompany a sinful people, and not a surrogate, is by God speaking forth his name, "The LORD, the LORD, the compassionate and gracious God" (34:6). The name is presence and testimony to a specific shared history that will go on with this people.

BEING AND PERSON IN EXODUS 3:14

Understood in this way, it is clear that the name of God in the exodus narratives is as personal a disclosure as God can make. God's name is himself; God's name expresses his promise and his faithfulness to that promise, to his elected people.

As is well known, the Greek rendering of Exodus 3:14 produced a different nuance, and the reason for this has been sought within different conceptual priorities. The English translation, "I am who I am," especially when heard in isolation from the narrative movement of Exodus 3–14 and its governing logic revealed at 6:7 (an isolation now assisted by talking about discrete sources in the Pentateuch), could almost be heard as pointing to the Hebrew *'ani 'asher 'ani*, "what I am I am," or, encroach no further. Then we would be in the realm, not of disclosure, but of its opposite, the stuff of Rudolph Otto's *hin und her* (fascination/dread).[20]

But the rendering of the Hebrew behind "I am who I am" was picked up differently in the LXX, as a statement involving God's being (so also Maimonides).[21] "I am the One who is" (*ego eimi 'o on*) is the daughter rendering into Greek. It was this nuance, arguably different than the narrative direction of Exodus, that in turn influenced certain New Testament and subsequent theological statements, focused on being, rather than personality. It is a very small leap to see how *ousia* dominated the options for trinitarian confession. In my judgment, later trinitarian statements would be wrongly judged antiexegetical or philosophical, rather than scriptural. Instead, their scriptural location was either detached or obscured, given the climate of exchange, or the Hebrew tradition in place in Exodus was wrongly assessed to begin with because of the LXX rendering. In the case of Exodus 3:14, we are not learning something about God's substance or essence but something about a personal identity and history he is about to make good on at Sea and Sinai.

HANDING OVER THE NAME

In recent years, scholars have paid special attention to the role of the holy name in christological coordination and have focused their attention quite rightly on the confession of Philippians 2:6–11. David Yeago and Richard Bauckham have drawn important attention to this hymn. Yeago does so to underscore that a divide between the church's theological speech and exegesis is a false one and that even the phrase *homoousia* ("of one substance") in Nicene confession is exegesis, not desire for extrabiblical coherency.[22]

The argument goes like this. Chapters 40–48 of Isaiah speak quite frequently about the LORD being God alone, and they also insist that the nations come to discover this reality and confess it, "God is with you alone, and there is no other; there is no god besides him" (45:14). At 45:23, God swears by himself "a word that shall not return" that "to me every knee shall bow, every tongue shall swear." The content of their pledge is given in 45:24, "Only in the LORD, it shall be said of me, are righteousness and strength."

What is contemplated here? It is nothing less than that all creation will give honor to God, will know his name, speak forth his name, and give honor to the LORD, in whom alone are righteousness and strength; that is, what has been true of Israel's experience of God, in name and in holy presence, will, according to God, be true for all creation, with God's righteousness and his election of a people affirmed (45:25). And this promise is sealed by an oath that cannot be revoked. It is sworn by God in his own name. The name of God, as revealed to Israel, will be known throughout all creation. (Jehovah's Witnesses, for obvious reasons, take this text literally and quite seriously.)

In Philippians 2:6–11, we have a hymn to Christ, whom Christians are told to imitate. Then language of condescension is used. Christ was of the form of God, he relinquished this, and he died on a cross. Therefore, the text says, "God . . . gave him the name that is above every name" and reference is made to every knee bowing, "in heaven and on earth and under the earth," and every tongue confessing "that Jesus Christ is Lord, to the glory of God the Father" (2:9–11).

The intratextual connection to Isaiah 45 is unmistakable. The name above every name, to which every knee shall bow and every tongue confess is the holy name, YHWH. So what are we to make of Philippians's literal sense, and how does what it says inform our speech about God, our understanding of God's personal name, subsequent credal confessions, and a proper conception of God as three in one?

We begin with the reality of Christian speech about God, which is the topic of this essay. Christians do not name the name of God as was true in Israel, as the Old Testament reveals God was known and worshiped. The Old Testament promises that as God was known in Israel, by his name and in himself, all nations will also know God, and for that give praise. This promise takes the form of a solemn oath.

What has happened to this oath that will not be revoked? It is not the case that all nations know God by name, and those who in Christ claim to know him do not use his name or know his name, in the strict sense in which Israel knew his name. Has the oath fallen to the ground? In the case of the first question, Christians have answered with the production of Christian eschatology. The promises of God remain irrevocable, Christ's raising by God is a first-fruit of a larger harvest he remains committed to, and it is under his sovereignty that we must live now by faith, in Christ.[23]

The second question is answered by Philippians in the terse transition of 2:10, "that at the name of Jesus," not at the personal name of the LORD, the promises sworn by himself are being fulfilled. This is made explicit in the final verse of the hymn. The confession is that Jesus Christ is Lord. The name of Jesus Christ stands where the promise had said that the name of the LORD would stand. And this has taken place to the glory of God the Father.

CONCLUSIONS

The implications of this hymn for Christian talk are hard to overemphasize. I will begin with the most obvious ones and assume that the works mentioned previously provide additional elaboration.

First, the hymn clarifies the silence over explicit mention of God's name in ongoing Christian practice. The New Testament speaks of YHWH in ways that we have discussed already, but it never seeks to imitate in its literal sense the exact practice of the Old Testament. Neither do we have any efforts to reconnect with Israel's experience of God through the name by means of vocalizations of Hebrew, such as Jehovah or Yahweh.

Second, the hymn is quite clear that a handing over of something is taking place. It is not the case that the text seeks to conflate the name of Jesus and the name of "the LORD." The name of Jesus is not a vocalization of YHWH! God has a name, and it is the name above every name. He gives this name to Jesus. In so doing, the personal character of the exchange is preserved. It is not that we are discovering a deeper intention or a secret, lying below the plain-sense promises of God in the Old Testament. God really did swear by himself that his name would be confessed throughout creation; he was not being indirect or subtle in an ingenious sense.

Third, the giving of the name affects Jesus, but it also affects God. The giv-

ing of the name to Jesus is a complete vindication by God of Jesus, an acknowledgment that he has been perfect in his obedience and in complete congruence with God's will. The way this congruence is underscored is the only way
to make this absolutely clear, on the terms of the Old Testament's governing
center. The name of God is God's very self, and by giving it to Jesus, maximal
identity is affirmed. Jesus Christ is Lord. He who will be as he is, is this one
raised by God.

How does this affect God? Here we return to the trinitarian revival mentioned before. It should be clear that whatever else the Philippians hymn is, it
is *not* a philosophical effort to coordinate abstract trinitarian concepts. The
intimate connection with the Old Testament's language ensures that we are
talking about a personal God and his personal Son. This is clarified once one
sees the centrality of the name in the Old Testament and its transfer here.[24]
There is an actual transaction taking place, and it could not be more personal
than it is. Jesus gives up his life with God and in so doing becomes nothing,
even to the extent of dying on a cross. The trinitarian revival has done a good
job of focusing on Jesus, the dereliction given utterance to, and the love it
bespeaks within the eternal life of God. When trying to maintain a commitment to *perichoresis* at the moment of death and nothingness, we have been
asked to imagine the suffering of the Father, who truly loses his Son, and in
that loss has his own unique, differentiated personal life within the Godhead.

The hymn from Philippians, understood against the backdrop of the divine
name, gives us another alternative. The condescension of Jesus has its counterpart in the giving over of the name. God surrenders his name and himself
to his Son and his name, *that at the name of Jesus* every knee shall bow. The
identification is two-way, of Jesus with YHWH and of YHWH with Jesus. The
hymn concludes, however, that this identification of Jesus with YHWH is "to
the glory of God the Father."

To be given a glimpse at the life of YHWH through the lens of Jesus is to
see God from within, from inside the relationship, from the standpoint of the
Son. The consequence of this is to call God Father and mean by that YHWH,
as seen from the standpoint of his Son, to whom has been given the name above
every name. To name the holy name is for Christians to name the name of
Jesus, but this happens to the glory of God the Father. The "loss of the divine
name" is what it means for God, the LORD, the maker of heaven and earth, to
share himself with those outside Israel in the person of his Son. This constitutes the sacrifice of the Father in obedience to his own name and oath, as
delivered to Israel, on behalf of all creation. It is a sacrifice with its own
integrity, as God allows his forsaking of Jesus to be a truthful statement of
his wrath, without thereby diminishing his own sacrificial act of love in sending the Son. By giving the Son his name, we see the Father express in the most

intimate way possible his identification with Jesus Christ the Lord, an identification that involves what the Greek Fathers called *taxis*, the ordered life within God's personal self. This ordering is as much about obedience and sacrifice as it is about triumph and joy, for in God's holy self, mercy and truth have kissed each other.

It belongs to the most mature Christian confession that the name of God has been given to Jesus. Efforts therefore to reinstate the name run up against the likelihood of misunderstanding and miscommunicating this confession and the implications of it for our understanding of God: the Father, the Son, and the Holy Spirit. The effort should be made, instead, to reinstate the heart of the trinitarian life as that which is worthy of our praise and obedience, which has been shared with us out of Israel and its scriptures, for all God's creation, to the glory of the Father, the LORD, the maker of heaven and earth.

In practical terms, the identification of YHWH with Jesus means not that the attributes of God as rendered by the literal sense of the Old Testament have become lost in some transfer. Holiness, righteousness, justice, mercy, compassion, and jealousy, as these describe YHWH in the Old Testament, remain true of God in his essence, and *perichoresis* means they are true of the Son and the Holy Spirit in their eternal life as well. They have not been "handed over." For this reason, it will be important in Christian talk about God to retain meaningful links to God as he has been described in the Old Testament, in ways other than by his sacred name (YHWH). The traditional ways of speaking of God as God Almighty, Father, Lord God of Hosts, should be complemented and enriched, not corrected or abridged in the name of some false modalism, whereby God's "mode" in Jesus is truer or more worthy of Christian talk.

If the concern expressed by efforts to vocalize the name is to be addressed, then let the Old Testament lead the way with its own rich stock of terms. Nothing prevents the Christian community from addressing God as "Holy One" (so Isaiah), or Lord Most High, or God Almighty, or Maker of heaven and earth, alongside the predominantly christological "Father." In this way, it will be made clear that we are speaking of God in the same way as the Israel of old spoke to him in his holy name, now confessed by Christian tongues through the power of the Holy Spirit, "Jesus Christ, LORD, to the glory of God the Father."

11

The Old Testament, Mission,
and Christian Scripture

INTRODUCTION
AND DEFINITION

There is no direct Hebrew (or Greek) equivalent for the English word "mission." An English language concordance of the Bible will show no entry for the term. "Mission" comes into English from a Latin verb whose chief meaning has to do with "sending" (*mittere*).

The lack of correspondence is not of any particular significance, as such. It does, however, mean we shall need to define our terms afresh and be careful about how we are using a word whose background and range must be sought from, or extrapolated out of, other words and other conceptualities in the Old and New Testaments. If "mission" carries with it the primary nuance of sending, can it be said that this tallies with what we find in the Old Testament when we look for some equivalent notion? Just what does the Old Testament mean when it is placed in a context of missionary concerns, which, in mature form, lie somewhere out beyond its own more immediate range of vision?

I think, intuitively, when we consider a notion like mission, we gravitate toward the New Testament and the larger concern it displays for spreading a message and a way of life, by human and transcendent agency. The Book of Acts comes to mind. The image we carry for this in our mind's eye is largely if not wholly centrifugal, outward-moving. "Sending" (*mittere*), "mission," is not a bad way to capture the sense of this.

I suspect as well that intuitively we do not move to the Old Testament with such an expectation; that is, as Christian readers (the matter would, of course, look different to Jews, who are themselves not one group), the notion of sending or promulgating something (however one might describe this) is chiefly the consequence of Christian possession of a two-testament Bible, in which the theme plays a major role in part two and only a minor role, if at all, in part one.

Now, this minor role could be related to one of the several ways in which we intuitively understand the relationship between the testaments more generally—that is, as promise and fulfillment, shadow and type, law and gospel, or, perhaps, as national, racial, local, over against something more international, universalistic, or global.[1] Anyone with a cursory knowledge of the world of eighteenth- to twentieth-century high culture will know that this last—to call it Marcionite might not go far enough—way of understanding the relationship between the testaments threatened or succeeded in destroying the nuance of the others, and one outcome was the Holocaust. That is, whatever positive religious ideas or virtues might be said to exist in the New Testament, their radiance was best perceived by setting them in sharp contrast with what existed in the religious ideas, and especially the practices, of the Old.[2]

So, in the realm of mission, if that should be defined as sending out the good news of Jesus Christ, then by definition, because such a theme is absent in explicit form in the Old Testament (and recent historical approaches to scripture have been interested in a constrained type of explicitness), we should have to consider this one of the areas where the Old Testament was particularly impoverished, if not racist and particularistic. And whatever residue of such religious instinct and practice washed up in the New Testament, it, too, would have to be eradicated or bleached through the deployment of higher-critical acids, pruning Paul from the real Jesus and the like. The instinct, if not the genuine practice, is as old as Marcion, and for some this was and is a proud and enduring heritage.[3]

So, to speak of mission in the Old Testament is to speak more broadly of how the Old Testament functions properly as Christian scripture, the alternative being to understand its scriptural status as under review or as objectionable and forfeit. Moreover, to speak of mission in the Old Testament carries with it a special challenge and a special burden of responsibility, given the moment in which the providence of God has placed the Christian church at the threshold of a new millennium, one generation after Auschwitz.

MISSION AS CENTRIFUGAL EXPANSION

The notion of movement, expansion, and enlargement is not, of course, foreign to the Old Testament. Created humanity is to grow and expand numerically, to "be fruitful and multiply," and this is true for Israel, for all peoples, and for creation itself. To think otherwise is not just tautologous, given the reality of a populated world. A static or unpeopled world is an absurdity that the Old Testament would look on as it later does the sin of Onan (Gen. 38). "Onan in Eden" is a "vanity of vanities."

But natural expansion is not, of course, mission, anymore than procreation is manifest enlargement of the kingdom of God, a "sending forth" of peoples in the nature of the thing. Already in Genesis 3, procreation is a thick reality, fraught and painful, and termination of all life in Genesis 7 will become a solution for a problem deeply embedded in the human condition. On the other side of the Flood, the problem still exists, but the remedy will never be the same again, we are told. "For the inclination of the human heart is evil from youth" (Gen. 8:21). The point here is that natural expansion is not capable of correlation with what we will mean when the term "mission" enters our vocabulary.

Now we may be getting close to a definition. Mission is a correlate not only of sending something forth but also of addressing something awry. Mission, if it cannot be tracked in terms of natural growth, expansion, enlargement—and the Old Testament right away shows in its first pages that this is not possible—must then be understood on some other axis, indeed, on an axis defined over against this. To understand this other axis, we must look at the way the something awry, which cannot be eradicated by flooding the world and stopping growth altogether, is got at by God. *Mission means getting at the something awry*, when we look at the issue theologically and not sociologically. Stated differently, the notion of missionary "sending" is an earthly subset of a theological reality, and it is this theological reality that makes mission have a divine and not a natural or simply human mandate. Mission is God's address to humanity's forfeit. Understood in this way, it is an Old Testament theme as well as a New Testament theme. Indeed, it could be said to be *the* theme of the Old Testament as such.

BLESSING IN GENESIS: THE STATUS AND ROLE OF ISRAEL

The language of God's address to humanity's forfeit is in Genesis the language of blessing. Blessing is tied up with expansion and spreading out, as Genesis 1:28 makes clear: "And God blessed them, and God said to them, 'Be fruitful and multiply, and fill the earth.'"

After the Flood, Genesis describes an expansion, a sending forth of people, which can be understood as a moral fulfillment of the charge to be fruitful and multiply, now under the conditions of a covenant with creation after the Flood. Indeed, the populations that are said to come forth from the loins of Noah do so under the specific charge, repeated from Genesis 1:28: "be fruitful and multiply, and fill the earth" (Gen. 9:1). Both there and here, the charge is preceded by blessing: "And God blessed them" (male and female) (Gen. 1:28) and "God blessed Noah and his sons" (Gen. 9:1).

Now there is an acute problem in chronological flow from Genesis 10 to 11, which modernity has solved by appeal to sources, which here are sitting next to one another but manifesting a disagreement (which allows them to be posited in the first place). Genesis 11:1 reports that all the earth had one language, while the previous chapter had envisioned different languages and families on earth. Genesis 11:6 reports God himself saying, "Look, they are all one people, and they have all one language" and the consequence of this one people's folly is a scattering, which appeared already to have taken place in Genesis 10, "abroad on the earth" (11:9).[4]

It is not the purpose of this essay on mission to resolve the problem by assessing modern critical method. What we do have, by virtue of this juxtaposing of Genesis 11 and 10, is the emergence of the line from Noah, which leads up to Abram, in a so-called vertical genealogy. The effect of this is to draw our attention to the existence of a special lineage, on the other side of Babel. So, von Rad puts it in his fine commentary:

> The rigor with which he (P) first traces all the nations back through Noah to Adam and only then describes a particular line down to Abraham shows that he knew about the riddle of divine election and wanted to make its harshness theologically vivid in his history.[5]

So, when we hear the language of blessing again in Genesis 12, we can suppose that, just as before and after the Flood some residual condition remained, so, too, before and after Babel, God's plan for blessing would not be thwarted by human sin and folly. The blessing of Noah's sons perdures through the Babel episode to take up a refined form in the line leading to Abraham and his descendents after him.

As von Rad especially has insisted, it belongs to the theological achievement of the biblical writer he called J that here at Genesis 12:2–3 we have a profound highwater mark. That is, whatever is marring God's creative intent, be it rebellion in the Garden, murder, evil human imagination, or projects for overextension and totalitarian unity, God is planning a different way forward, which he means to protect and superintend. Election is the means by which sinful creation receives the blessing originally intended for it, for all nations and people. Mission understood in Old Testament terms, then, is the address of blessing to the deficit and forfeit brought about by rebellion, in its many forms. It is required now to tease out the implications of blessing further.

One added benefit of close reading with attention to the theme of blessing, not highlighted in von Rad's own focus on J in Genesis 12, is making clearer the lines of continuity backward and forward in Genesis as a whole. What Genesis 12 says about God using Abram and his descendents as a blessing is said with an eye most explicitly to the innate human tendency to thwart and disrupt God's design for his people, as this has been described in manifold ways in Genesis 1–11, both before and after the covenant with Noah. Von Rad has seen this with respect to J, but it belongs to the design of the final form of Genesis 1–11, its canonical shape, as well. Attention to the canonical form shows the theological significance of the juxtaposing of episodes that are said to exist in different sources, especially in the movement from Flood to national dispersion to Babel to Abram's lineage. Blessing will come through election, and mission—God's word of blessing to the nations—will be the means by which God uses Israel to accomplish this in a special vis-à-vis toward all peoples.

Consequently, it is important to stress the forward-moving direction of the theme of blessing as well. Genesis 12 makes lavish promises regarding the descendents of Abram, in the same manner as all the sons of Noah were blessed. But of those sons, Genesis 11 makes clear only one line leads to the man Abram, whatever the original blessing may have entailed and may continue to entail for all humanity. The same holds true for Genesis 12, as the later chapters of Genesis will make clear; that is, God will hold in special regard Ishmael and Hagar, but it is with Abram become Abraham, Isaac, and Jacob that his promise of blessing for the nations finds its focus and its direction.

This can be demonstrated by simply tracking the word "bless" in the Book of Genesis. It is the proper reaction to Abraham, Isaac, and Jacob, and then also Joseph, whereby nations find blessing in the Book of Genesis. So when the book draws to a close in Egypt, we find Israel becoming fruitful and multiplying even in a foreign land (47:27), exceedingly. Moreover, we also have Joseph becoming a blessing to Pharaoh and all Egypt, and his father Jacob pronouncing a blessing over even the Pharaoh himself (47:7–11).

I stay with this appeal to larger context for a minute because of the difficulty of understanding the precise meaning of Genesis 12:2–3, where the theme of blessing is heaped up upon itself. Von Rad is right to see the centrality of election and blessing in Genesis, and indeed in the Old Testament itself. He makes several important observations, several of which can be filed here:

> . . . blessing concerns Abraham first of all; but it also includes those on the outside who adopt a definite attitude toward this blessing. (159)

> In the "name" (here referring to verse 3) that Yahweh (*sic*) will "make great" has been seen correctly a hidden allusion to the Story of the

Tower of Babel: Yahweh now intends to give what men attempted to secure arbitarily (160) [and consider that the effort in Babel was depicted as that of *all* humanity].

The promise given to Abraham has significance, however, far beyond Abraham and his seed. God now brings salvation and judgment into history, and man's judgment and salvation will be determined by the attitude he adopts toward this work God intends to do in history. (160)

In this last comment, von Rad draws a figural link to Luke 2:34, where Simeon's blessing of Mary and Joseph includes the solemn conclusion, "this child is destined for the falling and the rising of many in Israel, and to be a sign that will be opposed so that the inner thoughts of many will be revealed."

That is, God's blessing of Abram is a repeat of the charge to humanity in creation, and it involves his becoming many. God's blessing involves Abram's getting what humanity as a whole sought in tower building, here because God says so, not because Abram so seeks. The blessing of Abram entails blessing for others (so the passive form of the verb in verse 2), "so that you will be a blessing." And all those who bless Abram are contrasted with the third person singular, "he," who curses. The final (fifth) use of blessing appears to be a summary: "by you all the families of the earth will find blessing."

Now how does one relate this dense and profound theological promise with mission, understood as sending out, as a centrifugal outreaching, covering the geographical ("to the ends of the earth"), the temporal ("until God is all in all"), and the numerical ("all nations, peoples and tongues") spheres of God's creation? The promise to Abram is similarly unbounded, and in that sense it can be correlated with all of these spheres and with the way the New Testament more explicitly speaks of them, as the final goal of the gospel of Jesus Christ. So, von Rad rightly uses the language of prophecy when he says,

This prophecy in 12:3b reaches far out toward the goal of God's plan for history, but it still refuses any description of this final end. It is enough that the goal is given as such and that with it is suggested the meaning of the road that God has taken by calling Abraham. This prophecy . . . was especially important to the retrospective glance of the New Testament witnesses. (160–161)

But in what sense is Genesis 12:2–3 a text about mission as centrifugal, as a sending out, as a forward-moving and outwardly directed activity of Abraham? And in what sense do the variations on this theme of election and blessing for the nations, such as we find them elsewhere in the Old Testament, also entail what one might call Israel's active missionary outreach, toward all peoples, places, and times?

In Genesis, blessing (or cursing) appears to be not mere serendipity, but neither is it a self-conscious, willed activity on the part of Abraham and his descendents. Rather, it comes in the course of affairs as Israel is fruitful, multiplies, and moves about, encountering this or that family of the earth. In that sense, Israel's mission, if one can call it that, is neither centrifugal nor centripetal (though it does favor the latter). Instead, mission has to do with the simple existence of Israel and the charge that gives its existence sense and purpose, a charge entailing election and promise. The way its possession of this truth about its destiny affects its relationship to others, and them to it, informs the way the narrator relates the events and the encounters of Israel with the nations in the Book of Genesis. That is, the narrator relates omnisciently matters that occur in the course of Israel's movements and provides for them theological commentary, entailing blessing or curse, which cannot always be read off the events themselves, even by those for whom the events are present-tense realities.

Melchizedek, king and priest of Salem, blessed Abram in gratitude for his military deliverance. Sodom and Gomorrah receive curse. Abimelech inadvertently encroaches on the people of promise, in the affair with Sarah and Abraham, and Abraham prays for and accomplishes his healing (for, the narrator tells us, "the LORD had closed fast all the wombs of the house of Abimelech, because of Sarah, Abraham's wife" [Gen. 20:17]). At the juncture between each generation, the promise of blessing is repeated, and blessing plays a prominent role in the story of Joseph and Jacob in Egypt.

Perhaps typical of this theme is the story of Isaac and Abimelech in Genesis 26:26–32. This Abimelech (of Gerar) seeks to quell a disagreement over the possession of certain wells in the region shared by the people of blessing and his people. Generously, in verses 28–29, he proclaims, "We see plainly that the LORD has been with you; so we say, let there be an oath between you and us, and let us make a covenant with you so that you will do us no harm, just as we have not touched you and have done to you nothing but good and have sent you away in peace. You are now the blessed of the LORD." Though Pharaoh makes no similar statement of conviction about the LORD, the narrator tells us that Jacob blessed him, presumably on the strength of his positive treatment of Joseph, and Joseph's of him and his people, "So Joseph bought all the land of Egypt for Pharaoh" (Gen. 47:20).

It is the appearance of these accounts of given and received blessing that urged one commentator to speak of Genesis as conveying an impression of "ecumenical bonhomie."[6] We do not see "conversion" to the God of Israel. We see blessing given and received, as the nations encounter the people of blessing. Von Rad has cautioned against speaking of (in his words) a "magically effective manistic 'state of mind' which is poured out like a fluid" (159) in describing the place of election in Genesis, referring to the notion as "pre-Israelite." At another place, he speaks of "a remnant of the magical-dynamic notion of blessing" which Genesis 48:20 and later Zechariah 8:13 display in part. Instead, following the Jewish interpreter Benno Jacob, he speaks of the charge of Genesis 12:2–3 as "a command to history." Or, summarizing the view of Procksch, he states, "The extent of the promise now becomes equal to that of the unhappy international world."[7]

I think what von Rad is rightly at pains to avoid is the notion that the divine charge to Israel, which constitutes its ontological status in creation, holds God's own sovereignty hostage, on the one hand, and creates a people who magically conjure up reactions of blessing or cursing, on the other. And this occurs fully independent of any activity or bearing of obedience on Israel's part.

Here is another place where the story of the binding of Isaac demonstrates its centrality to the theological logic of Genesis. God takes away the child Isaac, only to give him back again, as the consequence of Abraham's willingness to let him and his own be fully at God's disposal. Genesis 22 serves the purpose of grounding the election of Israel and its capacity for bringing promise in God's sovereign will. It is for this reason that Genesis never schematizes Israel's encounters with the world into simple consequences of now blessing or now curse. Genesis 12:2–3 is a promise and, as such, remains within God's power to realize or turn back.

In the same manner, even Jesus in his earthly life does no mighty work here and there, and mission of any sort cannot be reduced to simple presence, on one side, or formulaic action on the other. If blessing is the means by which God restores and brings into proper relationship the families of the earth, it remains the case that he uses Israel for this purpose in ways neither Israel nor the nations fully comprehend. What is required of Israel is faith and obedience to the promise, which constitutes its only ground of existence in the world. Obedience to this promise allows blessing to occur, but it does not ensure it. Even the centripetal mission status of Israel in creation is subject to God's control and God's freedom, and in that sense it is indeed wrong to speak of a magical effectiveness. The biblical narrative and narrator never smooth out the edges of Israel's election and its utility in God's purposes.

THE NATIONS AND BLESSING IN ISAIAH

For the remainder of the chapter, I shall be looking at the theme of the nations in the Book of Isaiah. I do this for the following reasons.

1.   The theme of the nations stands at the heart of the Old Testament's understanding of mission; this is clear from the Book of Genesis and espe-

cially its language of election and blessing in Genesis 12; if von Rad is concerned about a "magical" understanding of election and blessing, Isaiah massively demythologizes any such conception, as we shall see.

2. As G. Davies has said, "(I)f any one of the prophetic books deserves the title "the prophet to the nations" it is Isaiah[8]—as against the explicit description of Jeremiah along these lines in Jer. 1:5. Because the book is concerned with the nations, it is concerned with our theme.

3. Recent appreciation for the unity of Isaiah means that a concern for Israel and the nations, a theme running across all chapters of the book, has been reinstated. In some ways the nineteenth-century conservative stance of Keil has been vindicated. About the literary movement of the whole book, he said, Isaiah speaks of "a test sent from God for Judah and the house of David, in which it was their duty to decide in favour of faith and confidence simply in the omnipotence and grace of the Lord; instead of which they placed their confidence in the earthly worldly power of Assyria, and, as a punishment, were drawn into the secular historical process of the (heathen) nations, in order that, being purified by severe judgements, they might be led through deep sufferings to the glory of their divine calling."[9] It will be the purpose of this section to elaborate in more detail this summary of Keil, with attention to its implications for mission in the Old Testament.

It may appear arbitrary to limit our discussion to Isaiah, but it is easy to note similar concerns with the nations beyond Israel in other prophetic literature and in the Psalms; our selection of Isaiah is not arbitrary but will help to focus the topic. In particular, I want to examine the way in which mission in Genesis has been adapted in the Book of Isaiah. The patriarchal promises play a central role in Isaiah the latter, as I will call chapters 40ff. But now we are not in a period of ecumenical bonhomie. Indeed, we are in a period of something like its reversal. But as Keil notes, God has a purpose within the international and cosmic judgment of Isaiah, for a purified Israel brought "to the glory of their divine calling." And this purpose, this plan of YHWH, as Isaiah refers to it, involves the completion of the promises to Abram, that the nations will find blessing in him—now, not through centripetal encounter alone but through trial and judgment and what latter Isaiah means when he speaks of Israel "light of, to, or for the nations."

The nations play a prominent role in former Isaiah. Isaiah 2 speaks of the nations coming to Zion, in latter days, to learn the ways of Israel's named LORD (2:3). The law given to Moses will go forth for all nations, from Zion.

Isaiah sets forth a grand tableau, involving the serial use of the nations Assyria, Babylonia, and the Medeo-Persian empire, as agents of his just bidding. Israel is addressed somberly in the opening vision, which appears calibrated to the entire sweep of former and latter Isaiah, as a sinful nation, one of the *goyim* it was to be a blessing for in Genesis. Instead, Israel has become like Sodom and Gomorrah. Election and separation appear to be cast-off notions.

In what is called the Isaiah apocalypse (chapters 24–27), the covenant with Noah would appear broken, as the world crashes into chaos and void under the weight of God's dramatic deployment of the nations in judgment. Can Zion remain the bulwark promised by the Psalms, when such mighty waters and such earthly rulers rage, or have the promises of Psalm 2 and Psalm 46 (among others) proven *tohu wevohu*, nothingness and void? Toward what end does this letting loose of judgment, this hardening of hearts and deafening of ears, serve in God's purposes?

In latter Isaiah, this sentence of judgment and deployment of the nations is addressed. Zion received double for its sins. The plan and purpose of God was punishment for its own lack of faith and confidence in God's promises and election.

In chapters 40ff., the cast-off and judged Israel—blinded and deafened by God's word spoken of old through Isaiah—is reconstituted and reaffirmed, according to the promises made to the ancestors in Genesis. Israel is, through this judgment and purified by it, "my servant, Jacob, Israel, whom I love." The promises to the patriarchs, to Abraham, Jacob, Sarah, and, even earlier, to Noah, are called out as the supreme firewall of God's deep concern for and protection of his servant, Israel.

As servant, Jacob-Israel also has a second Moses purpose for a second exodus, described in terms of the first coming forth of Abram from Ur of the Chaldees but now a return of the dispersed and judged Israel from every corner of the earth and not just the dungeon of Egyptian bondage. Servant Israel communicates, in the paradoxical silence of its witness, the instruction, the Torah of God, as did Moses. But now, we are told, this is not for Israel only but for the nations, "and the coastlands wait for his law."

This statement of Isaiah 42 is made within the context of a huge courtroom drama, as the heavenly council of God and the earthly courtroom of its manifestation are one, in chapters 40–48. The litigants are the despondent Israel and the confident nations. The evidence: the former things. The witnesses: an Israel, deaf but with ears, blind but with eyes, on the other side of Isaiah's preaching. The jury: the very corners of the world; heaven and earth; and the heavenly voices and retinue introduced in Isaiah 6 and reintroduced in Isaiah 40. The verdict: judgment over Babylon and all it represents, wherever such as it is represented in the nations, who cannot speak and have no recourse to evidence from no-gods and idols, as does Israel from its sovereign YHWH. Israel's evidence: God's formerly uttered word of prophecy, involving God's single plan and purpose for the whole earth, and that included the judgment of his people through the agency of the same nations without evidence— even of their own deployment by the Holy One of Israel.

And like any good courtroom drama, there is surprise testimony. A new thing, uttered only now, not before. Judges do not allow surprise testimony from lawyers and try to contain this. But the LORD is judge and defense and prosecution in this court. The surprise has to do with the end or purpose of the judgment, and it is that Israel is servant and has inside its own judgment the unchanged and insistent capacity to be "light to the nations." Inside Israel's judgment and its forgiveness, inside the trial with the nations, there is a verdict alongside one of judgment. In the recognition of Israel's just sentence, in presentation of the evidence, within the nations' own trial sentencing, they will come to acknowledge, "surely thou art a God who hidest thyself, O God of Israel the savior."

We see in Isaiah 40–48 actual foreshadowings, depicted with the rhetorical force that constitutes prophecy in pure form, of this national recognition. But the larger recognition remains eschatological in character in much of the proclamation of these latter chapters.

In Isaiah 40–48, the suprise testimony is servant Israel, "light to the nations," the very nations who in the midst of their sentencing and silencing, we are told, are to be recepients of the Torah, as did Israel from Moses. This was promised in Isaiah 2, but the "how" of its outworking we learn involves the work of the servant. The recognition by the nations of the LORD and their acknowledgment of him and receipt of his law, constitutes God's missionary act. The something awry that it is God's missionary purpose to address, God addresses through the judgment of his own people.

Now is this missionary act of God through Israel centrifugal or centripetal? In what sense is it what we have seen already in Genesis?

In the Book of Isaiah, it is neither and both. The nations come to Zion, and in the trial they see Israel vindicated. They bring offerings to bedeck Zion. They confess, "The LORD is God alone." The new sanctuary is not constructed with Israel's gift offerings, brought on the other side of golden calf sin and forgiveness, including the plunder of the nation Egypt. The nations bring their own offerings. Cyrus builds the temple (The Book of Ezra has him pay for it). And we are told that their coming to Zion in this way will mean confession and worship.

But the mission is also centrifugal, though in a deeply paradoxical sense. It is by virtue of being hauled into exile in judgment that contact with the nations comes about. Israel goes forth in a missionary activity whose deeper purpose it knows not. It is purificatory, as Keil has seen, but it is also missionary. In Israel's curse, to use the language both of Genesis 12 and Deuteronomy, there is God's missionary act of blessing. By becoming the sinful *goy* in judgment, by being sent forth into the hands of the nations who carry them away, there stands the paradoxical and unexpected fulfillment of the promises to Abraham.

The prologue to the confession and tribute to the suffering servant shows the kings and nations "seeing and hearing" what they had not understood. This mirrors the deafness and blindness, formerly of Israel in Isaiah's day, being transformed by God into their seeing and hearing in a latter day. By the end of the book, we see the nations coming to Zion. They bring gifts. They see and know the God of Israel. They then go forth as missionaries, to the survivors of the nations. They tell of the Lord of Israel, and they bring the dispersed of God back to the elected place. Some from the nations become priests and levites. We see a similar tableau in Zechariah 8.

But we also see in these final chapters a cleaving of the servant Israel community into two. The servants who suffer in imitation of their master, the one called to be the Israel after God's own heart in chapter 49, are separated from their persecutors within the household of God. The categories, Israel and nations, servant and *goyim*, are not undone in God's final missionary act of conjoining. But both undergo massive transformation, within what the prophet can call only a new creation, a new heaven and earth. The end of Isaiah returns to the beginning and speaks of a new day and a new created order of affairs. This ending vision is what one might call the eschatological completion of God's missionary act: His willed and sovereign intention to put what created humanity makes awry good and in full accordance with a design nothing in heaven and earth can thwart. He will get his way with his world, through the plan of election and its final transformation through the suffering and death of his servant Israel.

CONCLUSIONS

It would require another essay to show how this Isaianic depiction of Israel and the nations works itself out in later Christian scripture. A brief word, however.

The trajectory goes two ways. One is christological. It involves seeing in Jesus what he himself saw: the according and final act of God, in whose person and work is the life and death of servant Israel, so that all nations and peoples might confess, overhearing Israel confess, "he was wounded for our trangressions, crushed for our iniquities, upon him was the punishment that made us whole" (Isa. 53:5). So that which was not told us Gentiles, we might see and know.

The other is ecclesial and it would take us into Romans 9–11. The persecution of the servant who is Israel—both confessed and tragically prolonged—is the very means by which the nations come to the knowledge of the One God. So too, the rejection of Israel means "the reconciliation of the world," to use the language of Paul in Romans 11:15.

But there is a second level to this ecclesial typology, and it derives in part from Paul's other cautionary word: he has consigned all to disobedience so that he might show mercy to all. Does the church as the body of Christ and the Israel of God bring light to the nations by bearing witness to God's judgment over it, as well as to God's blessing, as did Israel of old? This is the sort of deep question posed by Ephraim Radner in his dense and provocative book, *The End of the Church*.[10]

If the Genesis-Isaiah portrait is a type both for the work of Christ and for the church, we will have to take into account mission as, always and inevitably, centrifugal and centripetal. The church must live out its own destiny within its own life, as the body of Christ, not allowing itself to be metamorphized to this world, again to quote Paul. This is its elect missionary act, or, non-act! And yet this alternative, transforming work of God the Holy Ghost in the church has a purpose that propels the church, both in blessing and in judgment, into the world to witness to the one author and giver of life.

The Old Testament reminds us just how intimately connected are these two aspects of divine missionary action. We talk about God's address of our something awry as his first missionary act, and, in so doing, we allow his healing and saving act to find its way home, where what is awry rules with tyranny, outwith the church. This broken world, like the church itself broken in judgment and in blessing, God has sent his only Son to claim, to love and to transform, in accordance with the (Old Testament) scriptures.

12

Prayer in the Old Testament
or Hebrew Bible

I approach this chapter with a mixture of envy, liminality, and contentment. I am envious of many of my colleagues who have also written on this topic and have wisely restricted themselves to a study of prayer within a specific New Testament book or tradition. I, however, will treat the topic far more globally here. I sense liminality because the study of prayer that I provide here, based as it is on the Old Testament, serves to set the boundaries for a complete study. I do not want this study to be a mere anteroom or foyer that one passes quickly through to a "real" study of the prayer which the New Testament alone provides. Finally, I feel a degree of contentment, because a chapter on "Prayer in the Old Testament" demands something of a wide-angle lens—and this is precisely the sort of approach that I believe is most needed today within the discipline.

The prevailing tendency in biblical studies is to divide things up and put them into separate bins, thereby creating an ecology where historical differentiation is seen as a goal unto itself and axiomatic of good biblical scholarship. Frequently missing from such a division of labor, however, is an ecology where synthesis and interconnections are prized as goods that must guide the discipline of exegesis and inform our interpretation of the biblical witness and not just left to what an onlooker may or may not be able to provide.

My particular assignment invites either integration or yet one more effort at a new taxonomy. I have settled for the former. Furthermore, because such integration must attend to the maximal limits of the Old Testament canon, it becomes immediately clear that this sort of approach must face the question of integration within the larger scope of the Christian scriptures as well. To speak of "integration" and "comprehensiveness" carries with it an obligation to be clear regarding the nature of the literature under scrutiny and the basic assumptions of interpretation—that is, whether for Christians, for Jews, or

159

for the merely curious (including biblical historians from various tribes with their representative sachems or chieftains).

Any treatment of prayer in the Old Testament that is sensitive to its canonical shape and full scope, therefore, invites reflection from the very start on how such prayer functions in relation to prayer in the New Testament and as a datum of the Christian faith. Or, to change the architectural metaphor, prayer in the New Testament must be seen as a fleshing out of a scaffolding that has already been fully raised and is intact in the scriptures of Israel.

At the moment that Jesus uses the first-person plural "our" in response to a question about how to pray (cf. Matt. 6:9), the shoe should drop! Understood from the context of the scriptures of Israel, Jesus is enclosing believers into a relationship that he has with the Father, whose name is "the name above every name." And that name is sounded forth and responded to in prayer, in all its rich variety, in one place only—that is, within the scriptures of Israel.

It is for the most central theological reason, then, in accordance with the theological logic that governs both testaments of Christian scripture, that any treatment of prayer must begin with prayer in the Old Testament. This is no anteroom but the very place where the logic of God's unfolding plan with humanity—including the intimate speech with God that is called prayer—is set forth. The New Testament does not recalibrate these bearings. Rather, it operates within them, setting them out in an eschatological display of first-fruits that is more familiarly referred to as "the gospel."

A WORD ABOUT PROCEDURE

In what follows, I look at numerous examples of prayer and praying in the Old Testament—from Enosh to Job, to Moses, to David, to Hezekiah, to Jonah, to the sailors who throw him overboard, to Sennacherib, and finally to the man called the "suffering servant." I am not going to attempt to deal with all of this material in detail. Rather, I will sketch out matters in broad brush and try to give a comprehensive picture of prayer in the Old Testament. So I will be moving at a fast clip and assume when I mention one line of scripture that the entire story will rise up in all of its rich detail within the reader's imagination.

But I am not giving such a sweeping treatment for its own sake. What I want to do is to say something about how prayer points to a theological truth about God. What I want to do is to set forth how the canon of Christian scripture, in its older first part, presents prayer for a reader it has already anticipated. In other words, the examples of prayer in the Old Testament are not just lying around like seams of ore in the ground, raw and in need of refining (if, in fact, they are to be used at all). Prayer—like prophecy, law, creation, worship, or wisdom—is presented in the Old Testament in such a way as to give the reader clues as to its abiding significance. To study the Old Testament, therefore, is not like visiting a museum (however much the historicism in vogue since the late nineteenth century has encouraged such a view). Rather, to open the Old Testament is to encounter the living God!

Often, in trying to comprehend the role of the reader in the interpretation of scripture, scholars, of late, have spoken about a "hermeneutics of suspicion" or a "hermeneutics of trust." Such language signals that the Bible is provocative literature, which makes claims on its readers—that the Bible is not to be taken as simply inert sherds dug up from the past to be scrutinized as one would study fossils. But neither suspicion nor trust are options on offer for our choosing if we are to understand the character of the narrative's sacred disclosure and appreciate our privilege in being able to glimpse beyond the veil at all. In effect, to overstate the Bible's historical character is all too often to understate its theological dimension from the start.

PRAYER AND THE NAME OF GOD (YHWH)

Our discussion of prayer is based on one major assumption: that prayer turns on an intimate knowledge of the named God of Israel, who revealed who he is to a particular people at the Red Sea and at Mount Sinai—and who, on these terms and this ground, is accessible in prayer. Prayer in the Old Testament is not special content, particular technique, or the quality of a person's spirituality. Rather, it is talk with the living God! And to talk with the living God is, for Israel, to know God's name.

By convention, I will in what follows refer to this personal name of God (YHWH) as "the LORD." I am, however, mindful of the inadequacy of this convention for expressing what the divine name expressed in Israel—however much we may be told that the convention is traceable to a reverential move designed to protect God's name against misuse (which, in turn, reveals how much the name was the virtual "real presence" of the person of the Holy One of Israel; cf. Exod. 34:6–7). Indeed, the existence of this convention makes it extremely difficult to emphasize how much prayer in the Old Testament is tied to the personal dimension of God as this is carried in God's name, for the modern and late-modern use of the name Yahweh can recapture none of this personal dimension. It may, in fact, even produce the opposite effect—not to mention the manifold problems for Christian theology that such a neologism introduces, whether of modalism or of an unacceptable confusion about relations among the persons of the Godhead in an "immanent Trinity."

It should not be forgotten, as well, that alongside this reverential convention was also a conspiring factor from another quarter, which is presupposed and carried over into the New Testament—that is, the emergence of the sacred name of Jesus and the implications of the sanctity of Jesus' name for Christian belief and worship. God gave his "name above all names," as the early Christian confession contained in Phil. 2:6–11 has it, to the One he exalted to his right hand (v 9).

In the Old Testament, it is God's personal name and the disclosure of his name to Israel that, in the very first instance, makes prayer possible. Prayer is fundamentally about God's holy, named self being made accessible to humans by God and on his own sovereign terms. However we are meant to understand the character of this disclosure before Israel's experiences at the Red Sea and Mount Sinai, Gen. 4:26 insists that prayer is, at bottom, a calling on "the name of the LORD." Underlying this third-person use of "the LORD" there is a first-person clarification in the form of a solemn self-introduction made in Exodus 3 and 6, which is capable of being paraphrased as: "I am the LORD, who will be as I will be in the events that I bring about"—as expressed in God's deliverance of his people at the Sea, before Pharaoh and all creation, and his revelation of the Torah at Sinai. Prayer is possible only on the strength of these disclosures.

Yet prayer also can imply a general access to God, which is what we mean when we speak of "prayer" in its own inherently general sense. How can this be so? How can God be accessible to those he discloses himself to, and only them, and yet also be accessible and meaningful in general terms?

Our treatment of prayer, therefore, will be in two main parts. The first will reflect on prayer within and outside the covenant. It will consider the theological significance of this "inside and outside" reality of prayer. Part 2 will look at prayer within the covenant relationship in the strict sense. The emphasis in this second part will fall on the "one and the many" as essential to prayer's intercessory logic.

Though many Old Testament figures will be treated in passing, in the final section I focus on three who pray: Moses, David, and the man called "the suffering servant." Just as there is a complex relationship between generic and specific prayers in the Old Testament or Hebrew Bible, so, too, there is within Israel a complex relationship between the prayers of the one and the prayers of the many. This relationship between the one and the many is taken up bodily in the New Testament. It represents the governing type or figure with which earliest Christian confessions were keen to correlate the actions and identity of Jesus the Christ. The New Testament refers to this figural correlation by using the expression "in accordance with the Scriptures" or "in fulfillment of the Scriptures" (cf. 1 Cor. 15:3). The theological truth conveyed by such language is as follows: who Jesus was and is—that is, the New Testament's adaptation of the divine name, "I am who I will be," which is fitted for the logic of its incarnational presentation—is known in relationship to the God who revealed himself to Israel and through Israel to the world, both in blessing and in curse.

Therefore, if prayer is to be understood rightly, it must be situated within the reality of God's disclosure of himself, which is the central revelatory truth at the heart of the Old Testament. And here, even though expressed in dialectical relationship to Israel's Torah, is to be found the explanation for Paul's phraseology in referring to the Scriptures as "the oracles of God" (i.e., the One Named and Holy God), which oracles had been entrusted to the Jews (Rom. 3:2).

PRAYER AND CHRISTIAN SCRIPTURE, OLD AND NEW

Two facts about prayer in the New Testament are basic: that Jesus prayed and that Jesus taught his disciples to pray. One might conclude from this that Christian prayer involves an understanding of (1) the manner of Jesus' praying, (2) the content of his prayer, and (3) how these features have been passed to the church, whose self-understanding is to be governed (at least in some measure) by (4) depictions of the followers of Jesus at prayer in the New Testament and (5) teachings of the New Testament writers on the subject of prayer. All of this would justify a study of prayer that focuses primarily on the New Testament witness.

At the same time, however, Christians always need to be aware that prayer did not begin with Jesus. All sorts of people have prayed, to all sorts of gods, and from time immemorial. Prayer, in fact, could well be as universal an instinct as eating or sleeping. And in that witness called the scriptures of Israel, prayer begins very early with Enosh in that lapidary statement of Gen. 4:26: "At that time people began to invoke the name of the LORD."

This Enosh was distinctly a pre-Abraham, pre-Israelite son of Adam. His name literally means "humanity"—that is, the genus of human beings broadly considered. Prayer emerges, therefore, together with the offerings of Cain and Abel, as soon as the flaming sword is set down east of Eden. It does not only first occur at that time when God chooses a special people who will be the means of blessing to all the nations—a people who will come to see that they have direct-dial service, and not just a party line, into God's presence (and will pay a higher surcharge for it, too).

Still, it is noteworthy—even if, ironically, often underappreciated by many gentile interpreters—that the scriptures of Israel tell us things about prayer that are not exclusively tied to Israel. Indeed, it will be a thesis of the first main section to follow that what is true about prayer, as these scriptures relate it, only comes to full realization as one grasps the universality of prayer as a human instinct.

Because prayer takes place both within and outside God's covenant relationship with his people, it has the capacity to show us something about God's
double-edged life with Israel—that is, his love and commitment, on the one
hand, and his jealousy, on the other. And, by figural extension, it expresses also
something about his relations with both the Christian church and Judaism.
Seen from Israel's own unique perspective, as the canon reveals this, this means
that prayer can become a means of imitating those outside that covenant relationship and so result in idolatrous and vain pleadings. Such "praying" drives
God to silence or to withdrawal, as in the Book of Isaiah. Or prayer can bring
about a more quotidian demonstration of God's judgment, as when pagan
sailors pray to Israel's LORD and not to their own gods, while Jonah, God's
prophet, hides below deck, silent and in judgment for being so. Both perspectives exist in the Old Testament: Israel becoming, in prayer, like the nations
and the nations doing what is appropriate in prayer, as this has been vouchsafed to Israel. In this dialectic of "inside-outside," the significance of prayer
as having to do with God's special revelation and election is underscored.

The Old Testament tells us that Moses prayed, that David prayed, and that
Israel as a people prayed. Measured against the prayers of Jesus, are we meant
to conclude that theirs was likewise a special praying with a special content—
in the same way (though, of course, in some preliminary or underdeveloped
way) that the praying and prayers of Jesus are central and special and exem-
plary? Is there something special about the manner of praying and the content
of what is prayed in the Hebrew scriptures that justifies the inclusion of such
a discussion within the ecology of prayer, the main loci of which are taken
to be found in the New Testament? I believe not. Rather, a discussion of
prayer in the Old Testament vis-à-vis prayer in the New Testament makes
sense only if it shows how prayer is about the basic theological truth of both
testaments—that is, about the identity and disclosure of God as he truly is. And
an interest in this theological truth means that our concern will be not only
with historical and descriptive matters but also primarily with the abiding and
constructive features of prayer as the Old Testament or Hebrew scriptures
present them.

To this end, it will first be established that the witness of the Old Testament
is not to prayer as an anthropological distinctive that somehow marks off Israel
as God's people. The Old Testament is not a project that sets out to tell us
things about Israel as a pre-Jewish *anthropos*, whether in the realm of prayer or
in other matters religious. That would make it a handbook of religious practices and ideas, which a people from another period (particularly Jews and
Christians today) can open and learn from as one might study (whether out of
curiosity or for edification) a certain religion or a body of religious beliefs. This
is not to deny that the Old Testament can be read in this way—and, indeed, is

generally read this way by many people today, especially by Christian readers who possess a second testament. The very existence of the dual phraseology "Old Testament" and "Hebrew Bible" points to a deeper ambiguity or dialectic that governs the inquiry and must be faced right up front.

To state matters somewhat differently, the very first question facing any inquiry into prayer in the Old Testament or Hebrew Bible is form-critical. Just what kind of depiction are we talking about when we turn to a set of scriptures that was once called by those with a "New Testament Scripture-in-the-making" one thing—that is, "the oracles of God," "the law and prophets," or "the scriptures"—and then, increasingly, by Christians, by Jews, and by others something else—that is, "Old Testament," "Tanak," or "Hebrew Bible"? What sort of book is this book, which is paired by Christians with another witness, by Jews with another distinctive interpreting lens, and by the simply curious with their own modern or late-modern spectacles?

Given such different perspectives, the opening statement that must be made about prayer is that the depiction of prayer in these scriptures is not riveted to Israel as a people but entails a broader, yet more intensive look at a more privileged reality: the identity of God as he truly is. To say this is to highlight the fact that these scriptures are making theological statements on the basis of religious ones—that is, they are speaking of Israel's religious experience and the religious experiences attributed to the nations as the means by which to offer testimony to God's very self. And because prayer lies at the heart of all such depictions, the Hebrew scriptures, which speak most specifically about prayer, are the best place to begin when we want to see how such general religious phenomena have become the media for theological truth about God as he is.

PRAYER AS UNIVERSAL
AND PRAYER IN ISRAEL'S EXPERIENCE

It is bracing to consider how far-reaching and fraught with theological meaning are the depictions of prayer in the Old Testament or Hebrew Bible, particularly when ranged alongside depictions of prayer in the New Testament and the Talmud. If we fail to take into consideration those Old Testament depictions, we will miss the perspective that governs the New Testament's own angle of vision. But there also exists, right alongside what can be said about Israel's experience, a universal aspect of prayer that guides the self-consciousness of Jesus and forms, under the authority of the Holy Spirit, the early church's emerging identity. And it is this universal understanding of prayer, over against the particular understanding of the scriptures, that supplies an important key to the portrayals of prayer in the New Testament and sets the mode within which the proclamation of the New Testament plays out its notes and makes it music.

Portrayals in Isaiah and Jeremiah

The universal or generic reality is—like much else in the Old Testament—that prayer can become deeply ironic in God's use of it. For when Rabshakeh, the Assyrian general, standing outside the city of Jerusalem with the most powerful army of the day, asked, "Is it without the LORD that I have come up against this land to destroy it?" (Isa. 36:10), he could have been quoting the prophet Isaiah, "Ah, Assyria, the rod of my anger . . . against a godless nation I send him" (Isa. 10:5). The word of the prophet had, it seems, become genericized. And on the lips of this Assyrian official, it constituted a blasphemy calling for divine judgment.

Likewise, prayer may be something of a generic reflex that simply ricochets off God's closed counsel and so becomes idolatrous. This was God's judgment on Isaiah's generation: "When you stretch out your hands, I will hide my eyes from you; even though you make many prayers, I will not listen" (Isa. 1:15). Israel had become a "sinful nation" (Isa. 1:4; a *goy* or gentile-like people), with prayers to match. Thus, a generic "Israel" with generic "prayers" gets a generic "god" (*elohim*)—one comparable to the plural "gods" so boasted about by Rabshakeh (Isa. 36:18) but unworthy of the dignity of God's name and self.

By contrast, the prayer of a righteous person can reverse the destruction and disgrace of Zion. This is what happened when Hezekiah prayed to God concerning the invasion of Sennacherib and his mocking, defiant letter (Isa. 36:1–37:20). In response, the prophet gives God's verdict: "Because you have prayed to me concerning king Sennacherib Assyria, this is the word that the LORD has spoken concerning him" (Isa. 37:21–22a)—with, then, a divine oracle of doom uttered against Sennacherib (Isa. 37:22b–29).

Prayer can also be denied to doom an entire generation, as with God's charge to Jeremiah: "Do not pray for this people!" (Jer. 7:16; 11:14; 14:11). Or it can go forth with the seeds of its own destruction, as in the case of Sennacherib, who was not killed by an avenging angel outside the city of Jerusalem but in an act of worship "in the house of his god Nisroch" (Isa. 37:38). The drama of the siege of Jerusalem, as portrayed in Isaiah 36–37, is a drama not of military might but of prayer. The story does not end with the dramatic defeat of an army of 185,000 men, as presented in 37:36, but with the defeat of one man in the silence of his own blasphemous sanctuary, as depicted in 37:38.

The Story of Jonah

The opposite depiction comes in the story of Jonah. When worried for their lives, pagan sailors tell Jonah to "call on his god." In a moment of unparalleled self-absorption, Jonah asks to be thrown into the sea (Jon. 1:12; cf. 4:9). The sailors oblige him. But they do so only after offering a prayer that brings about their own salvation—a prayer offered not to their god, or even to Jonah's god (who, presumably, from their standpoint, was another small "g" god), but to God, the LORD. Under examination, Jonah had earlier, ironically, borne witness to this god as "the LORD, the God of heaven, who made the sea and the dry land" (1:9). Jonah's subsequent prayer in the fish is to "the LORD his God" (2:1–9), who then directs the fish to spit him out when he does, at last, what he was told to do by the sailors (cf. 1:10).

One can see in this story a narrative that conveys a deeply theological truth about prayer: that prayer is not about technique or content, as such, but about naming the name and declaring the honor due that name, by witnessing before the nations to the one God, the LORD, maker of heaven and earth. If Jonah, who is acquainted with God's name, shirks from such a witness, then the nations will bear witness themselves—before God and before Jonah and before heaven and earth, prior to chucking him overboard. It matters not for the sake of the narrative that we be able to assess the moral qualifications of the sailors, their spiritual fitness, or the sheer dice-rolling character of their decision. What matters for the theological force of the narrative is that prayer is about calling on the one God and calling on him by name. Even on the lips of worried sailors with no knowledge of God's ways, God's name is God's self. All prayer begins with this reality, even if under—and for this narrative, precisely when under—forced circumstances. If Jonah persists in his strange piety and religious bearing, it would be just as well if he knew not God's name or called not on God. The consequence would be the same. Any prayer without God's name is as effective as silence. And Jonah tried both before he fell back on what he knew to be true about prayer and what others learned from his stubbornness to be the truth about prayer.

Prayer, therefore, is to address God by name. And to name God's name is to deal with God as he truly is, without remainder—yet always under the obligation of having invoked the one holy and jealous God. In the story of Jonah, that holiness and jealousy spill out in judgment and salvation, as God sees fit.

The Story of Balaam

Israel's depiction of the generic as testimony to the specific, through the vehicle of prayer, also comes in modified form in the story of Balaam, the hired gun who was called by Balak, king of Moab, to curse Israel (Num. 22:4–6). Although the story is not about prayer as we usually understand it, it is clearly about the reality of God's identity. In the course of the narrative, we see the generic god (22:9–12) become the named LORD God (22:13); become the LORD's angel (22:22); become "the LORD" on the lips of Balaam, the man from the land beyond the Euphrates (23:15); and become acknowledged as "the LORD" even by Balak, his Moabite employer (23:17).

When Balak hired Balaam, a famous foreign curser, to invoke God for his purposes, he did not have it in view that the God who brings judgment on mortals (for a fee) would reveal himself as "the LORD" and make that revelation of himself an occasion for the blessing of Israel and Balaam and the cursing of Moab and Balak. Here, again, we have a story told by Israel about the way that the invocation of God by the nations comes with rather startling and unexpected consequences.

The Story of Job

Job, too, was also not an Israelite, standing as he did on the other side of Sinai. He was a contemporary of Noah and, like him, was renowned for his intercession (cf. Ezek. 14:14). He was a man from the east, whose "friends" were like him in being removed from the circle of the fully named and known God, as revealed in Exodus 3 and 6.

It is striking that a man renowned for intercession does so little praying on his own behalf. Form-critically, there is very little in the long dialogue section of chapters 3–26 of the Book of Job that counts as prayer, strictly speaking. Some of that omission may be explicable because of the constraints of the section's form, which is more talk about God than talk to God. But even when Job lays down his famous oath of innocence in chapter 31, while we have talk about God and at God, it is still not prayer. It is not "Thou" speech to God in prayer.

Only once does Job name the name of God. "The LORD gave, and the LORD has taken away; blessed be the name of the LORD" (1:21). But it is not clear what the narrator means to say by that naming, particularly in view of the full revelation of God's name to Moses in Exodus 3:13–15. At the beginning of the story, the narrator tells his readers that the LORD is the God confronted by Satan within his court (1:6–2:6), who forced God to show in the case of Job the possibility of serving God without reward (1:9). And the reader also knows that this LORD is the God who appears in the whirlwind (38:1; 40:6).

But, as the true finale of the contest between Sennacherib and Jerusalem in Isaiah 36–37 did not come until a moment much later than the august military defeat, so, too, the true finale of the Book of Job does not come in chapters 38–41 with the speech of God from the whirlwind. The wager on Job was not determined by sheer divine extrusion into the world of suffering. Rather, it was settled when Job became who he was all along, even on the ash heap—that is, a man of prayer (cf. 42:1–9). So it is at this point the narrator comments: "And the LORD restored the fortunes of Job when he had prayed for his friends" (42:10). And though the narrator does not say it himself, the response of Job to God implies that he had learned something about God in the experience of the whirlwind that he did not know before (42:5), which knowledge was for him akin to the way that God is the same (yet more fully to be known in the events of Sea and Sinai) as the LORD.

Here, then, is a further instance in the Hebrew scriptures where God demonstrated in a universal manner his sovereignty over how and when he could be known. The consequence in Job's case, however, was overwhelming and compelling. He became a man of prayer—even for those who had not heard his cry. And in so doing, he defeated the evil whose face is hidden but whose presence is parasitic on all of life.

Here in the Hebrew scriptures—on the border between the generic and the specific, between the man from the east and God's covenant people at Sea and Sinai—prayer is the place where the truth of God's most essential self is grasped. This truth is that God's self is to be worshiped without any hope for reward. And in Job's confession of 42:5 ("now my eye sees thee") and prayer of 42:8–9, the forces of evil were rendered mute and helpless—until another man and another day and another prayer, to the glory of the one LORD.

A Summation

The Old Testament and Hebrew scriptures reveal that prayer has the widest possible base in God's dealing with the world. What is essentially at stake in prayer is knowledge of God's name. And that knowledge can be mysteriously conveyed, if God so chooses, as with Balaam. It can also be inadvertently and even desperately disclosed, as with Jonah's overtly selfish expostulation to the sailors, which became the means of salvation for them. Prayer, however, is fundamentally about learning that God can be known, as in the case of Job, and that he is one, as he revealed himself to Israel—but that he is also sovereign over his own disclosures, and so is revealed only as he sees fit.

Prayer is not humanity's effort to reach God from below by crying out to him. Rather, it is the consequence of his having made himself known and our faithful response to that prior knowledge. True prayer, therefore, means discourse with the one LORD, and that cannot be taken for granted as covered under some generic deity.

It remains true, however, that naming God's name in prayer, even within Israel, stands under God's sovereignty as well. If Israel becomes a nation like the other nations, prayer to him will not be heard. In the prophecy of Isaiah, becoming like the other nations (cf. 1:4; a *goy* or "gentile-like nation") has the consequence of producing—at least externally—a more prayerful rather than less prayerful people (cf. chapter 1)—that is, of turning to a proliferation of gods to make up the difference for calling on God by name and not being heard. God holds out his hands all day (65:2), but the people have forsaken him (65:11). And so they become more religious to fill up the void, not less religious.

PRAYER WITHIN THE COVENANT

When one looks at prayer within the covenant relationship, what is striking is what one does not find. There is no handbook on prayer, as there is on sacrifice and offerings. The elaborate details that governed Israel's worship have not a single specific word about how to pray or what to pray for. Here, again, one is thrown up against the reality that prayer in the Old Testament is distinctly nonreligious. Spirituality is religious, phenomenal, and self-conscious, but prayer in the Old Testament lacks the dimension of self-consciousness.

Moses and the Pentateuch

Staying within the realm of Israel's worship and focusing on Moses and the Pentateuch, three things can be said about prayer: first, that the prayer or "Song of Moses" of Exod. 15:1–18 emerges as critical to God's patience and forbearance—not just in the wilderness but in a much wider sense. Moses intercedes and puts God in mind of his promises to Israel's ancestors. It would not be too much to say that God is blackmailed (in a manner of speaking) by Moses, insofar as his suggestion to build a nation out of Moses or send an angel instead of himself is held hostage, Moses insists, to his own prior promises. Here, again, we see that prayer involves no special techniques beyond simple truth-telling. Moses does this. God responds. He will build a nation out of the children of the murmurers, and he will go in presence and in name with them, to fulfill his promises to their ancestors.

Second, and akin to this, Deuteronomy, amid its many worship statements, speaks of prayer in the context of judgment. At the end of the book, blessing and curse are set out before the new generation poised to enter the promised land. Yet the book looks even further into the future, to a time of exile and curse (29:22–29; cf. also 4:25–31; 9:4–5); that is, it reckons with a breaking of the covenant. How can there be a future for God's people? It is prayer, Deuteronomy insists, that reestablishes the relationship (30:1–5). Here we touch on the fundamental sacrificial reality, which lies just below or alongside the unitive character of sacrificial offering: a broken and contrite heart.

Finally, prayer is understood in Exodus and Deuteronomy as that which interprets and makes clear the unitive, purposeful nature of sacrificial offering (Exod. 34:29–35; cf. 1 Kgs. 8:22–53). This keeps Israel's cult from devolving into generic religiosity. Why was the worship of Aaron and the people, which they initiated at the foot of the mountain, any less sincere, heartfelt, celebrative, or earnest than what God himself set out? The answer is that their worship was wrong because God has not been called on as he is. And so we return to the fundamental reality that lies behind all prayer: the lifting up of the name of God, which is the sine qua non of prayer. Without God's name being lifted up, religion and prayers can flourish and multiply. But curse, not blessing, will ensue—stopped only by the prayer of Moses, which puts God in mind of his prior commitments and of the broken and contrite heart of the people (Deut. 30:1–5; cf. 1 Kgs. 8:35–53).

Prayer, it would seem, belongs to the realm of truth, from the standpoint of human beings within the covenant, and concerns God's holy self, from the standpoint of the divine. Certain individuals are better at staying with the truth than others. This truth has a twofold character: (1) truth about God's character and self and (2) truth about the situation of judgment and God's absence or withdrawal from the covenant relationship for a season. The latter is due to the sins of those who pray and/or the realization that a generation has so turned away from God that he has withdrawn to protect his own name and holy covenant.

Within the covenant, a dialectic exists between the prayer of everyman and the prayer of the one man. Israel retained in its memory the singular role of Moses as one who prays. This role cannot be underestimated as one looks at prayer more generally.

David and the Psalms

The role of the specific and the general is explicit within the Psalter. Martin Luther worked with an almost modern attitude toward the character of the Old Testament as Christian scripture, which attitude bears some resemblance to what would later emerge and be called "historical criticism." In the Psalms, however, he recognized what he called "the faithful synagogue." The anachronism "synagogue" may be telling as to Luther's modernity. But more important was his sensitivity to the abiding witness of the Psalter to prayer. The Psalms did not tell Luther something about the way a certain people prayed before Jesus showed up. Rather, for Luther the Psalms show us prayer as it eternally is—which is an important corrective to the pernicious habit, whether motivated by practical or mercenary concerns, of printing New Testaments by themselves (though, thankfully, such an inclination often halts at omitting the "Psalms of David").

The faithful synagogue and the Psalms of David? Can both be true? Can the Psalms be prayers of David and prayers of Israel and prayers of Christians all at the same time? The question, of course, is heuristic, because the psalms are manifestly these things anyway. How, then, are they this?

Jesus interpreted Psalm 110 as David's word regarding him (cf. Mark 12:35–37; par.). So the dimension of fulfilled prophecy comes to the fore in many instances of the use of scripture in the New Testament. And so the Psalms of the Hebrew Bible have become prayers for others than Jews. Stated negatively, there are no Psalms that represent the wisdom of praying and are universally available in the same way as the Book of Proverbs includes words from Agur or King Lemuel. Unlike the presentation of the Book of Job, the God addressed in the Psalter is not a veiled YHWH. Rather, the God of the Psalms is Israel's God in holy unveiling.

At the same time, it should not be forgotten that the question of "why" Jesus uttered Psalm 22 on the cross is a question that often bypasses a matter of deeper consequence in a Christian apprehension of the Old Testament as scripture for the Christian church. That God was absent and forsook Jesus in the manner declared by Psalm 22 is a recognition that God—both for Jesus and for Israel before him—could be said to be "my God" in the very strict sense of that term. The heart of Israel's praying is not wrecked on the shoals of either the complete presence or the complete absence of God for his people. Rather, this heart of Israel's praying is broken open and made accessible by virtue of the relationship that Jesus has with God, thereby tearing open a veil and giving those outside the covenant a relationship to God—and so, by the work of Jesus and being "in him," allowing Gentiles to enter the sanctuary of the "faithful synagogue" (to use Luther's metaphor) and, further, even to enter into the heart of David himself.

The Suffering Servant and the Prophets

I want to conclude this overview not with Moses or David but with another figure from the Book of Isaiah who is commonly called the "suffering servant." As we will see, a look at the servant brings us back full circle to Moses, whose prayers saved Israel in forfeit in the wilderness.

That there is a relationship between the movement of thought within the Book of Isaiah and the movement of thought within the Psalter is a thesis that is highly defensible. For our purposes here, however, it is sufficient to note that Isaiah 40–48 (a subsection of so-called Deutero-Isaiah) is as concerned with the kingship of God and his sole rule over nations and creation as is Book 4 of the Psalter (Pss. 90–106) and that both sections appear at a similar location in their respective canonical presentations. Furthermore, in both Isaiah 40–48 and Book 4 of the Psalter, an explicit mention of God's Messiah falls into the background.

Many have noted also the close association between God's servant in Isaiah 49–53 and the man Moses. Ernst Sellin and Gerhard von Rad are two recent defenders of this view; likewise, Klaus Baltzer pursues this position in his new Hermeneia commentary on Isaiah 40–55.[1] Such a view is also consistent with the depiction of Psalm 90, in which Moses, in prayer on behalf of David and Israel, is brought back, as it were, from his days as intercessor in the wilderness.

In the movement of thought in Isaiah 40–48, the servant is introduced before the heavenly council in chapter 42. The servant is to have a specific role in relation to the nations. As it is clear in this part of Isaiah that Israel is the servant, we should also expect the role to the nations described in chapter 42 to be that of none other than Israel.

But a change seems to be registered in chapter 49. A more individual figure appears to be commissioned. Moreover, this servant has a role vis-à-vis not just the nations but also Israel. Jeremiah was commissioned to be a prophet to the nations, and the language that appears here is very similar to what appears in Jeremiah 1. Here, however, the text refers to discouragement and seems to speak of a past vocation that has been frustrated, not one that lies in the future.

Jeremiah was considered by those who shaped the traditions associated with him to be a "prophet like Moses."[2] Such a prophet had been promised in Deut. 18:16 ("I will raise up for them a prophet like you from among their own people"), and Jeremiah's fulfillment of such a role seems clear. Yet, ironically, with this fulfillment, we may also see a distinctive interpretation of the language of Deuteronomy. Although Jeremiah is a second Moses, he is also the final prophet. With his return to Egypt, the curses of Deuteronomy are brought upon an evil generation. And his command not to intercede is styled on that of Moses—but with the obvious consequence that, without Mosaic prayer, the people are doomed.

Against the backdrop of these experiences of Jeremiah, the language of Isaiah 49 seems to take its bearings. Yet the servant of Isaiah 49 is not discouraged. Like Jeremiah, he suffers and endures persecution, which is described in the third servant poem of 50:4–11. In like manner as Jeremiah, he is assaulted by his own people, as well as by others. But the servant's legacy is not lament, as in Jeremiah 11–20, nor is it a withdrawal from the office of prayer, which occasioned such lament. And in the final, dramatic poem of 52:13–53:12, the servant is described as one who "made intercession for the transgressors."

There is every reason to believe that the servant of Isaiah 49–53, unlike Jeremiah, was one whose prayers were salvific because God was doing a truly new thing through him. Intercession was not denied the servant. Even more, the servant gave his life, as well as his petitions, on behalf of the people. That is the explicit verdict rendered by the final tribute of 52:13–53:12.

Now, it had been a loosely developed theme that Moses had suffered innocently, which is a theme that one can see especially in the Deuteronomic traditions. The people sinned in the wilderness, but Moses interceded and saved them. God said he would make a people from Moses only, but Moses rejected this and assured through his prayer Israel's ongoing life with God.

Later, however, when the spies returned with a report of giants in the land, God's patience with the people ran out (cf. Numbers 13–14). Again, Moses interceded for them (14:13–19). But God decreed that only the little ones, a new generation, would enter the Promised Land as a result of Moses' saving intercession. He himself would bear the sins of the people and would suffer God's judgment on a wicked and deserving generation. Yet he would see the Promised Land from afar and then die in the wilderness, with no one recalling the place of his burial (cf. Isa. 53:9).

The depiction of the servant's saving work in Isa. 52:13–53:12 has been clearly modeled on Moses. He, not Jeremiah, is the awaited "prophet like Moses." Unlike the death of Moses, however, the death of the servant is seen as atoning and bearing sins in the most explicit sense—even to the extent of occasioning an eschatological confession by the nations (52:13–15). Thus, through death, the servant of Isa. 52:13–53:12 brings to fulfillment the promise made to Jeremiah and to the righteous servant of Isaiah 42 and 49.

CONCLUSION

The Old Testament focuses on key individuals in its presentation of prayer within the covenant. It establishes a clear connection between the election of certain people who pray and the people at large. They who pray and their prayers have the capacity to restore or tear down. In Isaiah, the "one and the many" relationship is extended, quite specifically, to the nations outside God's covenant. The use of Moses suggests an awareness of his ongoing, figurally real presence. Yet the "new thing" of Isaiah points to an enlargement of thought: that the servant is a man of prayer. We see into his heart of anguish and find firm resolve there (50:7). His prayer is but the utterance of his life itself, which is given up in obedience—like Moses before him. But his intercession, even though very similar to that of Moses, costs him his life, brings life to a whole generation, and removes their iniquity—something that Moses did not do. And in the context of this vocation, the servant of Isaiah 49–53 sees the final eschatological moment released for a split second in the confession of the nations (cf. 52:15).

It is striking, however, that the content, technique, or spirituality of the servant's prayer is hidden. His intercession is known by its results and by its ongoing, dynamic character. Its fruit ("he shall see seed") is encountered in the final chapters of Isaiah in the "servants" who follow where he once walked.

This figural reality—involving the one and the many, the prophet like Moses, the interceding servant, the prayer that unleashes an eschatological reality regarding those outside God's covenant—is crucial to the way that the New Testament forms its central confessions, which are configured in accordance with the literal sense of these scriptures. To speak of prayer in the Old Testament, therefore, is to speak of God's intimate disclosure and the way that disclosure penetrates to the heart of prayer as presented in the New Testament.

13

"Our Help Is in the Name of the LORD, the Maker of Heaven and Earth"

Scripture and Creed in Ecumenical Trust

This essay discusses the exegetical-theological significance of Article One of the Nicene-Constantinopolitan Creed. I will set the context; discuss the meaning of the phrase "the maker of heaven and earth" and what was at stake in its selection; discuss the phrase within the context of the entire first line of the creed; and conclude with five reflections on what is still at stake when we use this language in our present context. Much of what I have to say will involve a proper appreciation of God's name, the relationship between language and truth, and saying what we mean and meaning what we say.

SETTING THE CONTEXT

As organizer of a conference on Nicene Christianity, I had decided to divide Article One of the creed into two sections, rather artificially, so as to use John Zizioulas, the lead speaker of the conference, to best advantage. I was also protecting a selfish concern. I have been much interested in the phrase "the Maker of Heaven and Earth" in its own right. If you had a concordance at hand, you would very quickly see that this phrase appears again and again in the Old Testament. It is a fixed formula, and it often appears right next to the divine, personal name, as in "Our help is in the name of YHWH, the Maker of Heaven and Earth" (author's translation, Ps. 124:8).

Some time ago, this got me thinking that more is at stake in the creed's use of this phrase than a metaphysical declaration about creation, true though that is. The phrase rivets a statement, not to an abstract concept, but to a person, Adonai (the LORD, YHWH), the maker of heaven and earth, and that fact ought not be run by too quickly. Moreover, its usage confirms an insight pressed on us recently by David Yeago, that the creed and scripture represent a far more natural and happy marriage than some scholars of early church and doctrine have allowed.[1] Creed is more than putting out theological brushfires. It is letting scripture come to its natural, two-testament expression. Just as the Old Testament leaves its father and mother and cleaves to the New, so the scriptures cleave to the creed, and the creed to them, and they become one flesh.

I want to dedicate these remarks to my father, Thomas Seitz, and to his father, William Clinton (little did he know) Seitz. My grandfather taught, among other things, doctrine at Bexley Hall. He had a clear influence on my father as priest and teacher. When Genesis speaks of generations, it includes this sort of influencing, from one age to the next. "These are the generations of the heavens and the earth" (Gen. 2:4) or "This is the book of the genera-tion of Adam. When God created man, he made him in the likeness of God. . . . Adam became the father of a son in his own likeness; after his image" (Gen. 5:1–3). "From generation to generation," as the Old Testament puts it, God's word of instruction goes forth.

I received from my father's library a classic Anglican exposition of the creed, by John Pearson.[2] In reviewing it as I brought this chapter to completion, I was struck at the great learning of the author. I was also struck at the sort of writing that was possible at this time, before the rise of the higher biblical crit-icism and its adoption into the Anglo-Saxon world (ironically, it was the same Anglo-Catholic movement that revived interest in Pearson in the mid-nineteenth century that also conceded quite broadly to biblical criticism at the century's end, so, e.g., the volume of essays published in 1889 as *Lux Mundi*). Pearson moves from scripture to fathers to creed in an enormously effective, wide-ranging, and subtle way. The sort of method that Yeago, Frances Young, or Richard Bauckham might now argue for, given the rise of historicism, con-sists for Pearson as self-evidence.[3]

The other lesson I take away from Pearson, and from my father and his father, is that the work was completed in the context of parish instruction. The book opens with an appreciative address to "the right worshipful and well-beloved parishioners of St Clements, Eastcheap." Pearson is put in mind of Jude's concern for the faith once delivered. Absent from his concern is pride or self-righteousness. Pearson speaks simply of the responsibility before God, as a parish minister, to teach the faith of the church. Here is a model for min-istry today.

Pearson says, "If it were so needful [for Jude] and for them to whom he wrote to contend for the first faith, it will appear as needful for me now to fol-low his writing, and for you to imitate their earnestness, because the reason which he renders, as the cause of that necessity, is now more prevalent than it was at that time, or ever since." Then, quoting Jude (my adaptation of RSV), "For admission has been secretly gained by some . . . ungodly persons who pervert the grace of our God into licentiousness, denying the only Lord God and our Lord Jesus Christ."

In our situation, the difference is that we are not talking about a "secret admission" into the household of God but of public and proud pronouncement by church leaders. Both Jesus Christ but more deliberately "Our Lord God" have been deconstructed, the latter proclaimed dead, parochial, in need of regendering, reimaging, or replacement.

I recently read a news report of a national conference, "God at 2000," held at Trinity Church Wall Street.

> One of the most celebrated speakers was [Marcus] Borg, who advocates a brand of pantheism that rejects notions of a personal God in favor of a broader universal spirit. "I grew up in a time and place where it was taken for granted that Christianity was the only true religion and Jesus the only way to salvation," Borg recalled with distaste. "That's why we had missionaries. . . . I find it literally incredible to think that the God of the whole universe has chosen to be known in only one religious tradition."[4]

Compare the remarks of St. Augustine.

> What are you then, my God—what, but the Lord God? For who is Lord but the Lord? Or who is God save our God? Most high, most excellent, most powerful, most almighty, most merciful, and most just; most hidden, yet most present; most beautiful, and most strong; stable, yet mysterious; unchangeable, yet changing all things; never new, never old; making all things new and bringing age upon the proud, though they know it not; ever working, yet ever at rest; still gathering, yet lacking nothing; sustaining, filling and protecting; creating, nourishing, and maturing; seeking, yet possessing all things. You love without passion; you are jealous without anxiety; you repent, yet have no sorrow; you are angry, yet serene; change your ways, yet your plans are unchanged; recover what you find, having never lost it; never in need, yet rejoicing in gain; never covetous, yet requiring interest. You receive over and above, that you may owe—yet who has anything that is not yours? You pay debts, owing nothing; remit debts, losing nothing. And what have I now said, my God, my life, my holy joy—what is this I have said?[5]

At least one Trinity Conference speaker got it right when she said, "Surely there is no one participating in this conference who really believes that this conference is about God at 2000. This conference is about us at 2000."

There you have it.

By contrast, Pearson settles to have as his task both the plain exposition of the words of the creed for God's own sake and "also the truth thereof, and what efficacy and influence they have in the soul" (a topic ably pursued by Fitz Allison in *The Cruelty of Heresy*). Pearson concludes that his responsibility is "by collection of all, briefly to deliver the sum of every particular faith, so that everyone, when he pronounceth the Creed, may know what he ought to intend, and what he is understood to profess, when he so pronounceth it."[6] I can think of no better statement of purpose than that.

The one inadvertent piece of Christian wisdom at the Trinity Conference was supplied by a follower of the faith of Islam, "If you accept that your religion is relative you will not follow it. There must be something of absoluteness within religion. . . . Otherwise, there will just be languages that don't mean anything."

I thank my father for passing on Pearson's clear teaching volume. I especially prize his handwritten notes, which I suspect he made in the context of teaching ordinands, which as an examining chaplain it was his responsibility to discharge, in the course of parish ministry, now fifty years in the undertaking.

WHAT DOES "MAKER OF HEAVEN AND EARTH" MEAN, AND WHAT WAS AT STAKE?

When we say the words "I believe in One God, the Father Almighty" and then "maker of heaven and earth," we are right to believe we are describing a specific activity of God. God made the heavens and the earth. He made all things visible and invisible, in the creed's restatement of this.

The reference to this activity comes as the very first sentence of scripture. "In the beginning when God created the heavens and the earth" (Gen. 1:1).

The Old Testament refers to this activity in its own creedal-like formulations. God as creator is the subject of the Psalms of enthronement (see 92–99) and hymns to God as creator are not uncommon (so Pss. 8, 104). Then again, the phrase may appear of itself, as in, "I lift up my eyes to the hills: from whence comes my help? My help comes from the LORD, the maker of heaven and earth" (Ps. 121:2; cf. Ps. 134). Lengthy descriptions of God as creator can be found in Job and Deutero-Isaiah. In the long prayer of David at the dedication of the temple, we hear, "Yours, O LORD, are the greatness, the power, the glory, the victory, and the majesty; for all that is in the heavens and on the earth are yours" (1 Chron. 29:11), establishing the logic of pantocrator (the almighty) alongside creation, alongside praise of God's name. Paul before the gentile Athenians proclaims, "What therefore you worship as unknown, this I proclaim to you. The God who made the world and everything in it, he is the Lord of heaven and earth" (Acts 17:23–24). This is but a modest sample from a large range of usage.

What we see in these examples is the description of God as the one who, amid various other activities, created the heavens and the earth. More than this, we would be right to say this is a special activity of God. As such, it sits alongside other such special activities. For example, the solemn phrase "I am the LORD who brought you out of Egypt" is notable for its frequency in the Old Testament; so, too, "The LORD, the LORD, compassionate and merciful." Phrases like this get repeated and reused until their rough edges are worn off. They are moved from being episodic statements of an activity, making or bringing out or having compassion, and begin taking on appositional or predicative character. So, in a context of psalm petition and not the act of creation itself, we hear "Our help is in the name of the LORD, the maker of heaven and earth" or "May the LORD bless you from Zion, he who made the heavens and the earth" (Ps. 134:3).

The activities to which such phrases refer are irreplaceable and nonuniversalizable. They are single events whose doer, whose author or agent, has no substitute. Deutero-Isaiah makes explicit what is everywhere assumed. "For thus says the LORD, who created the heavens (he is God), who formed the earth and made it. . . . I am the LORD and there is no other." No one else brought Israel out of Egypt. No one else is gracious and compassionate. No one else created the heavens and the earth. Just this agent and no other agent can be connected to an activity humanity later will speak about independently of him, when they speak of creation, the making of the universe, and all created matter, some visible and some invisible (is there water on Jupiter?). We now talk about an activity and use various names for this—creation, evolution, cosmology—without using God's name, detached from his sovereignty into rival modes of rationalism.

There can be no doubt that at Nicaea, swirling about, were various rival understandings of God and creation. Was God by himself, or were there demigods? Did one god create a good heavenly or spiritual reality and another an earthly or carnal realm? That this discussion took place is undeniable, and the statements of the creed live and have their being within a climate where they are statements canceling out rivals. They are counterfactuals, the saying of "No" to alternatives.

The Old Testament also presents a world where rival understandings of god exist, together with rival views of a single deity's or several deities' relationship to the created order. Yet the primary mode of speech on this matter in the Old Testament is not argumentative or persuasive, but declarative. In the sentence to which we have just referred, it is important to take account of the order,

"I am the LORD, who brought you out of Egypt, you shall have no other gods before me." The LORD's existence and sovereignty are not conclusions to be drawn after one assesses alternatives. We only know about creation or deliverance or compassion because the One God demonstrates these, speaks them forth, and gives us speech in return to refer to him. God speaks his word, and he fulfills what he says, faithfully. In this way, he establishes his sole Lordship, from which we learn that he is Lord, he alone, the maker of heaven and earth.

So, if we ask what was at stake at Nicaea, in the very first instance, it was the declaration that the God and Father almighty of the Lord Jesus was this named LORD, and none other. Jesus is not related to Godness. Nor is Jesus known independently of the LORD's speech in Israel, which accords or figures his coming. This properly named LORD gave the name above every name, his own name, to Jesus, that at his name every knee would bow, to the glory of the Father. "Our help is in the name of the LORD, the Maker of Heaven and Earth" (Ps. 124:8) is a statement in which the two phrases, as is typical of Hebrew poetry, seek to fill out what can be said in one only partially. This might be called an OT version of *homoousia*. The name Adonai is "of one being" with maker of heaven and earth. To say "maker of heaven and earth" is to say "the LORD." It is just as specific a denotation as "he who brought Israel out of Egypt," "he who raised Israel from the dead of dry bones," "he who raised Jesus from the dead." Jenson treats this matter with great clarity.[8]

When Paul says to the Athenians (in Acts 17) that the unknown god is the Lord of heaven and earth, he is not in the first instance arguing something about creation on the basis of common assumptions. Rather, he is asserting that the maker of heaven and earth is the sole Lord is the LORD who brought Israel out of Egypt is the Lord who has appointed one to judge the earth. Paul's reference to God's making all nations from one man and determining generations and boundaries finds its source in Genesis 1–11 alone, where the one God speaks these matters forth.

To be sure, among the many, many gods Paul was sickened by seeing at Athens, one was likely in charge of one realm, heaven, and another, earth, and so his statement was canceling out some false and idolatrous things. But his was not a statement about the character of creation as an independent matter that the Athenians were in the dark about (which they were) and needed to be corrected about (which they did). In the first instance, Paul was stipulating that the Lord of heaven and earth was not the summation of all the other gods (a high God) or an alternative with a more compelling account of creation (a better god) but an unknown and unknowable God, without his own speaking or sending, without his own self-declaration. Paul was virtually enacting the logic of Isaiah 45 at Athens. Isaiah reads "They [the nations] shall come to you . . . saying, 'God is with you only, and there is no other. Truly thou are a God who hidest thyself, O God of Israel, the Savior'" (45:14–15). Paul announces, "What therefore you worship as unknown, this I proclaim to you" (17:23), filling Isaiah's promise to its fullest measure.

In sum, the phrase "maker of heaven and earth" functions to point explicitly to the named God of Israel, about whom certain understandings of creation and sovereignty can be known only by reading these—not off nature itself with something called unaided reason—but off the Old Testament's account of the creator, who rules by his word and his name in Israel, and by his sovereign mystery—his almighty rule—over the nations and in creation, shutting the mouth while opening the eye of that grateful gentile Job.

"MAKER OF HEAVEN AND EARTH" AND ARTICLE ONE AS A WHOLE

The first thing to note is that "maker of heaven and earth" exists within a bundle of expressions that speak of God. It is the fourth in a series: "One God," "the Father," "Almighty" (*pantocrator* in Greek; cf. the Hebrew Shaddai, LORD of hosts, and rabbinic use of "Eternal" [*ha'olam*]) and only then "maker of heaven and earth."

Two parenthetical notes: In the seventeenth-century exposition of Pearson, the judgment was made to treat God as Father and God as Almighty as separate, while also discussing their meaning conjoined as "the Father Almighty." This is right. Second, we note in passing that the final phrase of the first article of the creed, "and of all things visible and invisible," is a virtual restatement of "maker of heaven and earth"; it does not seek to say anything different. This discussion, however, belongs in part to a technical inquiry into the relationship of the Nicene to the Constantinopolitan creed.[9] More on this cannot be said here. A separate treatment of "of all things visible and invisible" could imply that maker of heaven and earth needed greater precision, which it does not. Both are virtual restatements of each other, as the history of the creeds shows. Colossians 1:15 is only making clear root understandings from the scriptures, correlated with the revelation in Christ.

For the phrase "I believe in One God" we look of course to the foundational language of the Decalogue, "you shall have no other god," which follows directly upon the solemn self-declaration, "I am the LORD your God who brought you out of Egypt." The reflexes of this phrase in the Old and New Testament are too numerous to list. Consider only, "And this is eternal life, that they may know you, the only true God" (John 17:3) and "Thou shalt worship the Lord thy God and him only shalt thou serve" (Matt. 4:10). These are, in turn, based on the logic of Deut. 6:4, 5, "Hear, O Israel, the LORD our God is one God." "No one can serve two masters" (Matt. 6:24). Tertullian in *Against Marcion* puts it thus, "If God is not one, He is not" (*Deus, si non unus est, non est*; Bk. 1. Chap. 3).[10]

In this context, it is important that Christians rightly grasp that God was known in Israel by his personal name, "the name above every name." Based on a process already at work in the Old Testament, the name is rendered from Hebrew *adonai* into Greek *kyrios*, "the LORD," but specifying a personal name and not a mere title. This name God gave to Jesus, so that at the name of Jesus, every knee should bow. He did not transfer an office only (lordship); he transferred his name, of himself. As David Yeago has pointed out, this confession from Philippians 2, heard in conjunction with Isaiah 45, establishes the pivotal judgment of Christian scripture that will give rise to the judgment of *homoousia*, even while the conceptual systems may and do differ (handing over a name and saying "of one substance or being").

So, God's name is not a phoneme known by those he has elected and withheld from others (abracadabra; a code word). Exodus tells us God's name is the disclosure of God's faithfulness in time, by speech in promise and fulfillment: "you shall know that I am who I am when I demonstrate the sovereignty of my promise and self" is the gist of Exodus 3–15. "I am who I am" is God's history and identity, his *ehyeh aser ehyeh* when he says it and *adonai* when his people say it back or the nations confess it. As such, God's name encloses a particular history with a particular people, providing them with particular memories and particular understandings of their future in God's time. God's name declares a specific identity with a providential purpose. "He who brought Israel out of Egypt" is he who made the heavens and the earth, he who has sworn by himself, to him shall every knee bow and every tongue confess a solemn oath, to the ends of the earth (Isa. 45:22–25). This is the one who is as he is, in revelation to his people.

To believe in one God and no other god is to believe in this God, whose name is spoken not only by a particular people in recollection and promise but also by those who now, having been enclosed in a covenant of blood, name Jesus Christ Lord (*kyrios*) to the glory of his Father. Barth once said, Christian (trinitarian) doctrine "neither is nor claims to be anything else" than an explanatory confirmation of the name, YHWH-*kyrios*.[11]

"The Father" is somewhat rare language for God in the Old Testament. It would appear to emerge within a specific set of constraints. First, it appears when multiple, connected covenant promises are threatened, including those to Noah, Abraham, Moses, David, and Zion (so Isaiah's final chapters). "For you are our father, though Abraham does not know us," the prophet says in 63:16, "you, O LORD, are our father; our Redeemer from of old is your name." In 64:8, the appeal is more explicitly to God's act of creation. "Yet, O LORD, you are our Father; we are the clay, and you are our potter."

Here is the second constraint. The logic of Genesis 1–5 is: as Seth is in the image of Adam, so mortal man and woman are in the image of God. God is not a male deity. He is not human fathering projected upstairs. God is "our Father" when his created and chosen people so cry out in uncreation and rejection. Genesis speaks of "the generation of heaven and earth" in a pregnant phrase (2:4) and then tells of Adam being formed from the earth by God, who is Father in something of the way Adam is father to Seth. According to Pearson, "The title of Father is given unto divers persons or things, and for several reasons unto the same God" (pp. 40–41). Then, quoting Genesis 2:4, Pearson comments, "So that the creation or production of anything by which it is, and before was not, is a kind of generation, and consequently the creator or producer of it a kind of Father" (p. 41). Moving from this basis in Genesis, he can commend Job 38:28, "Has the rain a father?" alongside Malachi 2:10, "Have we not all one Father? hath not one God created us all?" en route to 1 Cor. 8:6, "for us there is one God, the Father, from whom are all things." The proximity to creedal confession is obvious.

God is "our Father," that is, "ours" outside Israel, when his Son teaches us so to pray. In so doing, our unelection and estrangement, in the language of Ephesians, our "without God in the world" status, is eternally and providentially altered, in accordance with the promise of those same scriptures in which God's name was named and known and praised. God is "the Father" and, because of Jesus' restorative work as the new Adam, begotten not made, "Our Father in heaven, hallowed be his name."

"The Almighty" is yet a further gloss, or virtual metonym, for the name that is to be hallowed (Adonai). "Thus says Adonai, the LORD of Hosts, I am the first and I am the last, besides me there is no god" (Isa. 45:5). As though reflecting on Genesis, "I form light and create darkness, I make weal and create woe; I Adonai do all these things" (Isa. 45:7). God is almighty over creation, over time, over holiness and moral order. We know that as the divine name began to recede in use (probably out of fear of misuse by Gentiles "brought near"), metonyms were deployed to refer to God. So, "Almighty" (ha'olam), to which, for example, the predications of David's prayer would logically point, "Yours, O LORD, are the greatness and the power and the glory and the victory and the majesty," etc. So, too, the psalmist's simpler "Our help is in the Name of the Lord, the Maker of Heaven and Earth." Father, almighty, and maker of heaven and earth each in its own way bespeaks the divine and sacred name.

WHAT DOES "I BELIEVE IN THE MAKER
OF HEAVEN AND EARTH" MEAN TODAY?

First, Jesus makes no sense without the Father, without the prior "I believe in one God, the maker of heaven and earth." Childs puts it thus: "The faith of the Christian church is not built upon Jesus of Nazareth who had a Jewish background, but its faith is directed to God, the God of Israel, Creator of the world, the Father of our Lord Jesus Christ."[12] James Barr states, "It is an illusory position to think of ourselves as in a position where the New Testament is clear, is known, and is accepted, and where from this secure position we start out to explore the much more doubtful and dangerous territory of the Old Testament. . . . In so far as a position is Christian, it is related to the Old Testament from the beginning."[13] From the standpoint of the New Testament, Lee Keck states, "The point is that no one can deal with Jesus of Nazareth without confronting the question of God, because his concentration on God and his kingdom is what was constitutive of Jesus."[14]

Three challenges must be resisted: The pursuit of a true Jesus behind the witness, to be called after the fashion of our day "historical Jesus"; the reduction of a doctrine of God to the *beneficia Christi* (so, e.g., Melanchthon in Barth's estimate); and measuring of the work of Christ according to a virtue or religious asset he brings, especially as this is to be contrasted with the assets and virtues of the Old Testament or Judaism.

I have written at length on the first and last items, so I wish here to highlight only the middle: the problem of our understanding of God being fundamentally related to Christ's benefits, as received by us.

A recent expositor misses the mark badly when he states: "We do not start, save in long retrospect, with article 1 of the church's creeds: 'I believe in God the Father.' Rather, our starting point is article 2: 'I believe in Jesus Christ, his only son our Lord.'" This is an unfortunate distinction, and the problem is compounded when the declaration is made that "theology is unable to start from God as the creator of the universe." Then, issue is taken with Barth (and, one might also say, with Augustine, Thomas, Calvin, and a list too long to begin) in a sweeping conclusion: "Barth did not start with Jesus. He started with the electing or sovereign God who said 'Let there be light!' and there was light (Gen. 1:3). He started with God's electing choice in general rather than God's grace in Christ in particular. Barth's God was too removed, too other. This is because we live here!"[15]

Obviously, a Christian apologetic must make strategic decisions. But I think we would have to conclude that what is at issue is not Barth's God, but God as he is portrayed in scripture and in creed, as the starting point from which condescension and enclosure gain their logic in salvation. When the first line of the creed can be called a "long retrospect," we must consider whether the logic of Nicaea is being renegotiated in the name of a diagnosis of culture, well intended, which is itself mistaken.

Let us stay with the matter of the removed or "too other" God. The problem here is to do with matters associated with so-called natural theology. If one were to assume that we begin with vague apprehensions of Godness such as these are supplied by nature, God could indeed be viewed as detached or remote (so Locke; Kant). But just as surely he or she could well become too proximate, too naturally derived. Such was the situation of late antiquity that Athens had an unknown god ranged alongside gods of every description, regulating this or that aspect of the material world.

The otherness or remoteness of God lacks precision in this formulation. God's otherness (or holiness in the lexicon of the Old Testament) is not to do with natural theology but turns on election and God's own essential character as holy. God is not remote in Israel; he comes as judge! Moses sees him face to face. He speaks his word. Because he has chosen Israel, he enforces his will directly with this people. Israel's times are in his hands. Israel has been told. "Have you not known?" could not be said with more urgency. The Scottish expression "I didda nae ken. Well Ye kenn noo!" cannot apply to God's way and word with Israel.

The nations stand in another relationship. Israel insists God governs them in ways they do not know (Cyrus) or in ways they come to learn in judgment (so Sodom; so the nations in Amos 1–2; so Sennacherib in Isaiah 38) or awe (so Job). Here is a remoteness, of sorts, in nature: an estrangement from God, without the creator laying direct claim to us in his son, his servant Israel in whom he is well pleased.

It is not possible to speak of Jesus as this savior without speaking of the God who sent him. This is the whole force of the creed's logic and order. There is no Jesus Christ apart from the prior electing, creating "maker of the heavens and the earth." There is no "for me" that can be said before first is said, "The maker of the stars and sea became this child on earth" and then "for me."

Second, the creed is not lacking in its affirmation of the witness of the entirety of the Old Testament's presentation of God. Neither is it a "long retrospect," but instead it is a pithy, telegraphic recapitulation, which focuses on God's self and identity to lay claim to the complete sweep of Israel's witness. One God, the Father almighty, the maker of heaven and earth—these phrases intend to comprehend the vast range of Old Testament witness, in law, prophecy, wisdom, and praise.

Kendall Soulen has recently worried about what he regards as omissions in the Christian creeds and in Christian dogmatic theology: "Following the creeds, countless works of Christian theology set forth the dogmatic content of Christian belief almost wholly without reference to God's way with Israel. The first and largest part of the Bible possesses no doctrinal locus of its own, nor is it often materially decisive for any other locus."[16] And "Indeed the background can be completely omitted from an account of the Christian faith without thereby disturbing the overarching logic of salvation history. This omission is reflected in virtually every historic confession of Christian faith from the Creeds of Nicea and Constantinople to the Augsburg confession and beyond" (32) ("the First Scottish Confession [1560]" being a recent exception).

But as von Campenhausen has stated (in a paraphrase from Childs), "the problem of the early church was not what to do with the Old Testament in the light of the gospel, which was Luther's concern, but rather the reverse. In the light of the Jewish scriptures which acknowledged to be the true oracles of God, how were Christians to understand the good news of Jesus Christ?"[17] What this means theologically is that the Old Testament presentation of God is the fixed point toward which the creed seeks to correlate the church's understanding of Christ and the Holy Spirit. It does not belabor the point by listing the mighty acts of God in the Old Testament; to do so would suggest that a defense or apologetic was required. The phrases one God, Father almighty, and maker of heaven and earth unequivocally point to this God, known in the Old Testament. The very lack of expansion is testimony to the givenness of this witness from the bosom of Israel, such that the stock phrases function to encapsulate the whole.

It is another thing, rightly I believe, to worry with Soulen about the church's present confusion on this front. The correction does not come from filling out lacunae in the creed, however, which do not in fact exist. The correction comes from making clearer what the language means.

Third, the insistence on the rootedness of this description of God in the Old Testament must guard against another tendency, however. The God of the Old Testament has fully identified himself with Jesus Christ. He does not continue to exercise some separate, untameable, unpredictable rule prior to, and perduring after, what he has made clear in Jesus. The New Testament does not introduce a great parenthesis outside which God retains an unruly and undomesticated authority. The mystery and sovereignty of God the maker of heaven and earth are guarded precisely as these attributes are true of Christ, who raises the dead and walks on water, and of the Holy Spirit, who blows as he will—not over against them. The creed does not seek to isolate the Father to ensure his majesty. It points us to the God of Israel and asks us to see in his life with the world as shown there, that which comes to expression in complete terms in his Son. To speak of the Old Testament as Christian scripture, and not as Hebrew Bible, is not an offense to Judaism, which takes this selfsame literature and hears it through the testimony of tradition, just as Christians hear it in conjunction with the testimony of a second testament. Stressing the Jewishness of God, by reinstating his name or enumerating his Israel-specific life untouched by his condescension in his Son, makes sense for neither Jew nor Christian. Again, Childs puts it succinctly in his review of Brueggemann's recent Old Testament theological exposition.

> By juxtaposing Israel's core testimony with his so-called counter-testimony, Brueggemann sees the task of interpretation to be a never-ending activity of negotiating between conflicting voices. There is never a final testimony, but every interpretation is described as provisional and shaped by shifting 'socio-ecclesial-political-economic contexts' within the process of disputation (p. 711). The result is the God of Israel is both gracious and merciless, truthful and deceptive, powerful and impotent which is constitutive of the very nature of this deity.
>
> In spite of Brueggemann's constant reference to the 'Jewishness of the Old Testament,' the irony emerging from his description of God is one that no serious, religious Jew can tolerate. Israel's faith in God rests on Torah, covenant, and eternal promise which are non-negotiable because of the truth of God's Word. The stability of God in relation to his people sets Israel's faith apart from all the arbitrariness and confusion of paganism. Of course, there remain continuous threats, demonic terrors, and persistent evil, but these do not alter God's unswerving commitment to the Patriarchs. Israel continues to suffer because of its confession that God has not, and will not, change toward his people in spite of experiencing life on the very edge of distinction."[18]

My fourth point builds upon the work of Robert Jenson. He writes:

> Precisely being able to turn from their gods to the true God occasioned the joy, with which the apostles' gentile converts . . . received the word. In the act of faith, gentile believers recognize themselves as those who have worshipped or might have worshipped Moloch the baby-killer or Astarte the universal whore or *Deutsches Blut* or the Free Market or the Dialectic of History or the Metaphor of our gender or ethnic ressentiment, and on through an endless list of tyrants. Only a naiveté impossible for the apostolic church, which fully inhabited the religious maelstrom of late antiquity, can think that religion as such is a good thing or that gods are necessarily beneficent.[19]

Jenson makes several observations here, but I want to focus on two in conclusion. We are living in a time of religious naïveté. Culture's claim, "we all worship the same god," points to the issue at stake. If God is not one, he is either many or he is not (to quote Tertullian). To say that God is one is not to say he resides in a Jesus of past history or somewhere behind or above the language about him in the scriptures of Israel. God cannot be worshiped through a veil of imperfect language about him. That is naïve, and here antiquity was far more honest. It spoke of an unknown god but was unable to maintain such a stoic courage and so filled shrines with gods with names and specific language known to be about them, and them alone.

Pearson is right to say that a speaker of the creed should expect to know "what he ought to intend, and what he is understood to profess, when he so pronounceth it." This claim about language is not one Pearson is importing to the creed. It belongs to the scriptures' most fundamental claim about creation, that our language can reliably and specifically name God, address God, and speak of him as he is truly.

Out of the Babel of religious talk, "You shall worship the Lord your God and him only shall you serve" sounded a genuine alternative. God is one, and his creation can speak of him, because he has given it to be so, not because we need it or desire it. "I believe in One God, the Father Almighty, Maker of Heaven and Earth" is language God has given us to use, so that we can call upon him and know that he knows himself to be addressed. In so doing, we move into a personal relationship to him, akin to what it meant for Israel to call on his name in their day, and to guard the name against all common use or vain speculation, "god-talk." To be brought into this relationship is what occasioned the joy of the first apostles.

Fifth, Christian talk about God begins with his holiness, his oneness, his majesty in creation, his speech in Israel, in order to understand the depth of his mercy and kindness toward us in Christ. It begins with his holiness because this is where he begins, in his eternal life with the Son and the Spirit.

Christians are brought near in Christ to learn the extent of his love, and of our estrangement, in one fell swoop. To share his name and self with us, to make us new again in him, requires the bestowal of his holiness, the character of which P. T. Forsyth has described as, "the eternal moral power which must do, and do, till it sees itself everywhere."[20] He gives us speech to say back to him, "I believe in One God, the Father Almighty, Maker of Heaven and Earth."

A fitting conclusion is Augustine's opening prayer in the Confessions:

> Grant me, Lord, to know and understand which of these is most important, to call on you or to praise you. Or again, to know you or to call on you. For who can call on you without knowing you? For he who does not know you may call on you as other than you are. . . . Let me seek you Lord by calling on you, and call on you believing in you as you have been proclaimed to us. My faith calls on you Lord, the faith you have given me.

Part Four

Conclusion

14

Conclusion

What has been our intention in this book?

We have sought to provide examples of serious exegesis and interpretation of Christian scripture from three related standpoints: (1) mindful of the shadow cast by the historical-critical quest for a certain kind of "literal sense"; (2) seeking, however, to contest a thin understanding of such a sense, which was fostered by the concerns of historicism, strict referential reading, and single authorial intention; and most importantly (3) approaching the reading of Christian scripture as a single witness to the triune God, through the dual testimony of prophets and apostles (Old Testament and New Testament).

In each of the essays of Part Three, we have self-consciously sought to read one testament in the light of the other, as this is urged by the text itself: either due to the way the judgments rendered by one scriptural witness match another, or because the New Testament witness itself makes no sense without attention to its literary dependence upon a prior witness it assumes will continue to sound forth as Christian scripture.[1] We have also tried to take seriously the final form of the literary witness, as theologically crafted to make sense of prior traditions and to comprehend these traditions from a distinct angle of view. This angle of view, we have argued, often has its focus on the wider shape of the canon. We have provided seven examples.

First, John's ending is cued to the fourfold Gospel collection and comments upon it from the standpoint of concern with revelation through a literary witness; in doing this, its "judgments" find kindred expression in the Book of Ecclesiastes. Second, the earthly Jesus, we argued, must be understood from the perspective of prior scriptural attestation, such as is found in the canonical Isaiah. Third, the decisions of the Council of Jerusalem did not turn on creative "Holy Spirit taboo-toppling work" detached from the witness to Israel; rather, these decisions match the judgments of Leviticus seen from the perspective of the New Testament's understanding of the work of the Holy Spirit (and Acts takes its cue both from Luke and from the intervening witness of the Fourth Gospel). Fourth, to understand the logic of Philippians 2 and the mature statements of "homoousia" in the later life of the church, one must understand the way the literal sense of the New Testament derives from the literal sense of the Old and assumes its ongoing word to the church. Fifth, for the church rightly to speak of "mission" (which on the face of it seems to be a theme detachable from Old Testament speech), it is necessary to comprehend the logic of key Old Testament notions of blessing. So too, sixth, prayer must be considered with an eye toward God's revelation as YHWH within and outside the covenant with his people Israel, before we are in a position to speak more broadly about how prayer functions for a people engrafted by Christ in a new covenant in which prayer is so obviously central. And last, the logic of Nicene confession is not truncated or supercessionistic when it speaks in such compressed fashion about theological and historical givens from the Old Testament. Rather, statements like "I believe in One God, the Maker of Heaven and Earth" must be given the widest possible capacity to gather to themselves all that the Old Testament means when it speaks of a named God YHWH who has revealed his faithfulness, sovereignty, and promise within a people of election, and then, finally, in Christ, to a creation redeemed and blessed by Jesus. In this sense, Jesus is both the new Adam and "my servant Israel in whom I am well pleased" (Isa. 49:3).

These examples are, of course, not exhaustive. They are meant only to provide a sample that will give indication of the sort of reading which the church, in academic, theological, ethical, and liturgical expressions, needs, in my view, to recover.

Two matters are at stake here, and these were the subject of the analytical chapters of Part Two.

First, historical-critical reading so valorized the past and itself as the arbiter of a new reading unsullied by the prior readings of the church and synagogue, that it succeeded in marginalizing or destroying another sort of history: the history of biblical interpretation. By its own strictures, it was virtually required to do this. The consequence was a proud severance of modern readings, which themselves demanded novelty and more novelty, from the insights of other ages (the exceptions prove the rule). This severance was demanded by a notion of inspiration that focused on a retrievable but lost authorial voice, below the canonical form of the witness. Not surprisingly, forfeited in the exchange was a notion of plenary inspiration within the canonical process, whereby a "historical Jeremiah" or "historical Isaiah" became subservient to the authority of the word spoken by them both, which in turn gave rise to fuller revelation within the community of faith; that fuller revelation is now represented by the

Book of Isaiah or the Book of Jeremiah (even in its several ancient forms!). The culprits in this attenuation of inspiration are found on right and left sides of the theological spectrum.[2]

The second consequence flowed from the first. The testaments of Christian scripture could only be considered as related in any meaningful sense from a specific historical point of view, which had to be critically reconstructed and then defended from within a range of alternative views. Not surprisingly, if the testaments were not revelations of the One God in any intrinsic sense, as scripture, two effects would be and were immediately registered. First, the revelation of God would become a matter of unveiling the true or historical Jesus and setting forth his understanding of God, quite independently of assessing such a revelation as stable and as vouchsafed as such to Jesus himself, from the canon of the Old Testament. And second, the detachment of the testaments on historical grounds rendered the subsequent history of Christian thought difficult to handle, not least because the earliest Christian proclamation was itself the setting forth of theological truth on the basis of a single literary witness to God—that is, our present Old Testament.

The damage wrought by this approach to the canon and the history of tradition was the focus of Part Two. It would require a separate treatment to evaluate, theologically, the attenuation of a doctrine of inspiration which rendered the history of interpretation a separable category of reflection, and which located inspiration in a narrow sense within the mind of an author below or behind the witness of sacred Scripture. We can say this much, however. When the Holy Spirit is appealed to as the broker of new truths in the new age, against the witness of Scripture's final literary sense, and against the historical teaching of the church, it should be clear that we are indeed in a new age. That such a new age requires a New Spirit as the endorser of its theological and ethical judgments should not cause surprise; all distortion of theological truth uses theological language and concepts, in the nature of the thing.

What should be acknowledged, however, is that such a decision to cloak modern and late-modern innovation in theological dress comes at the price of introducing gaps in time—that is, the forfeiture of any meaningful appeal to providence, as is implied in the psalmist's confession, "'Thou art my God.' My times are in thy hand" (RSV Ps. 31:15). Providence of this sort depends on particular revelation which is itself grounded in particular election ("in Judah God is known" [RSV Ps. 76:1]). Election is the warrant for the Christian turn to the Old Testament as truthful witness to God, validated by the teaching, life, cross, and resurrection of its Lord.[3] This teaching, life, cross, and resurrection are confessed as accorded and "typed" or "figured in" Israel's canonical scripture. Pull any of these stable pillars apart, and the entire edifice is threatened. The Scriptures will be figured out, with the effect of the loss of collaborating convictions regarding election, providence (within Israel, the apostolic circle, and the late-modern and divided church), and the twofold character of scriptural witness, from a figurally united Old and New Testament Christian Bible. The confusions of our age regarding time, history, and revelation will simply be projected onto God himself, who in the exchange becomes the Divine Warrant for an altogether different notion of God-talk, time, history, and general revelation (if the term is warranted at all).

The intention of this book will have been met if it satisfies one final criterion. Do the various judgments, to use Yeago's category, that it seeks to render collectively and individually, match those of the vast witness of Christian hymnody and worship, as the church has sung and praised God throughout its long history? If what I have written permits the reader to move into traditional worship practices of the church without stumbling over a ditch of historicism or a scriptural legacy now "figured out," my goal will have been met.

Consider, for example, the great sixth-century Lenten hymn text, "The Glory of These Forty Days." In the first verse, we are presented with Christ's forty-day trial in the desert. This trial moves the author directly back to Moses and his forty days of communion with God without bread or water (Exod. 34:28), and to Elijah in the desert, in verse two. Verse three gives equal time to Daniel, whose mystic sight delivered him from the might of lions, and to John the Baptist, the bridegroom's friend. Now the author is ready in verse four to figure us into this two-testament story, involving Law (Moses), Prophets (Elijah), Writings (Daniel), and Gospel (John the Baptist). The prayer is offered that we might find our place alongside them all, with Christ typing and mapping out the way. The point is not merely to do with desire for exegetical symmetry or equal time for various biblical figures. Rather, there is an assumption that God has providentially ordered his word and witness, in such a way that we are anticipated by these writings from Moses, the prophets, and apostles. Our spirits are thus to be strengthened, and we too are to have a share in the joy of seeing God's face. All that is left to do, then, is to praise God in his threefold name, who from age to age is one and the same LORD. The final verse shows the theological logic from which flows prayer, praise, fasting, and the wondrous confession of providential order and design throughout God's time and God's history, from Moses to Elijah to Daniel to John to Jesus to the church.

Without moving into a nostalgic or pre-modern mode, I have sought in this book to diagnose the way in which, for various reasons, the two-testament witness of Scripture has been "figured out" in academic and other theological settings. I have then sought, again fully mindful of my own location in time, to offer some tentative alternative readings of Christian scripture. These engage recognizably modern and late-modern debates, but they also seek to provide an alternative angle of vision.

If, at the end of the day, the logic of "The Glory of These Forty Days" (or, "The Lion of Judah" or "These Are the Days of Elijah," to choose two modern praise-hymns) is seen and appreciated for the way it respects the judgments of Christian scripture and its figural witness to God, my concerns in writing this book will have been met. It is time to learn again how to read the witness of a two-testament scripture, armed with all the tools supplied by the science of biblical scholarship. Obviously, what is more difficult to learn is the discipline of Moses, Elijah, Daniel, John, and Jesus. Yet without this, no deployment of new reading instincts or new ways of asking older questions will bear the fruit God desires, such that with joy we might see his face and praise his threefold name, from age to age the Only Lord.

Appendix

The Virginia Report: "Preface" and "Origins and Mandate" Sections*

SECTION 1: PREFACE

This Report is the work of the Inter-Anglican Theological and Doctrinal Commission which comprises theologians and church leaders who themselves represent the diversities of the Anglican Communion. Their task was to respond to the call of the Lambeth Conference of 1988 to consider in some depth the meaning and nature of communion. This response was to be set within the context of the doctrine of the Trinity, the unity and order of the Church and the unity and community of humanity. At the heart and center of the Anglican pilgrimage lies the concept of communion. From it we derive so much of our belief and practice. It is not itself a static concept. It has become with our pilgrimage a living and developing reality. Yet that fact alone demands understanding which cannot be tied to any one period of our history or to any single cultural approach.

This Report is offered to the Anglican Communion as one more step in the process of seeking greater understanding of what communion means to the Body of Christ. In particular it seeks to suggest ways in which our Communion can respond in practical ways which touch and concern how we order our corporate life and lives as individuals.

I wish to acknowledge with sincere gratitude the generosity and support given to the Commission by the Right Reverend Peter Lee, Bishop of Virginia, the Diocese of Virginia and the staff of the Virginia Theological Seminary. Their practical assistance and encouragement made the production of this Report possible.

It has been a great privilege to chair the Commission and I acknowledge the support and work of all its members.

—Robert Eames
Archbishop of Armagh

SECTION 2: ORIGINS AND MANDATE

In 1988 the Lambeth Conference was faced with a question that challenged the unity of the Communion: the proposal by the Episcopal Church of the United States of America to consecrate a woman to the episcopate. In the light of its deliberations the Lambeth Conference passed resolution 1 on the ordination or consecration of women to the episcopate. In response to this resolution of the Conference the Archbishop of Canterbury, in consultation with the Primates, established a Commission on Communion and Women in the Episcopate under the leadership of the Most Revd Robert Eames, Archbishop of Armagh.

a. to provide for an examination of the relationships between Provinces of the Anglican Communion and ensure that the process of reception includes continuing consultation with other Churches as well;

b. to monitor and encourage the process of consultation within the Communion and to offer further pastoral guidelines (The Truth Shall Make You Free, The Lambeth Conference 1988. Resolution 1, page 201).

The Eames Commission, as it came to be known, met five times and produced four reports which were published together in December 1994. Its last meeting was in December 1993 and its report will be presented to the 1998 Lambeth Conference. During its lifetime the Commission engaged in theological reflection on the nature of koinonia. It offered guidelines on how Anglicans might live together in the highest degree of communion possible while different views and practices concerning the ordination of women continued to be held within the Communion. The Eames Commission saw this as a way of enabling an ongoing process of reception both within the Anglican Communion and the wider ecumenical fellowship. Its guidelines are intended to support graceful and charitable relationships and to ensure proper pastoral care for one another. Before its last meeting, five women had been consecrated as bishops. Also in that period the ordination of women to the priesthood had received the necessary consents in the Church of England and over 1000 women were ordained as priests, and by then women had also been ordained as priests in Australia, Aotearoa, New Zealand and Polynesia, Brazil, Burundi, Canada, Hong Kong and Macao, Ireland, Kenya, the Philippines, Scotland, Southern Africa, Uganda, the USA and West Africa.

The Eames Commission between 1988 and 1993 provided a model of how Anglicans can remain together in the highest degree of communion possible while endeavoring to come to a common mind on a matter which touches the fundamental unity of the Communion.

The 1988 Conference recognized that there was a need to describe how the

Anglican Communion makes authoritative decisions while maintaining unity and interdependence in the light of the many theological issues that arise from its diversity. To address this need, the Conference resolved that there should be:

As a matter of urgency further exploration of the meaning and nature of communion with particular reference to the doctrine of the Trinity, the unity and order of the Church, and the unity and community of humanity (Lambeth Conference 1988, Resolution 18, page 216. See Appendix I).

Resolution 8 on the Final Report of the Anglican Roman Catholic International Commission also had a direct bearing on the exercise of authority in the Church. It encouraged ARCIC to explore the basis in Scripture and Tradition of the concept of a universal primacy, in conjunction with collegiality, as an instrument of unity, the character of such primacy in practice, and to draw upon the experience of other Christian Churches in exercising primacy, collegiality and conciliarity.

In implementing Resolution 18 of Lambeth 1988, and at the request of the Primates of the Communion, the Archbishop of Canterbury invited a group of representative church leaders and theologians to meet in December 1991 at the Virginia Theological Seminary at Alexandria, USA to begin the exploration. The Consultation's report was called Belonging Together. The Report was circulated widely within the Communion between 1992 and 1994 with a request for critical comment. A number of Anglican member churches responded officially. There were also responses from theological institutions and individuals.

All the responses were considered by the Inter-Anglican Theological and Doctrinal Commission, the successor of the 1991 Consultation, when it met in December 1994, and again in January 1996, on both occasions at the Virginia Theological Seminary. This report is the product of its consideration and further reflection on the issues.

* From http://anglicancommunion.org/documents/virginia/. The references to documents can also be followed up at this Internet site.

Notes

Preface

1. "The tunnel was dug from both ends at once; the joining at midpoint was an engineering feat" (R. B. Coote, "Siloam Inscription," *The Anchor Bible Dictionary* (vol. 6; New York: Doubleday, 1992) 23.
2. H. Frei, *The Eclipse of Biblical Narrative* (New Haven: Yale University Press, 1974). N. MacDonald, *Barth, Wittgenstein and the "Strange New World" of Scripture* (Carlisle: England: Paternoster, 2000).
3. The names of Lampe, Woolcombe, R. P. C. Hanson, and Danielou come to mind. Such a position is now challenged by Louth, Crouzel, Young, Childs, and especially Torjesen.

Chapter 1

1. From the book of the same title, *The Crucified God* (R. A. Wilson and J. Bowden, trans.; London: SCM, 1974).
2. *God Crucified: Monotheism and Christology in the New Testament* (Carlisle, England: Paternoster, 1998).
3. See especially volume 1, *Systematic Theology: The Triune God* (New York: Oxford University Press, 1997). A critical assessment of Moltmann's proposal can be found in part 2 of this book. My review of Bauckham's book appeared in the *International Journal of Systematic Theology* 2 (2000) 112–116.
4. "Thus 'the one who rescued Israel from Egypt' is confirmed as an identification of *God* in that it is continued 'as he thereupon rescued the Israelite Jesus from the dead'" (Jenson, *Systematic Theology*, 44).
5. C. Seitz, "'In Accordance with the Scriptures': Creed, Scripture, and 'Historical Jesus,'" in *Word without End: The Old Testament as Abiding Theological Witness* (Grand Rapids: Eerdmans, 1998) 51–60. See also "The Divine Name in Christian Scripture," in A. Kimel, ed., *This Is My Name Forever* (Downer's Grove, Ill.: InterVarsity Press, 2001) 23–34.
6. For a fuller discussion, see chapters 10 and 13 in this book.
7. E. Radner, *The End of the Church: A Pneumatology of Christian Division in the West* (Grand Rapids: Eerdmans, 1998). For a good summary of Radner's thesis, see J. Magina, "Review Essay," *Pro Ecclesia* 9 (2000) 490–496.
8. The most insightful treatment of the movement was provided by B. S. Childs, *Biblical Theology in Crisis* (Philadelphia: Westminster, 1970). Also, L. Gilkey, "Cosmology, Ontology, and the Travail of Biblical Language," *JR* 41 (1965) 194–205.

9. A rare exception to this sort of preoccupation was the essay by Childs, "The God of Israel and the Church" in *Biblical Theology in Crisis*, 201–219.

10. See the discussion of Pusey, Gore, and the Anglo-Catholic accommodation of historical-critical work in chapter 2 of this book.

11. The quotations are from pp. 149, 153–155 of *Old and New in Interpretation* (New York: Harper and Row, 1966). See also my discussion in *SJT* 52 (1999) 209–226.

12. See R. Greer, *Broken Lights and Mended Lives: Theology and Common Life in the Early Church* (University Park: Pennsylvania State University Press, 1986); P. M. Blowers, "The *Regula Fidei* and the Character of Early Christian Faith," *Pro Ecclesia* 6 (1997) 199–228; K. Greene-McCreight, *Ad Litteram: How Augustine, Calvin, and Barth Read the "Plain Sense" of Genesis 1–3* (New York: Peter Lang, 1999).

13. See the discussion of "scope" and "mind" in relationship to the rule of faith in F. Young, "Exegetical Method and Scriptural Proof: The Bible in Doctrinal Debate," *Studio Patristica* 19 (1989) 291–304, and "The Mind of Scripture," in *Biblical Exegesis and the Formation of Christian Culture* (Cambridge: Cambridge University Press, 1997) 29–45; compare T. E. Pollard, "The Exegesis of Scripture in the Arian Controversy," *BJRL* 41 (1958–59) 414–429; H. J. Sieben, "Herméneutique de l'exégèse dogmatique d'Athanase," in C. Kannengiesser, ed., *Politique et théologie chez Athanase d'Alexandrie* (Paris: Beauchesne, 1974) 195–214; C. Stead, "Athanasius als Exeget," in J. van Oort and U. Wickert, eds., *Christliche Exegese zwischen Nicaea und Chalcedon* (Kampen: Kok Pharos, 1992) 174–184. The Arius-Athanasius debate is illuminating because of the literalism of Arius, which "disfigured" scripture. The cause of this also involved his starting point outside the "rule of faith" or "ecclesiastical scope," this latter referred to by Athanasius in discourse 3 of his essays against the Arians. Irenaeus had referred to scripture's "hypothesis"—that hermeneutical key, or stance, without which the Gnostics could produce only strange pictures instead of the true unifying portrait and portrayal of the two-testament Christian witness to God.

14. R. Greer, *Theodore of Mopsuestia: Exegete and Theologian* (Westminster: Faith Press, 1961); K. Froehlich, *Biblical Interpretation in the Early Church* (Philadelphia: Fortress, 1984); J. Kugel and R. Greer, *Early Biblical Interpretation* (Philadelphia: Westminster, 1986).

15. See the penetrating analysis of Origen as reader of the Psalms in K. Torjesen, *Hermeneutical Procedure and Theological Method* (Berlin: de Gruyter, 1986). She shows how the literal sense is a single theological sense for Origen.

16. C. Stephen Evans, "Methodological Naturalism in Historical Biblical Scholarship," in C. Newman, ed., *Jesus and the Restoration of Israel: A Critical Assessment of N. T. Wright's Jesus and the Victory of God* (Downer's Grove, Ill.: InterVarsity Press, 1999) 180–205.

17. B. S. Childs, "The One Gospel in Four Witnesses," in E. Radner and G. Sumner, eds., *The Rule of Faith: Scripture, Canon, and Creed in a Critical Age* (Harrisburg, Pa.: Morehouse, 1998) 51–62. From a different angle, see R. Bauckham, ed., *The Gospels for All Christians: Rethinking the Gospel Audiences* (Grand Rapids: Eerdmans, 1998); also, the brilliant analysis of the New Testament canon by David Trobisch, *The First Edition of the New Testament* (Oxford: Oxford University Press, 2000).

18. See chapters 3 and 8 in this book.
19. See S. Fowl, *Engaging Scripture* (Oxford: Blackwells, 1998). For a textbook taxonomy, see K. Vanhoozer, *Is There a Meaning in This Text?* (Grand Rapids: Zondervan, 1998). Somewhat more peripherally, N. Wolterstorff, *Divine Discourse: Philosophical Reflections on the Claim That God Speaks* (Cambridge: Cambridge University Press, 1995).
20. See F. Young, "Exegetical Method" and "The Mind of Scripture."
21. See Radner, *End of the Church.*
22. This is the language used by Archbishop of Canterbury George Carey in reviewing the American Episcopal Church's revisionary stance toward homosexuality.
23. See chapters 4 and 9 in this book.

Chapter 2

1. Kevin J. Vanhoozer, *Is There a Meaning in This Text?* (Grand Rapids, Mich.: Zondervan, 1998); Nicholas Wolterstorff, *Divine Discourse: Philosophical Reflections on the Claim that God Speaks* (Cambridge/New York: Cambridge University Press, 1995). See also the work of Stephen Fowl, *Engaging Scripture* (Oxford: Blackwell, 1998).
2. F. Watson, *Text, Church and World: Biblical Interpretation in Theological Perspective* (Edinburgh: T&T Clark, 1994); *Text and Truth: Redefining Biblical Theology* (Edinburgh: T&T Clark, 1997); see also my review, "Christological Interpretation of Texts and Trinitarian Claims to Truth," and his response in SJT 52 (1999), 209–32.
3. The distinction I am drawing here is seen at once when one looks at the older German works of Westermann or Reventlow, and compares these with Vanhoozer and Wolterstorff. In these earlier volumes, one cannot talk about hermeneutics without the difference between the two Testaments of Christian Scripture being registered as of historical and theological significance, in the nature of the thing. See C. Westermann, ed., *Essays on Old Testament Hermeneutics* (Atlanta: John Knox Press, 1963); H.G. Reventlow, *Problems of Old Testament Theology in the Twentieth Century* (Philadelphia: Fortress, 1985) followed by *Problems of Biblical Theology in the Twentieth Century* (Philadelphia: Fortress, 1986).
4. *Hermeneia—A Critical and Historical Commentary on the Bible* (Minneapolis: Fortress) utilizes a common preface for all its volumes, written by Frank Moore Cross and Helmut Koester, in which it is said: "The editors of Hermeneia impose no systematic-theological perspective upon the series (directly, or indirectly by selection of authors). It is expected that the authors will struggle to lay bare the ancient meaning of a biblical work or pericope. In this way the text's human relevance *should become transparent, as is always the case in competent historical discourse*" (emphasis added).
5. For a critical appraisal, see the 1998 issue of *Ex Auditu* on "The Theological Significance of the Earthly Jesus."
6. Claus Westermann, ed., *Essays on Old Testament Hermeneutics* (Atlanta: John Knox Press, 1963).
7. S. E. Fowl, *Engaging Scripture: A Model for Theological Interpretation* (Oxford: Basic Blackwell, 1998); S. Hauerwas, *Character and the Christian Life: A Study in Theological Ethics* (San Antonio: Trinity University Press, 1985).
8. Watson, *Text, Church and World.*
9. See the author's *Word Without End* (Grand Rapids, Mich.: Eerdmans, 1998).

Also, Paul van Buren, "On Reading Someone Else's Mail: The Church and Israel's Scriptures," in *Die hebraische Bibel und ihre zweifache Nachgeschichte* (FS R. Rendtorff; Neukirchen-Vluyn: Neukirchener, 1900), 595–606; Jon Levenson, *The Hebrew Bible, the Old Testament, and Historical Criticism* (Louisville, Ky.: Westminster John Knox, 1993); Brevard S. Childs, *Biblical Theology of the Old and New Testaments: Theological Reflection on the Christian Bible* (Minneapolis: Fortress, 1992).

10. B. S. Childs, *Introduction to the Old Testament as Scripture* (Philadelphia: Fortress, 1979), 612.

11. E. B. Pusey, *Daniel the Prophet* (Oxford, 1865).

12. Childs, *Introduction*, 612.

13. See the assessment of Stuhlmacher and his challenge to a "hermeneutics of suspicion" in "'And Without God in the World': A Hermeneutic of Estrangement Overcome," in *Word Without End* (41–50).

14. C. Gore, *Lux Mundi: A Series of Studies in the Religion of the Incarnation* (London: John Murray, 1889).

15. George Lindbeck, *The Nature of Doctrine* (Philadelphia: Westminster, 1984). See also, Ronald Thiemann, *Revelation and Theology: The Gospel as Narrated Promise* (Notre Dame: The University of Notre Dame Press, 1985). For a different take on "the expressionist (Romantic) view" see Wolterstorff (*Divine Discourse*) and a further response by Lindbeck, "Postcritical Canonical Interpretation: Three Modes of Retrieval," in C. Seitz and K. Greene-McCreight, eds., *Theological Exegesis: Essays in Honor of Brevard S. Childs* (Grand Rapids, Mich.: Eerdmans, 1998), 26–51.

16. "The appeal to 'experience' in religion, whether personal or general, brings before the mind so many associations of ungoverned enthusiasm and untrustworthy fanaticism, that it does not easily commend itself to those of us who are most concerned to be reasonable. And yet, in one form or another, it is an essential part of the appeal which Christianity makes on its own behalf since the day when Jesus Christ met the question 'Art thou He that should come, or do we look for another?' by pointing to the transforming effect of his work" (315). This is how the essay begins, and the paragraphs which follow proceed along a similar path.

17. Gore, *Lux Mundi*, 329.

18. Ibid., 354.

19. Ibid., 360.

20. Ibid.

21. E. G. Selwyn, ed., *Essays Catholic and Critical* (London: SPCK, 1926).

22. Ibid., 99.

23. Ibid., 100.

24. Ibid., 98.

25. Eichrodt, *Theology of the Old Testament*.

26. Lothar Perlitt, *Die Bundestheologie im Alten Testament* (WMANT 36; Neukirchen-Vluyn: Neukirchener, 1969).

27. O. Eissfeldt, "Israelitisch-judische Religionsgeschichte und alttestamentliche Theologie," *ZAW* 44 (1926) 1–12.

28. R. Bultmann, "The Significance of the Old Testament for Christian Faith," in *The Old Testament and Christian Faith: A Theological Discussion* (B. W. Anderson, ed.; New York: Harper and Row, 1963) 8–35.

29. Compare my analysis in "The Historical-Critical Endeavor as Theology" in *Word without End*, 28–40.

30. Gerhard von Rad, *Genesis: A Commentary* (OTL; Philadelphia: Westminster Press, 1972).
31. R. Rendtorff, *The Old Testament: An Introduction* (London: SCM, 1985).
32. W. Knox, "Authority," in Selwyn, *Essays Catholic and Critical.*
33. Walter Brueggemann and H. W. Wolff, *The Vitality of Old Testament Tradtions* (Atlanta: John Knox, 1975).
34. Fowl, *Engaging Scripture.*
35. A. MacIntyre, *Whose Justice? Which Rationality?* (London: Duckworth & Co., 1988).
36. E. B. Pusey, *Daniel the Prophet* (Oxford, 1865) xii.
37. Ibid., xi.
38. P. R. Davies, *Whose Bible Is It Anyway?* (JSOTSup, 204; Sheffield: Sheffield Academic Press, 1995).
39. Childs, *Introduction,* 608–623.
40. Reventlow, *Problems.*
41. T. C. Vriezen, "The Old Testament as the Word of God, and Its Use in the Church," in idem, *An Outline of Old Testament Theology* (Oxford: Basil Blackwell, 1958), 79–96.
42. See above all, Radner, "Absence," 355–394; and W. J. Abraham, *Canon and Criterion in Christian Theology: From the Fathers to Feminism* (Oxford: Clarendon, 1998).

Chapter 3

1. *Word without End* (Grand Rapids: Eerdmans, 1998). The essay in question is chapter 3, "The Historical-Critical Endeavor as Theology: The Legacy of Gerhard von Rad" (28–40).
2. See my summary of von Rad's views on typology in ibid. (34–38).
3. Hartmut Gese, "Tradition and Biblical Theology," in Douglas A. Knight, ed., *Tradition and Theology in the Old Testament* (London: SPCK, 1977) 301–26. Peter Stuhlmacher, *Historical Criticism and Theological Interpretation of Scripture: Towards a Hermeneutics of Consent,* trans. Roy A. Harrisville (London: SPCK, 1979); and volume 2 of his New Testament theology, *Biblische Theologie des Neuen Testaments (Band 2): Von der Paulusschule bis zur Johannesoffenbarung* (Göttingen: Vandenhoeck & Ruprecht, 1999).
4. See the discussion of Childs and von Rad on pp. 342–345 of Stuhlmacher's *Biblische Theologie.*
5. See above all the discussion of Stuhlmacher, "Historical Criticism and the Protestant Principle," in *Historical Criticism* (63–75).
6. Gerhard von Rad, *Old Testament Theology* 1 (Louisville: WJK, 2001), 105.
7. J. Trebolle Barrera, *The Jewish Bible and the Christian Bible,* trans. W. G. E. Watson (Leiden/Grand Rapids: Brill and Eerdmans, 1998).
8. S. B. Chapman, *The Law and the Prophets: A Study in Old Testament Canon Formation,* Forschungen zum Alten Testament 27 (Tübingen: Mohr Siebeck, 2000). Chapman conceives of a process of mutual development and reciprocity, which rules out a simple "law then prophets" formation of the canon. In this, he develops, inter alia, the suggestions of Clements and others (Childs, *Biblical Theology,* 57).
9. A particularly insightful essay on this topic was read at the 2000 SEAD conference by Kathryn Greene-McCreight, "The Hermeneutics of Suspicion and a Doctrine of Scripture." She was responding to an exchange between myself and Richard Hays and others at an annual Society of Biblical Litera-

ture meeting, where we discussed a "hermeneutics of consent." My contribution appears in chapter 4 of *Word without End*, "'And without God in the
World': A Hermeneutic of Estrangement Overcome" (41–50).

10.   See my discussion in chapters 7 and 8 of this book.

11.   Childs sees the implications of this clearly when he writes, "If the New Testament used such freedom in respect to its Jewish heritage, does not the
Christian church have a similar right to develop its own form of scripture in
a manner different from that of the synagogue?" (65). Stuhlmacher responds
accordingly, "Angesichts der enormen Bedeutung der Septuaginta für das
neutestamentliche Christuszeugnis muss der Neutestamentler kanonge-
schichtlich anders urteilen als Childs und von *einem* veilschichtigen kanoni-
schen Traditionsprozess denken, *dem die Hebräische Bibel einerseits und der
zweiteilige christliche Kanon anderseits entstammen*" (*Theologie*, 343; this last
emphasis mine).

12.   Stuhlmacher, *Theologie*, 343.

13.   Childs (p. 56) summarizes the conclusion of T. Swanson as "the third section
of the Hebrew canon, the Writings, may have been a secondary canonical
subdivision which was effected long after the scope of the non-Mosaic books
had been fixed within the comprehensive category of the 'Prophets.'" See
Swanson, "The Closing of the Collection of Holy Scripture: A Study in the
History of the Canonization of the Old Testament" (Diss. Vanderbilt, 1970;
University Microfilms, Ann Arbor, Michigan). See also the discussions of R.
Beckwith (*The Old Testament Canon of the New Testament Church* [London:
SPCK, 1985]) and J. Barton (*Oracles of God* [London: Darton, Longman &
Todd, 1986]).

14.   Note the extreme difference in formulation between Childs and Stuhlmacher.
The latter states that the NT and Church Fathers do not shy from quoting
apocryphal and pseudepigraphic writings from the LXX, and he gives as evidence James 1:19 ("quoting" Sirach 5:11) and Mark 10:19 ("quoting" Sirach
4:1). Childs states, "The early controversies with the Jews reflected in the New
Testament turned on the proper interpretation of the sacred scriptures (*he
graphe*) which Christians assumed in common with the synagogue. Although
there is evidence that other books were known and used, it is a striking fact that
the New Testament does not *cite as scripture* any book of the Apocrypha or
Pseudepigrapha. (The reference to Enoch in Jude 14–15 is not an exception.)
The use of the Old Testament by 1 Clement and by Justin Martyr is further
confirmation of the assumption of a common scripture between the synagogue
and the church, even if in fact a slight variation had begun to appear" (62). See
also the full discussion of E. Ellis in *The Old Testament in Early Christianity*,
WUNT 54 (Tübingen: J. C. B. Mohr [Paul Siebeck], 1991), 10–36.

15.   Beckwith, *The Old Testament Canon*. Qumran (4Q MMT) likewise witnesses
a reference to the canon that begins with Moses and ends with "the words of
the days" (Chronicles). See the discussion of Ellis (10) and E. Qimron and J.
Strugnell, "An Unpublished Halachic Letter from Qumran," *IMJ* 4 (spring
1985), 9–12.

16.   Eighty citations from Torah, 80 from the Prophets, and 55 from Psalms; he
quickly adds, "this cannot mean that the NT (as with Qumran) is unaware of
other books." This latter reservation is fine as far as it goes, but it lacks genuine evaluation and, moreover, the general sense of this is not lost on Childs
(see n. 14 here) and others.

17. See Markus Bockmuehl, "'The Form of God' (Phil. 2:6) and Variations on a Theme of Jewish Mysticism," *JTS* 48 (1997), 22. "The typological interpretation of the Song of Songs appears to go back at least to the first century, as the rabbinic and early Patristic evidence suggests; it may also be attested in what has been tenuously identified as a commentary at Qumran (4Q240, still unpublished). New Testament hints at such an interpretation include Rev. 3:20, 'Behold, I stand at the door and knock,' and perhaps 19:7 about the marriage of the lamb (cf. Cant. 5.2; see also John 7:38 with Cant. 4.15)" (22).

18. Richard Bauckham has a fine treatment in his essay on Acts 15 in *The Book of Acts in Its Palestinian Setting* (Grand Rapids/Carlisle: Eerdmans and Paternoster, 1995).

19. R. Bauchkham, "James and the Jerusalem Church," in *The Book of Acts in Its Palestinian Setting*, 452–62; B. Witherington, *The Acts of the Apostles: A Socio-Rhetorical Commentary* (Grand Rapids/Carlisle: Eerdmans and Paternoster, 1998) 457–8; R. Bauckham, "Jude's Exegesis," in *Jude and the Relatives of Jesus in the Early Church* (Edinburgh: T & T Clark, 1990) esp. 225–33. Stuhlmacher also sees this issue but draws different conclusions from it. The NT authors had no closed list. They relate instead to a "kanonisch noch unabgeschlossene Sammlung des Heiligen Schriften in hebräischer und griechischer Sprache" (*Theologie*, 292).

20. E. Ellis, *The Old Testament in Early Christianity*, Wissenchaftliche Untersuchungen zum Neuen Testament 54 (Tübingen: J. C. B. Mohr [Paul Siebeck] 1991), 10–36. Melito's list represents the canon of the Old Testament on terms consistent with *Baba Batra*; Epiphanius, Origen, Jerome, Augustine, and Athanasius are also examined. When asked to list books, they clearly distinguish between canonical and others and give the conservative listing as constituting genuine, undisputed canonical authority.

21. Ellis, *The Old Testament*, 3–36.

22. F. M. Cross, "The Evolution of a Theory of Local Texts," in *Qumran and the History of the Biblical Text*, ed. F. M. Cross and S. Talmon (Cambridge: Harvard University Press, 1975) 306–20; E. Tov, *Textual Criticism of the Hebrew Bible* (Minneapolis: Fortress; Assen/Maastricht: Van Gorcum, 1992); "The History and Significance of a Standard Text of the Hebrew Bible," in M. Saebo ed., *Hebrew Bible/Old Testament: The History of Its Interpretation* 1 (Gottingen: Vandenhoeck & Ruprecht, 1996) 49–66. Childs states, "The strongest evidence for a fixed Hebrew canon derives from the history of the stabilization of the Masoretic text. . . . The text of a book would not have been corrected and stabilized if the book had not already received some sort of canonical status" (60). And Stuhlmacher does concede that "recensional activity at Murabba'at (e.g., the 12 Minor Prophets Scroll) is only possible and logical if the Hebrew possessed some priority over the Greek" (291). In a very recent study, Al Wolters studies the Qumran finds and their impact on the history of the canon. He quotes Tov as follows, "The earliest Qumran finds dating from the third pre-Christian century bear evidence, among other things, of a tradition of exact copying of texts belonging to the Masoretic family, that is, the proto-Masoretic texts" ("The History and Significance of a Standard Text of the Hebrew Bible," in *Hebrew Bible/Old Testament: The History of Its Interpretation* (vol. 1; ed. M. Saebo [Gottingen: Vandenhoeck & Ruprecht, 1996], 57). Schiffman and van der Woude draw a similar conclusion. Tov believes that 60 percent of all texts at Qumran are "proto-Masoretic" and only 5 percent are "pre-Samaritan" and

"those approximating the LXX" (*Textual Criticism of the Hebrew Bible* [Minneapolis: Fortress; Assen/Maastricht: Van Gorcum, 1992).

23. "Die Childs leitende Sicht der Kanongeschichte ist ein Konstruction, bei der weder den Textfunden von Qumran noch der Geschichte der Septuaginta gebuhrende Aufmerksamkeit geschenkt wird" (343).

24. He and Childs agree that Ben Sira and Qumran confirm rather than challenge Josephus, Philo, and *Baba Batra*. The so-called Council of Jabneh belongs in the rubbish bin of the history of ideas.

25. Even Barr notes: "It is theologically meaningful that we do not pass without substantial temporal interval from the main body of the Old Testament into the New. There is, on the contrary, a time of ripening, as it were, in which the Old Testament is able to develop its effects historically within the life, history and thought of a historical people" (*Old and New in Interpretation* [New York: Harper and Row, 1966], 156).

26. See now the work of Stephen B. Chapman, *The Law and the Prophets* (Tübingen: Mohr Siebeck, 2000). Compare *Wisdom as a Hermeneutical Construct* (BZAW; Berlin: de Gruyter, 1980).

27. Justin's claim that the Jews had falsified the texts was proven wrong. Still, it would be a mistake to believe that his debate with Trypho was essentially hedged about by misinformation at a text-critical level. It is sufficient to conclude that Justin was wrong without concluding that he witnesses to a live theological debate over the status of the LXX for the early church over against the (proto-) Masoretic Hebrew tradition. See the discussion of Wolters cited in n. 22 here.

28. See my discussion in chapter 4 of *Word without End* (49–50).

29. See my discussion in *Pro Ecclesia*, reprinted in *Word without End*, "Hebrew Bible or Old Testament?"

30. "Christologial Interpretation of Texts and Trinitarian Claims to Truth" and "The Old Testament as Christian Scripture: A Response to Professor Seitz," in *Scottish Journal of Theology* 52 (1999) 209–32.

31. H. Hübner, "Vetus Testamentum und Vetus Testamentum in Novo receptum. Die Frage nach dem Kanon des Alten Testaments aus neutestamentlicher Sicht," in *Jahrbuch für biblische Theologie* 3 (1988) 147–62.

32. I follow here the treatment of Bauckham in n. 18 of this chapter.

33. The quote (in *Theologie*, 344) is taken from Childs's *Biblical Theology* (77).

34. Ellis, *The Old Testament*, 128.

35. Adolph von Harnack, *Die Mission und Ausbreitung des Christentums: in der ersten drei Jahrhundertene* (Leipzig: J. C. Hinrichs, 1902).

36. See the discussion in *The Formation of the Christian Bible* (Philadelphia: Fortress, 1972) and in chapter 5 ("In Accordance with the Scriptures: Creed, Scripture, and 'Historical Jesus'") of *Word without End* (51–60).

37. See chapter 12 in this book. On the debate between Athanasius and Arius, and especially their appeal to scripture, see the brilliant analysis of Frances Young, *Biblical Exegesis and the Formation of Christian Culture* (Cambridge: Cambridge University Press, 1997).

Chapter 4

1. The Lambeth Conference is held every ten years. The record of its proceedings is widely available on the Internet (see http://anglicancommunion.org/acns/).

2. The bishop made this statement at his diocesan convention, in light of the

fact of the Lambeth Conference's resounding vote against blessing same-sex relationships.

3. The statement was made in response to a question posed at a forum at Berkeley Divinity School at Yale. Frank Griswold had attended Lambeth Conference as the bishop of Chicago. The forum was held at Berkeley Divinity School just prior to his assuming the role of presiding bishop in the American Episcopal Church.

4. In actual fact, the resolutions of Lambeth Conference 1988 (and previous conferences) are misrepresented in Griswold's (rather awkward) analogy.

5. See W. L. Schoedel, "Same-Sex Eros: Paul and the Greco-Roman Tradition," in D. L. Balch, ed., *Homosexuality, Science, and the "Plain Sense" of Scripture* (Grand Rapids: Eerdmans, 2000), 43–72.

6. See my discussion in chapter 12. The bibliography of modern studies on exegesis, the literal sense, and constructive theological statements includes the work of Yeago, Greene-McCreight, Frances Young, and others.

7. It is striking how many Church of England bishops were trained at Ridley Hall, Wycliff Hall, or Cranmer Hall. There is no direct analogy in the Episcopal Church USA.

8. For a convenient description of the issues, see B. S. Childs, *Introduction to the Old Testament as Scripture* (Philadelphia: Fortress, 1979), 611–613.

9. For a discussion of the details of this period, see chapter 1.

10. *Lux Mundi: A Series of Studies in the Religion of the Incarnation* (London: J. Murray, 1889).

11. This Anglo-Catholic Wellhausenism would have given Wellhausen pause, as he regarded any such mooring as a simple failure to press on in the quest for scientific truth. Wellhausen resigned his church post in the university and went on to deconstruct the New Testament and then the Koran. See the treatment of John Rogerson, *The Old Testament and Criticism* (Philadelphia: Fortress Press).

12. Hans Frei, *The Eclipse of Biblical Narrative* (New Haven: Yale University Press, 1974).

13. E. G. Selwyn, ed., *Essays Catholic and Critical* (London: SPCK, 1926).

14. This is a twentieth-century spin-off (development?) of the Anglo-Catholic movement, once associated with Pusey, Newman, and Keble (whose roots are in the early to mid-nineteenth century). The movement has a Website at www.affirmingcatholicism.co.uk. One can find there an essay critical of the Lambeth 1998 resolutions against homosexuality, "Incompatible with Scripture: The Lambeth Resolutions on Human Sexuality." A sketch of their own sense of historical lineage is provided in "Varieties of Anglo-Catholicism in the Twentieth Century."

15. On the 1979 prayer book revision and its relationship to historicism, see chapter 5.

16. The Balch volume cited is one of the most recent discussions of homosexuality. Those authors who are in favor of some form of same-sex blessing usually argue that the Bible simply cannot see far enough off to be useful in assessing today's world. This is a different line of argument than what one found in early revisionist efforts.

17. "Love your neighbor as yourself" is a levitical injunction (genre: law). Intriguingly, it was the Book of Leviticus to which Henry VIII appealed for his annulment. According to this logic, a fundamentalist or legalist gave rise to Anglican Christianity.

18. See the discussion of Acts 15 in chapter 8. See also the insightful discussion of Richard Bauckham, "James and the Jerusalem Church," in *The Book of Acts in Its Palestinian Setting* (Grand Rapids: Eerdmans; Carlisle, England: Paternoster, 1992), 415–480.
19. See the report on the Internet.
20. A foundation reproduced in modified form by Stephen Fowl, *Engaging Scripture*.
21. I have in mind here those Christians who have understood themselves to be "homosexuals" but regard the exercise of that behavior sinful, capable of being healed, or an affliction like alcoholism.

Chapter 5

1. H. Frei, *The Eclipse of Biblical Narrative* (New Haven: Yale, 1994); H. Reventlow, *The Authority of the Bible and the Rise of the Modern World* (Philadelphia: Fortress, 1985); W. Abraham, *Canon and Criterion in Christian Theology: From the Fathers to Feminism* (Oxford: Clarendon, 1998).
2. See chapters 1 and 3. Also recall that a Lambeth Conference in the nineteenth century had to deal with the problem of the teaching of higher-critical methods.
3. See, above all, the trenchant essay of E. Radner, "The Absence of the Comforter: Scripture and the Divided Church," in C. Seitz and K. Greene-McCreight, eds., *Theological Exegesis: Essays in Honor of B. S. Childs* (Grand Rapids: Eerdmans, 1999) 355–394. Also, E. Radner, *The End of the Church: A Pneumatology of Christian Division in the West* (Grand Rapids: Eerdmans, 1998).
4. See J. R. Searle, *Speech-Acts: An Essay in the Philosophy of Language* (Cambridge: Cambridge University Press, 1969); N. Wolterstorff, *Divine Discourse: Theological Reflections on the Claim That God Speaks* (Cambridge: Cambridge University Press, 1995); K. Vanhoozer, *Is There a Meaning in This Text? The Bible, the Reader, and the Morality of Literary Knowledge* (Grand Rapids: Zondervan, 1998).
5. For the actual text, consult http://anglicancommunion.org/documents/virginia/.
6. John Zizioulas, "The Doctrine of God and the Trinity Today," in Alasdair Heron, ed., *The Forgotten Trinity* (London: BCC/CCBI, 1991).
7. See the very good treatment of Frances Young, "The Mind of Scripture," in *Biblical Exegesis and the Formation of Christian Culture* (Cambridge: Cambridge University Press, 1997) 29–45.
8. See chapter 2 above for a fuller discussion of these matters.
9. Trevor Hart, "Person and Prerogative in Perichoretic Perspective: The Triunity of God" and "Truth, Trinity and Pluralism," in *Regarding Karl Barth* (Carlisle, Cumbria, England: Paternoster, 1999).
10. Jame Torrance, *Worship, Community, and the Triune God of Grace* (Carlisle, England: Paternoster, 1996).
11. Zizioulas, "Doctrine of God."
12. Hart, "Person and Prerogative," 115.

Chapter 6

1. See the fine study of H. Graf Reventlow, *The Authority of the Bible and the Rise of the Modern World* (Philadelphia: Fortress, 1984), where the English Deistic and German theological tradition is explored.

2. Gregory Dix, *The Shape of the Liturgy* (London: Dacre Press, 1945).

Chapter 7

1. C. Stephen Evans, "Methodological Naturalism in Historical Biblical Schol-arship," in Carey C. Newman, ed., *Jesus and the Restoration of Israel* (Downer's Grove/Carlisle: InterVarsity and Paternoster, 1999) 180–205.
2. B. H. Streeter, *The Four Gospels* (London: Macmillan, 1924).
3. Paul Trobisch, *Paul's Letter Collection* (Minneapolis: Fortress, 1994).
4. The published findings of Trobisch are now available in *The First Edition of the New Testament* (Oxford: Oxford University Press, 2000). Compare also R. Bauckman, ed., *The Gospels for All Christians* (Grand Rapids: Eerdmans, 1998).
5. I am unpersuaded one can build a bridge from Barth to N. T. Wright, Richard Hays, or Luke Johnson, when it comes to how they approach the form of the Gospel record. Barth handles the Gospel form with great sophistication and never allows historicism to interfere with genuine history. His treatment of Judas is a classic example.

Chapter 8

1. I should like to thank Professor Gary Anderson for his comments on an ear-lier draft of this essay.
2. See my essay "In Accordance with the Scriptures," in *Word without End*.
3. C. R. Seitz, *Proclamation IV, Advent*, Series A, 1988.
4. F. Kermode, *The Genesis of Secrecy: On the Interpretation of Narrative* (Cam-bridge, MA: Harvard University Press, 1979).
5. See Hans von Campenhausen, *The Formation of the Christian Bible*, trans. J. A. Baker (Philadelphia: Fortress, 1972).
6. G. von Rad, *Old Testament Theology*, vol. 2: *The Theology of Israel's Prophetic Tra-ditions*, trans. D. M. G. Stalker (Edinburgh and London: Oliver and Boyd, 1965) 261–262; C. R. Seitz, "The Prophet Moses and the Canonical Shape of Jere-miah," *ZAW* 101 (1989) 3–27; R. Clements, "Isaiah 53 and the Restoration of Israel," in *Jesus and the Suffering Servant*, eds. W. H. Bellinger Jr. and W. R. Farmer (Harrisburg, PA: Trinity Press International, 1998) 39–54; Gordon P. Hugenberger, "Servant of the Lord in the 'Servant Songs' of Isaiah: A Second Moses Figure," in *The Lord's Anointed: Interpretation of Old Testament Messianic Texts*, eds. Philip E. Satterthwaite, Richard S. Hess, and Gordon J. Wenham (Carlisle, England: Paternoster; Grand Rapids: Baker, 1995) 105–140.
7. A. C. Coxe, ed., *The Apostolic Fathers with Justin Martyr and Irenaeus*, ANF 1, vii.
8. "Dialogue of Justin, Philosopher and Martyr, with Trypho," in *Apostolic Fathers*, 219.
9. C. R. Seitz, "In Accordance with the Scriptures," in *Word without End*, 51–60.
10. C. R. Seitz, "'And without God in the World': A Hermeneutic of Estrange-ment Overcome," *Word without End*, 41–50.
11. See the discussion in F. Watson, *Text and Truth* (Grand Rapids: Eerdmans, 1997).
12. G. A. Williamson, ed., *Eusebius, The History of the Church from Christ to Con-stantine* (Baltimore: Penguin, 1965), 38 n.1.
13. David S. Yeago, "The New Testament and the Nicene Dogma: A Contribu-tion to the Recovery of Theological Exegesis," *Pro Ecclesia* 3 (1994) 152–164.
14. B. S. Childs, *Biblical Theology of the Old and New Testaments* (Minneapolis: Augsburg Fortress, 1993). This is Childs's central contribution to the biblical theology discussion in late modernity.

15. "The First Apology of Justin," 87 (ANF, 1.186).
16. Of relevance also is my paper "Scripture, Spirit, God's Word to Culture: Acts 15 and Christian Theological Exegesis," which was delivered at the Scholarly Engagement with Anglican Doctrine conference in Toronto.
17. *Word without End.*
18. This is the sustained point of my several essays in *Word without End* and why a turn to the Patristic period of christological reflection is so illuminating; there one sees the centrality of the scriptures of Israel for doing Christology in the first instance.
19. "It is quite wrong to say that the Old Testament had no authority in its own right for the first Christians, and that it was taken over purely because people saw that it 'treated of Christ' or pointed toward him. The critical problem, to which Luther's well-known but misused formula supplies an answer, had not yet been posed. The situation was in fact quite the reverse. Christ is vindicated to unbelievers out of the Scripture: but the converse necessity, to justify the Scriptures on the authority of Christ, is as yet nowhere even envisaged" (*Formation*, 63–64).
20. N. T. Wright, "The Servant and Jesus: The Relevance of the Colloquy for the Current Quest for Jesus," in *Jesus and the Suffering Servant*, 283–299.
21. Ibid., "I think, in fact, that we have been too shortsighted in focusing on the fourth Servant Song and on the precise meaning of various phrases within it," 291–292.
22. Ibid., "I suggest, then, that the categories of the sixth or fifth or fourth centuries B.C.E., and those of the sixteenth or subsequent centuries C.E., are not necessarily good guides for our understanding Jesus. Listening to the debate between substitution and representation, in however sophisticated and nuanced fashion it may be carried on, leaves me as a historian with the same feeling I have when I meet people . . . for whom the key question in the New Testament is whether the Rapture comes before or after the Tribulation. The critical nest of meaning in the second-temple Jewish world did not focus on substitution and representation, but on exile and how it would be undone . . . not simply on isolated bits and pieces of text" (297).
23. Ibid., and "it is clear to me that if there is a lacuna in this conference it is at the point of discussing how Isaiah might have been read by Jesus' own contemporaries" (284).
24. See my brief treatment "Isaiah, Book of (First Isaiah), *Anchor Bible Dictionary*, ed. David Noel Freedman (New York: Doubleday, 1992), 3.472–488.
25. On this, see now the brilliant contribution of Robert Jenson, *The Triune God*, vol. 1: *Systematic Theology* (Oxford: Oxford University Press, 1998).
26. See my remarks in *Word without End.*
27. I was struck by J. L. Martyn's selective use of only one form of the former-latter refrain in order to ground his biblical theological reflections. See his "Listening to John and Paul on the Subject of Gospel and Scripture," *Word and World* 12 (1992) 68–81.
28. H. G. M. Williamson, *A Book Called Isaiah: Deutero-Isaiah's Role in Composition and Redaction* (Oxford: Clarendon Press, 1994).
29. For a typical treatment from this working perspective, see C. R. North, "The Former Things and the New Things in Deuter-Isaiah," *Studies in Old Testament Prophecy*, ed. H. H. Rowley (Edinburgh: T. & T. Clark, 1950), 111f. A minority view from the same period has frequently been overlooked; see

Douglas Jones, "Tradition of the Oracles of Isaiah of Jerusalem" *ZAW* 67 (1995) 226–246. See the discussion of B. S. Childs, *Introduction to the Old Testament as Scripture* (Philadelphia: Fortress, 1979), 328–330.

30. In preparation for *NIB*; see Benjamin D. Sommer's remarks in "Allusions and Illusions: The Unity of the Book of Isaiah in Light of Deutero-Isaiah's Use of Prophetic Tradition," *New Visions of Isaiah*, eds. Roy F. Melugin and Marvin A. Sweeney (Sheffield: Sheffield Academic Press, 1996), 156–186.

31. For a good survey of form-critical work of this passage, see R. Melugin, *The Formation of Isaiah 40–55* (BZAW 141; Berlin: Walter de Gruyter, 1976).

32. See Peter Wilcox and David Paton-Williams, "The Servant Songs in Deutero-Isaiah," *JSOT* 42 (1988) 79–102.

33. See "How is the Prophet Isaiah Present in the Latter Half of the Book? The Logic of Chapters 40–66 Within the Book of Isaiah," *JBL* 115 (1996) 219–240.

34. A convenient précis of his thesis can be seen in the essay cited above.

35. R. N. Whybray, *Thanksgiving for a Liberated Prophet* (Sheffield: University of Sheffield Press, 1978); D. P. Bailey, "Concepts of *Stellvertretung* in the Interpretation of Isaiah 53," in *Jesus and the Suffering Servant*, eds. William H. Bellinger and William R. Farmer (Harrisburg, PA: Trinity Press International, 1998), 223–250.

36. See above all the fine essays of W. Beuken, "The Main Theme of Trito-Isaiah: The Servants of YHWH," *JSOT* 47 (1990) 67–87; and "Isa. 56:9–57:13—An Example of the Isaianic Legacy of Trito-Isaiah," in *Tradition and Reinterpretation in Jewish and Early Christian Literature*, ed. J. W. Van Henton et al. (Leiden: Brill, 1986), 204–221.

Chapter 9

1. Charles C. Hefling (ed.), *Our Selves, Our Souls and Bodies: Sexuality and the Household of God* (Cambridge, Mass.: Cowley, 1996).

2. See Marilyn Adams's treatment in ibid., "Hurricane Spirit, Toppling Taboos," 129ff.

3. *Decision Making in the Church: A Biblical Model* (Philadelphia: Fortress, 1983).

4. It is striking to this reader that the "Spirit" is no longer the "Holy Spirit." "Holy" may, however, in the universe of "taboo" and social anthropology, imply separation and "taboo" itself in the logic of the argument. "Gospel" is not capitalized even as "Spirit" is. We are definitely in a "taboo-toppling" age of change.

5. *The Nature of Doctrine* (Philadelphia: Westminster, 1984).

6. R. Bauckham, "James and the Jerusalem Church," *The Book of Acts in Its Palestinian Setting* (Grand Rapids: Eerdmans; Carlisle, England: Paternoster, 1985) 415–480.

7. Johnson, *Decision Making*, 88; emphasis mine.

8. Ibid., 82.

9. Bauckham, "James and the Gentiles (Acts 15.13–21)," in B. Witherington ed., *History, Literature, and Society in the Book of Acts* (Cambridge: Cambridge University Press, 1996) 154–184.

Chapter 10

1. See my essays "The Call of Moses and the 'Revelation' of the Divine Name" and "The Divine Name in Christian Scripture" in *Word without End*. Also see

Michael Wyschogrod, *The Body of Faith: God in the People of Israel* (San Fran-
cisco: Harper & Row, 1983). "*The God of Israel has a proper name.* There is no
fact in Jewish theology more significant than this" (91; quoted from R. Jenson, *Systematic Theology*, vol. 1: *The Triune God* [Oxford: Oxford University
Press, 1997], 43 n.10).

2. As Jenson puts it, "Asked who God is, Israel's answer is, 'Whoever rescued us
from Egypt' and 'Thus "the one who rescued Israel from Egypt" is confirmed
as an identification of *God* in that it is continued "as he thereupon rescued the
Israelite Jesus from the dead"'" (*Systematic*, 44).

3. These include the special orthographic rendering of the tetragrammaton, in
Hebrew script.

4. Jenson says of the practical problem of using a convention, as he does in volume 1 of his systematic theology, "It is unlikely that the text of this work will
often be read aloud, but to cover the eventuality, where it seems desirable to
use JHWH in the text, the name will be spelled in that fashion, with only the
consonants" (44 n.12). If his text were read aloud, the reader would have to
use another convention for oral delivery, like "the LORD," thus illustrating
what is at issue.

5. Jenson's rhetorical power is on display as he makes this point in another context: "Precisely being able to turn from their gods to the true God occasioned
'the joy' with which the apostles' gentile converts 'received the word.' In the
act of faith, gentile believers recognize themselves as those who have worshiped or might worship Moloch the baby-killer or Astarte the universal
whore or *Deutsches Blut* or the Free Market or the Dialectic of History or the
Metaphor of our gender or ethnic ressentiment, and on through an endless
list of tyrants. Only a naiveté impossible for the apostolic church, which fully
inhabited the religious maelstrom of late antiquity, can think that religion as
such is a good thing or that gods are necessarily beneficent" (50–51). What
is said here of "religion as such" applies *a fortiori* to language for God cut loose
from connection with Israel's LORD, who raised Israel and Jesus from the
dead.

6. See n. 1. Jenson notes, "We probably will never be quite sure what JHWH
originally meant; since historical Israel did not either, the theological loss
cannot be great" (43 n.9). This likely overstates the matter. Israel probably
knew that the name had to do with God "being who he is in the events he
shares with Israel in deliverance from Egypt," but only Hebrew speakers living within the nexus of the scripturally attested universe of discourse could
be expected to feel the force of this.

7. "The discussion of the meaning and origin of the name Yahweh constitutes a
monumental witness to the industry and ingenuity of biblical scholars" is the
way Cross opens his own treatment; it is unclear as one reads on whether he
was being ironic (*Canaanite Myth and Hebrew Epic: Essays in the History of the
Religion of Israel* [Cambridge: Harvard University Press], 60ff.).

8. Interestingly, this extrusion of "Yahweh" into common parlance was soon
followed by "Hebrew Bible" as preferable to Old Testament or Tanak.
See my discussion in *Word without End* (61–74) and *Pro Ecclesia* 6 (1997),
136–140.

9. "Israel's and the church's God is thus identified by specific temporal actions
and is known within certain temporal communities by personal names and
identifying descriptions thereby provided" (Jenson, *Systematic*, 46).

10.   Again, Jenson captures this nicely in his compact sentences: "Asked about her
       access to this God, Israel's answer is, 'We are permitted to call on him by
       name'—just so, the name was eventually felt too holy for regular utterance
       aloud and was replaced by stated euphemisms, in reading Scripture by *Adonai*,
       'the Lord.' The name does not thereby lose its power; on the contrary, in rab-
       binic discourse the phrase *Hashem*, 'the Name,' is often used instead of
       'God'" (*Systematic*, 44).
11.   See the discussion by Kendall Soulen, "YHWH The Triune God," *Modern
       Theology* 15 (1999), 25–54.
12.   One explanation may entail Israel's extrusion into the gentile world and the
       attendant fear of breaking the Decalogue's commandment regarding keeping
       the name holy.
13.   See the fine treatment by David Yeago, "The New Testament and Nicene
       Dogma: A Contribution to the Recovery of Theological Exegesis," *Pro Eccle-
       sia* 3 (1994), 152–164.
14.   J. Moltmann, *The Crucified God*, trans. R. A. Wilson and J. Bowden (London:
       SCM, 1974).
15.   See my remarks on this in the review of Richard Bauckham's *God Crucified:
       Monotheism and Christology in the New Testament* (Carlisle, England: Pater-
       noster, 1998). The review will appear in the *International Journal of Systematic
       Theology*, forthcoming.
16.   "In the Scriptures . . . it is first among the Lord's attributes that he is 'a *jeal-
       ous* God'," Jenson writes with reference to Exod. 34:14 (*Systematic*, 47).
17.   See my several essays in *Word without End*. Zimmerli begins his Old Testa-
       ment theology with a discussion of the name of God (*Old Testament Theology
       in Outline* [Atlanta: John Knox, 1978]).
18.   The theological case for this has been made, e.g., by Hans Frei and George
       Lindbeck.
19.   For a full treatment of the argument summarized here, see "The Call of
       Moses and the 'Revelation' of the Divine Name," in *Theological Exegesis: Essays
       in Honor of Brevard S. Childs* (Grand Rapids: Eerdmans, 1998), 145–161.
20.   Rudolph Otto, *The Idea of the Holy*, trans. J. W. Harvey (London: Oxford Uni-
       versity Press, 1929).
21.   "This is, therefore, the expression of the idea that God exists, but not in the
       ordinary sense of the term; or, in other words, He is 'the existing Being which
       is the existing Being,'" that is to say, the Being whose existence is absolute"
       (Moses Maimonides, *The Guide for the Perplexed* [M. Friedlander, trans.; 2d
       ed.; London: Routledge & Kegan Paul, 1904], 95).
22.   Yeago, "Nicene Dogma"; Bauckham, *God Crucified*.
23.   See my treatment, "Creed, Scripture and 'Historical Jesus,'" in E. Radner and
       G. Sumner, eds., *The Rule of Faith: Scripture, Canon, and Creed in a Critical Age*
       (Harrisburg, Pa.: Morehouse, 1998), 126–135.
24.   Sadly, it must be regarded as a particularly Christian temptation to underes-
       timate the significance of God's giving to Jesus the "name which is above
       every name," because that name (YHWH) was not universally available but
       existed within the bosom of Israel and her faith. Gentile Christians (as in
       Philadelphia) may even view access to the LORD, granted through naming
       the name of Jesus, as nothing of the kind; rather, "lord" is a phoneme
       of oppression to be improved upon by address to "Sophia." Something has
       gone dreadfully wrong here. The root of the problem lies with a failure to

understand the self-disclosure by God of himself, in Israel, in the name above
every name, and hence a failure to understand what it means to call Jesus anything at all.

Chapter 11

1. On the use of tradition-history to link the testaments, see chapter 2 in this book.
2. On the problems of biblical theology for Jews, see J. Levenson, *The Hebrew Bible, the Old Testament, and Historical Criticism* (Louisville, KY: Westminster John Knox Press, 1993).
3. One thinks in particular of Rudoph Bultmann's essay "The Significance of the Old Testament for the Christian Faith" in B. Anderson, ed., *The Old Testament and Christian Faith* (New York: Harper & Row, 1963), 8–35. But at the same time, Bultmann was representative of a larger instinct.
4. For a classic treatment, see C. Westermann, *Genesis 1–11* (Minneapolis: Augsburg, 1983).
5. Gerhard von Rad, *Genesis: A Commentary* (Philadelphia: Westminster, 1974), 157.
6. See the fine discussion of ancestral religion by Walter Moberly in *The Old Testament of the Old Testament* (Minneapolis: Fortress, 1992). The phrase is that of Gordon Wenham.
7. The phrases are so rendered in von Rad's commentary (167).
8. "The Nations in the Book of Isaiah," in J. Vermeylen, ed., *The Book of Isaiah* (Louvain: Leuven University Press, 1989), 107.
9. Karl Friedrich Keil, *Manual of Historico-Critical Introduction to the Canonical Scriptures of the Old Testament* (trans. from the 2d ed. by C. M. Douglas; Edinburgh: T & T Clark, 1870–71), 286–287.
10. Grand Rapids: Eerdmanns, 1998.

Chapter 12

1. E. Sellin, *Mose und seine Bedeutung fur die israelitisch-judische Religionsgeschichte* (Leipzig: A. Deichert, 1922); G. von Rad, *Old Testament Theology* 2 (New York: Harper & Row, 1965) 261–62; K. Baltzer, *Deutero-Isaiah* (Hermeneia; Minneapolis: Fortress Press, 2001).
2. C. R. Seitz, "The Prophet Moses and the Canonical Shape of Jeremiah," *Zeitschrift für die alttestamentliche Wissenschaft.*

Chapter 13

1. "The New Testament and Nicene Dogma: A Contribution to the Recovery of Theological Exegesis," *Pro Ecclesia* 3 (1994), 152–164.
2. *An Exposition of the Creed by John Pearson, D.D.* (London: George Bell & Sons, 1902).
3. Frances Young, *Biblical Exegesis and the Formation of Christian Culture* (Cambridge: Cambridge University Press, 1998); Richard Bauckham, *God Crucified: Monotheism and Christology in the New Testament* (Carlisle, England: Paternoster, 1998).
4. "Apostasy at 2000: Episcopal Institute Promotes Pantheism, Syncretism," by Mark Tooley, *Touchstone* (January 2001).
5. Book 1, 4; *The Confessions of St Augustine*, Hal M. Helms, trans. (Brewster, Mass.: Paraclete, 1986), 3.

6. C. FitzSimons Allison, *The Cruelty of Heresy: An Affirmation of Christian Orthodoxy* (Harrisburg, Pa.: Morehouse, 1994).
7. John Betjeman, *Collected Poems* (compiled and with an introduction by the Earl of Birkenhead; London: John Murray, 1997). (The final two lines have been added for this context).
8. Robert Jenson, *Systematic Theology*, vol. 1 (Oxford: Oxford University Press, 1997), 42–60.
9. See Pearson's own discussion (75ff.).
10. Ibid., 38, n.4.
11. Barth, *CD* (Edinburgh: T. & T. Clark, 1936–77) I/1: 400.
12. B. S. Childs, *Biblical Theology in Crisis* (Philadelphia: Westminster, 1970), 217.
13. J. Barr, *Old and New in Interpretation* (New York: Harper and Row, 1966), 149.
14. L. Keck, *A Future for the Historical Jesus* (Philadelphia: Fortress, 1980), 213.
15. P. Zahl, *A Short Systematic Theology* (Grand Rapids: Eerdmans, 2000).
16. K. Soulen, *The God of Israel and Christian Theology* (Minneapolis: Fortress, 1996), 50–51.
17. Childs, *Biblical Theology*, 226; Hans von Campenhausen, *The Formation of the Christian Bible* (Philadelphia: Fortress, 1972), 62–102.
18. "Walter Brueggemann's *Theology of the Old Testament: Testimony, Dispute, Advocacy*," *SJT* 53 (2000), 228–233. Brueggemann's book was published in 1997 by Fortress (Minneapolis).
19. Jenson, *Systematic Theology*, 50–51.
20. P. T. Forsyth, *Positive Preaching and the Modern Mind* (London: Independent Press, 1907).

Chapter 14

1. The distinction between judgments and concepts is profitably set forth by David Yeago, "The New Testament and the Nicene Dogma: A Contribution to the Recovery of Theological Exegesis," *Pro Ecclesia* 3 (1994) 152–164.
2. See the comments on this in the specific context of lower (text) criticism and conservative biblical scholarship by Al Wolters, "The Text of the Old Testament," in D. W. Baker and Bill T. Arnold, eds., *The Face of Old Testament Studies* (Grand Rapids: Baker Books, 1999) 36–37.
3. This is what the thirty-nine Articles of reformed, catholic Anglicanism sought to assert in its language, "Wherefore they are not to be heard, which feign that the old Fathers did look only for transitory promises" (Article VII).

Index

intertestamental congruence, 19
Irenaeus, 106, 108
Isaac, 151, 152
Isaiah, 32, 63, 103, 108, 110–16,
  122, 136, 137, 184, 194–95
  appreciation for unity of, 153
  assessing in light of earthly
    Jesus, 110
  former-latter motif in, 111–13
  fulfillment in Acts, 124
  heard in period of earthly
    Jesus, 111, 113–16
  Lord as God alone, 141
  Messiah of Israel in, 107
  mission in Genesis adopted in,
    153
  plain-sense reading of, 113
  pointing to Messiah of Israel,
    105
  prayer in, 166
  problems with reading through
    historical-critical lens, 110
  revealing two-testament wit-
    ness to Jesus Christ, 104
  suffering servant and prayer,
    172–74
  theme of the nations in, 152–56
  type of Christian scripture,
    104, 111–16
Isaiah apocalypse, 154
Isaiah scholarship, 31
Israel
  challenge to sacred history, 25
  cleaved in two, 156
  God known by his personal
    name in, 184
  literary legacy, 25
  meaning of rejection of, 156
  plan for in Isaiah, 113–14
  reconstructing religion of, 29
  status and role of, 147–52
  as suffering servant, 114–15
  sympathetic participation in
    life of, 135
  unruliness of God, 26–27
  witness, privileged character
    of, 5

J

J, 25, 27, 83, 84, 148
Jacob, Benno, 149, 152
James, 41, 121, 127–28
"James and the Gentiles (Acts
  15:13–21)" (Bauckham), 126–27
Jehovah's Witnesses, 141
Jenson, Robert, 3, 131, 189
Jeremiah, 153, 166, 173, 194–95
Jeremias, 114

Jerome, 41–42
Jesus
  acceptance of Daniel, 21
  as according and final act of
    God, 156
  addressing as Lord, 132

appeal to as endorser of love
  and human acceptance, 59
approach to Old Testament,
  55–56
authority of law and prophets
  for, 46
characterizing, 106
chronicling actions, 92
comprehended by accordance
  with the scriptures, 104
demanding appraisal in accordance with scriptural witness, 110
dismissing Christians from the
  law, 57
distinguishing between earthly
  and risen, 103–4
earthly, 99–100
emergence of sacred name,
  161–62
fully identified with God of
  the Old Testament, 188
historicizing mental state, 114
identification with YHWH,
  143–44
inseparability from God, 187
making no sense without the
  Father, 186
as Messianic interpreter, 39
model for modern biblical
  interpretation, 29
name distinguished from name
  of God, 142–43
name given by God, 182
necessary presence of in God-
  talk, 44
perception of Old Testament
  witness to God and himself,
  43
religion of, 65–66
significance of raising, 107
silence on homosexuality, 9, 57
starting point for study, 186–87
theological significance of
  earthly, 105–10
use of scripture in his own
  time, 29
uttering Psalm 22 on the cross,
  172
warnings against viewing
  earthly history only, 105
words selectively chosen as
  "God," 59
Jesus seminar, 18
Job, 99, 168–69
Joel, 122, 124
John, 54, 62, 72, 92, 94–97, 99,
  137
  ending of, 193
  final words of Gospel, 92–97
  importance of placement, 92,
    94, 99
  plain sense of, 101
  relationship to prior Gospels,
    94, 99
  role of Spirit, 122

Johnson, Luke, 61, 119, 120–21,
  122, 123–24, 128, 129
Jonah, 164, 167, 169
Joseph, 149, 151
Josephus, 42
Joshua, 106
Josiah, 88
Jude, 179
judgment, brought into history,
  150
jurisdictional resolution, 49
Justin, 42, 43, 62, 104, 107–8,
  109, 111, 113

K

Käsemann, E., 39
Keble, J., 56, 64
Keck, Lee, 186
Keil, Karl F., 53, 153
kenosis, 22
kenosis surrender, 54
Kirk, Kenneth, 57
Knox, W., 26
koinonia, 72, 117
kyrie, placement of, 82, 85
kyrios, 184

L

Lambeth Conference (1988), 50,
  72–74, 75
Lambeth Conference (1998), 49,
  63, 64, 66, 67–68, 69
language-to-scope argument, 41
Law, relationship with Prophets,
  36
Laws of Ecclesiastical Polity, 73
Lessing, G. E., 109
letter-writing conventions, 93
Leviticus, 44, 57, 128, 193–94
Lewis, C. S., 86
Lindbeck, George, 19, 120
"Lion of Judah, The," 197
literalism, ruling out, 10
literal sense, 28, 29, 47
literary criticism, 25
literary-theological movement, 83
liturgical historicism, 82
liturgical renewal, 84
liturgical revision, 82–83
liturgical studies, effect of historicism on, 83–84
Locke, J., 75
Lord (kyrios), 131
  addressing Jesus as, 132
  oppressiveness of term, 132
  vagueness in speech, 132
lost ark, 87
Luke, 40, 42, 43, 83, 92, 94, 110
Luke-Acts
  Holy Spirit in, 121–22, 125–26
  structure of, 122–23
Luther, Martin, 172
Lux Mundi (Gore), 18–19, 24, 54,
  56, 178